THE ROLE OF INDEPENDENT DIRECTORS IN CORPORATE GOVERNANCE

an update of *The Role of Independent Directors after Sarbanes-Oxley*

BRUCE F. DRAVIS

AMERICAN BAR ASSOCIATION
Business Law Section

Cover design by ABA Publishing.

Page composition by Quadrum.

Printed in the United States of America.

Library of Congress Cataloging-in-Publication Data

Dravis, Bruce F.

 The Role of Independent Directors in Corporate Governance (an update of Role of Independent Directors after Sarbanes-Oxley) / Bruce F. Dravis.

     p. cm.

Includes an index.

 ISBN-13: 978-1-61632-053-9 (alk. paper)

 ISBN-10: 1-61632-053-2 (alk. paper)

 1. Outside directors of corporations—Legal status, laws, etc.—United States. 2. Corporate governance—Law and legislation—United States. I. Title.

 KF1423.D734 2010

 346.73'0664—dc22

2010044462

Contents

Acknowledgements

This author received significant assistance from many contributors to this project, both in the first edition and in the second edition.

Special thanks for the first edition goes to Stewart McDowell, Steve Dorian, Debbie Elder, Carrie Arnold, Megan Lane, Ilya Filmus, Joanne Tan, Ann Poole, Kelli Christiansen, and to Betty Barth for her work on the electronic version of the book.

For the second edition, special thanks goes to Sherry Tabaczynski, Elizabeth Jackson, Ashley Ray, Caroline Colangelo, and Justin Dela Cruz, and to the ABA's Susana Darwin, who provided excellent editorial guidance. I also thank my wife, Liane Anderson, for her patience, support and love.

Preface

This book is an update of *The Role of Independent Directors after Sarbanes-Oxley,* which was published in 2007. It is intended to provide independent directors and their advisors with an understanding of the primary legal and governance issues that have evolved in the corporate governance environment since the passage of the Sarbanes-Oxley Act in 2002. As this book went to press, not all of the additional SEC rulemaking mandated under Dodd-Frank was completed. Updates on the additional rulemaking can be found at http://sec.gov/spotlight/dodd-frank.shtml.

The printed text is intended to be accessible to attorney and non-attorney readers. Since the book covers legal matters and is written by lawyers, some "legalese" is inevitable, good intentions notwithstanding.

The references on the accompanying CD-ROM link lawyers (or interested non-lawyers) to legal source material, including statutory, regulatory, administrative, and case material underlying the text.

The source material is intended to be a useful starting point for deeper research, but it is not encyclopedic in scope and will not reflect developments after the date that this book and disc are published.

Footnote references are abbreviated, and not in legal bluebook style. For example, "Dodd-Frank Wall Street Reform and Consumer Protection Act of 2010, Section 951" is abbreviated as "Dodd-Frank 951;" "Sarbanes-Oxley Act of 2002, Section 301" is abbreviated as "SOX 301;" and a regulation such as "17 C.F.R. 240.10b-5" would be listed as "SEC Rule 10b-5." Tables of the cited underlying materials are provided at the conclusion of the book.

CHAPTER **I**

Introduction and Summary

"Corporations are legal devices for assembling and organizing capital, labor, and other resources to produce and sell goods and services. . . . [T]he broad policies, strategic plans, and day-to-day decisions in large publicly traded corporations are largely controlled by professional managers. These are typically individuals whose own at-risk assets are small relative to the assets they administer. Thus the central problem in any corporate governance system is how to make corporate executives accountable to the other contributors to the enterprise whose investments are at risk, while still giving those executives the freedom, the incentive, and the control over resources they need to create and seize investment opportunities and to be tough competitors."

—Margaret Blair, *Ownership and Control* (1995)

1

1. Independent Directors are Key Players in Corporate Governance

Since the turn of the millennium, independent directors have become the focus of corporate governance. In this still-developing corporate governance environment, the work, time commitment, and responsibilities of independent directors have increased significantly.

This increased focus started with the massive corporate scandals and failures of the early 2000s (Enron and Worldcom, for example), which propelled the passage of the Sarbanes-Oxley Act of 2002 ("SOX"). The financial crisis of 2007-08 resulted in the federal government adopting the nearly $1 trillion Troubled Asset Relief Program ("TARP"), and in a renewed focus on the role of independent directors in evaluating corporate strategy, risk, and compensation. The Dodd-Frank Wall Street Reform and Consumer Protection Act of 2010 ("Dodd-Frank") was developed out of the financial crisis, but included many corporate governance matters, including executive compensation and director nomination processes.

In this book, the term "governance" is used to refer to a combination of state and federal legal requirements and developing doctrines regarding the control of corporations. This guidebook addresses not only the laws affecting independent directors and corporations but also the broader context in which these laws have risen and will be interpreted.

The law sets certain minimum requirements regarding how directors and officers are selected, what decision-making processes they must use, and how corporate financial reporting systems are structured and their accuracy verified.

In addition, institutional investors and their advisors are advancing an evolving set of "best practices" governance recommendations that represent standards beyond the legal minimum.

Compared to governance practices prior to 2000, there is now more active oversight of corporate management by the board and by committees of the board. On some matters, such as the authority to engage the company's auditors, decisions have been taken out of management's hands entirely.

As boards actively monitor executive performance, the role of independent, non-employee directors has necessarily expanded. At the same time, independent, non-employee directors do not control the information or other resources of the corporation, including inside and outside counsel who are typically engaged by management.

Thus, one challenge for independent directors is to ensure that they have adequate information and resources for the jobs they are performing.

Moreover, boards and independent directors must deal with the issues raised by shareholder pressure to provide an increased voice in governance to investors and by the enforcement practices of the Securities and Exchange Commission ("SEC").

This guidebook addresses legal and governance issues from the perspective of the independent director, with the goal of helping independent directors navigate this new environment. Topics covered in this guidebook include:

- what the independent director should know, individually and from the company's perspective, to ensure his or her compliance with the law and to reduce his or her exposure to personal liability;

- individual securities law compliance actions;

- the roles and actions of key committees of the board;

- board evaluation processes; and

- the issues regarding conflicts of interest, litigation, investigations, and similar situations in which the independent director becomes a critical corporate decision maker.

This text is intended to be accessible to attorney and non-attorney readers, and the accompanying CD source book provides readers with links to full text statutory, regulatory, administrative, and case material underlying the text. Sample committee charters and self-evaluation materials are included to provide a point of reference for corporate boards and advisors. The book also includes a checklist on factors to determine the independence of a director.

2. What is Governance Good For?

Corporate governance describes a process but does not guarantee a result.

A board of directors with immaculate corporate governance processes might still make bad business decisions, and a board with weak governance processes might make excellent decisions.

Directors are not guarantors of the successful outcome of their business decisions. Such a burden would prevent anyone from serving on a board. Courts recognize this and do not second-guess business decisions by boards, if those decisions have been made with due care and without a conflict of interest.

The existence of good corporate governance practices permits members of a board to demonstrate that their decisions were made without the taint of real or perceived personal interest, with appropriate attention to the issues at hand and to the best interests of the shareholders.

The regulatory scheme under SOX and Dodd-Frank assumes that corporate managers require active oversight by individuals who are independent of management. The independence of directors, and of professional advisors such as accountants, attorneys, and financial advisors, is intended to prevent certain types of management abuses of corporate resources.

In addition, some commentators have observed that the independent review of key management decisions also may reduce the effect of potentially negative decision-making biases. For example, a management considering an acquisition might be so focused on the potential benefits that it dismisses potential negative elements (a "wishful thinking" bias). A management that has seen a strategy play out unhappily might be reluctant to admit the loss, redeploy resources, and move on (a "loss aversion" bias). Independent directors who can review decisions with a cold eye may have a better opportunity to overcome wishful thinking and loss aversion influences on decision making.

3. Issues for Independent Directors

This guide is intended to provide independent directors and their advisors with a general understanding of the laws and issues affecting corporations and directors. From this awareness, directors can be better positioned to recognize significant issues as they arise or to inquire into whether issues exist.

The accompanying CD source book is intended to provide significant additional detail that is not covered in the main text.

Because the guide contains broad descriptions of the duties of independent directors, it is not intended as legal advice. Moreover, the discussion is aimed primarily at U.S.-based operating companies and not foreign private issuers, asset-backed securities issuers, or mutual funds. Special situations, such as corporations emerging from bankruptcy or near insolvency, corporations conducting registered offerings of securities, change of control situations, or shareholder derivative litigation, also would require a level of detailed discussion that is beyond the scope of this guide.

Set out below are summaries of the topics contained herein.

A. The Definition of Independence

SOX and Dodd-Frank emphasize the importance of independent directors.

The underlying assumption is that, in the absence of oversight, management will be tempted to use corporate resources in its own self-interest. The board acts as a check on management, and it will perform its role more effectively if its members are not part of management or financially beholden in some way to management.

When a corporation provides direct financial benefits to a director, other than fees paid for service as a director, there is the potential for such benefits to compromise the director's judgment or the director's willingness to oppose management if management controls the benefits the director will receive.

The term "independent director," which means a director who does not have employment, family, or other significant economic or personal connections to the corporation other than serving as a director, is often used interchangeably with the term "disinterested director," which means a director who, for purposes of voting on a specific transaction or arrangement with the corporation, does not have an economic or personal interest in that transaction or arrangement.

The two terms overlap substantially, but they are not identical. Independent directors will be "disinterested directors," almost as a matter of definition, but not all disinterested directors will be independent. For example, it would be possible for the CEO, as a non-independent director, to be a "disinterested director" and to vote on a transaction in which another director had a financial or personal interest.

The basic definition of "independence" for directors is derived from SOX, Dodd-Frank, SEC rule making, and the listing requirements for the New York Stock Exchange ("NYSE") and NASDAQ. In some circumstances, however, such as participation on the audit committee or the compensation committee, or participation in a special litigation committee, independent directors have to meet additional independence requirements.

Chapter II.1 discusses director independence requirements.

B. Fiduciary Duty and Director Liability

Fiduciary duties of directors are governed by state law. The basic duties of due care (the requirement that directors make considered decisions) and loyalty (the requirement that directors not allow self-interest to taint the decision-making process) are simple to state. Application of those standards to individual situations, however, can be complex.

The use of good corporate governance processes gives directors the legal protection of the "business judgment rule" if their decisions are challenged.

In addition to the duties of due care and loyalty, there are sometimes judicial references to additional director duties, such as a duty of disclosure when shareholders are asked to make decisions affecting the corporation and a duty of good faith in order for a director to be able to receive indemnification from the corporation.

These topics are discussed in Chapter II.2.

C. *Governance Laws, Rules, and Recommendations*

Beyond the requirements set by law, the behavior of directors is also governed by other rules established inside and outside the corporation. Committee charters and corporate policies are not laws, although in some cases they are required by law, and directors need to abide by their provisions. The listing requirements of the market on which the corporation's stock trades are contractual requirements that bind the corporation and require specific behavior by the directors as well.

Finally, there is an ongoing discussion by institutional investors, advisors to institutional investors, and various other members of the business community about the best practices for corporation governance. None of those recommendations is a law or a rule, and yet they may be evidence of a standard of conduct that directors should consider when taking corporate actions.

These topics are covered in Chapter II.3.

D. *Shareholders and Governance*

Shareholders have the power to elect the board of directors.

Shareholders generally are not empowered to initiate significant corporate events, but key corporate decisions require shareholder approval. These include mergers or acquisitions, where the corporation would cease its independent existence or where significant equity would be issued; dissolution of the corporation; and amendments to corporate governing instruments.

While corporate law allocates and balances risks, benefits, and decision-making authority among management, the board, and shareholders, the economic, legal, and decision-making balances have undergone continuous evolution. During the 2000s the rate of change was particularly dramatic, driven by multiple factors, including major market declines following the "dot.com" bubble, the 9/11 attacks, and the financial crisis of 2007-2008, and the revelation of massive corporate misconduct at companies like Enron and Worldcom preceding the adoption of SOX.

Shareholders have been increasingly vocal on various governance issues, such as whether a majority vote should be required for the election of directors, participation in the director nomination process, and the way in which shareholder concerns are communicated to the board between shareholder meetings.

In 2010, the development of the "proxy access" rules by the SEC enhanced the traditional state law right of shareholders to provide nominations for board candidacies by permitting qualified shareholders to include information on their nominees in the company's proxy materials.

These topics are covered in Chapter II.4.

E. Committees

SOX set out in exhaustive detail the requirements for the audit committee. Dodd-Frank and SEC rule making have also established significant requirements for the compensation committee. Under SEC rules, there are also detailed requirements regarding operation of the nominating committee.

These core committees bear significant responsibility for corporate decision making. In all cases, these committees must be comprised of independent directors.

The board also may want to form other committees for specialized purposes or to consider specific transactions.

Key management decisions, such as CEO succession and executive compensation, are initially handled at the committee level, and such decisions can have far-reaching impacts on the corporation.

The use of committees by the board is discussed in Chapter III.1. Chapters III.2, III.3, and III.4 are devoted to the Audit Committee, the Compensation Committee, and the Nominating Committee, respectively.

F. SEC Enforcement

The SEC received expanded enforcement authority under SOX. It has levied substantial fines against companies for various securities law violations and increased the number of lifetime bans it has imposed on "unfit" persons serving as officers or directors of public companies.

In addition, the SEC has increasingly targeted individual directors and their corporate advisors for enforcement actions on the grounds that they are the "gatekeepers" who are responsible for effective corporate disclosure. The list of "gatekeepers" includes independent directors, attorneys, accountants, securities analysts, and credit rating agencies.

These enforcement procedures are one more element in the evolving corporate governance environment.

These topics are covered in Chapter IV.1.

G. Trading in Corporate Securities

Trading in corporate securities by corporate directors and officers is not automatically illegal, but it can be complex, and it is subject to significant regulation.

Directors and other corporate insiders are exposed to material information about the corporation in advance of its disclosure to the investing public. Securities laws impose restrictions on their ability to trade in corporate securities prior to the general release of such information and limit their ability to use and disclose this information for their own benefit.

A significant body of law developed around the interpretation of the insider trading prohibitions under SEC Rule 10b-5, including the definition of what information about a corporation is "material."

The determination of what information is material for securities law purposes is important not only for securities trading by directors but also for other securities law disclosure questions.

In addition to the limitations on insider trading under Rule 10b-5, directors must execute certain SEC filings in connection with their securities trades. Corporations also develop internal policies that are intended to prevent insider trading, and these policies also affect trading by directors. Under Dodd-Frank, companies must disclose whether employees and directors are permitted to "hedge" potential losses in corporate shares they hold or have been granted as compensation.

These topics are covered in Chapter IV.2.

4. Corporate Governance in Context

A. Ownership, Control, and the "Agency" Issue

The debate over corporate governance is not new and has its roots in the corporation's inherent division of the roles of owners and managers.

Unlike sole proprietorships, partnerships, or family businesses, where the owners tend to be the same people as the managers and the operators, corporations are owned by a dispersed set of investors, and managed and operated by a professional management group.

This gives rise to what is generally called the "agency" issue: the risk that the shareholders' agents, the corporate managers who have control over the corporate resources on a day-in, day-out basis, will be tempted to use those resources for their own gratification, rather than in the best interests of the investors, who are the owners of the corporation.

Contributing to this risk is the economic reality that even though investors acting together might obtain better returns from stronger monitoring of management, each investor has a relatively small stake in the corporation, and the cost to a single investor of monitoring management would likely outweigh that investor's increased return.

Given these circumstances, the board of directors is the obvious candidate to act as a source for control over management on behalf of the shareholders.

However, corporate management historically has had a significant hand in selecting the board. A board member who was supposed to hold management accountable for its operation of the business was at the same time beholden to management for the board position and in many cases for other business from the corporation as well.

To some degree, the concentration of shareholder wealth in the hands of institutional investors, the development of the proxy advisory and governance industry, changes in corporate governance law and practices, and the ability of investors to communicate have created greater ability in shareholders to address potential management abuses directly.

B. Corporate Governance Since 1980

The wave of corporate takeovers in the 1980s helped generate an increased focus on corporate governance issues. The justification for many corporate takeovers at that time was that corporate management was inefficient or complacent and not doing enough to create value for the shareholders, and that new ownership and management would do better.

In response, corporations and their advisors developed various defense strategies, such as the "poison pill" plans (or shareholder rights plans) that made takeovers more expensive, or payment of "greenmail" to repurchase shares from would-be raiders.

Institutional investors, such as the California Public Employees' Retirement System ("CalPERS"), reacted to the wave of takeovers and defensive measures by developing and promoting agendas to improve corporate governance, focusing on the board of directors' oversight of management and the independence of directors as means to improve corporate performance.

By the 1990s, the questions of corporate governance were receiving interest from business school academics and from the business community as well, culminating in the 1999 Blue Ribbon Committee on Improving the Effectiveness of Corporate Audit Committees (the "Blue Ribbon Committee"). The Blue Ribbon Committee consisted of leading executives and the heads of the NYSE and National Association of Securities Dealers ("NASD," now known as Financial Industry Regulatory Authority ("FINRA")).

The Blue Ribbon Committee was formed in response to concerns about the independence and adequacy of the oversight of the corporate audit process raised by then SEC Chairman Arthur Levitt. Its report recommended that the audit committee be comprised of independent directors, be independent from management, and act to ensure that the auditors were independent from management as well.

When Enron collapsed two years later as its fraudulent accounting was exposed, the Blue Ribbon Committee proposals were included in the congressional legislative response that ultimately became SOX, which was signed into law in 2002.

Notwithstanding the significant emphasis on financial statement accuracy and corporate governance under SOX, the financial crisis of the late 2000s generated massive economic damage, massive government economic intervention, and additional concern over the corporate processes used to compensate executives, assess risk, and elect directors.

The Dodd-Frank bill, adopted in 2010, provided that shareholders would be entitled to make non-binding votes on executive compensation, mandated certain compensation committee processes, and provided the SEC with authority to allow shareholders to include information on their own director nominations in the company proxy statement.

C. *Corporate Governance and State Law*

Corporations are created under state law, not federal law. State corporate law defines the duties of directors, but the general principle that directors have a fiduciary duty to act in the best interest of shareholders is consistent from state to state.

Matters such as when shareholders may, or are required to, vote on corporate transactions, or the qualification and selection of directors, are governed by state laws that are substantially similar from state to state but vary in detail depending on the state in which the corporation is formed.

The federal securities laws were first enacted in the 1930s and governed the disclosures required by corporations offering and selling securities, as well as certain corporations whose shares were traded on national trading markets. The SEC administers the securities laws and prepares rules implementing them.

Some of the SEC's disclosure requirements (such as proxy disclosures by the compensation committee) effectively required corporations to undertake specific actions, but prior to the adoption of SOX, the SEC did not historically have the authority to regulate internal corporate governance processes, which continued to be a matter of state law.

With SOX, and again with Dodd-Frank, Congress has effectively federalized certain elements of corporate governance for publicly traded corporations, particularly with respect to the organization and operation of the audit committee and the process by which shareholders can nominate candidates for election to the board.

Even though SOX was applicable only to publicly traded corporations, it affected private corporations and nonprofit organizations as well. The SOX standards have been incorporated into some state law requirements governing nonprofit organizations, for example.

Private corporations that target either an initial public offering or acquisition as "exit" strategies to achieve their investors' goals need to consider whether they are ready for the new public company environment or have enough structure in place to make a good "fit" for a public company. A potential target company that did not have adequate internal financial controls, for example, could find its valuation reduced because a public company acquirer would have to make expenditures to bring it up to SOX standards.

Measuring Director Independence

1. Introduction

Independence is a simple concept with complicated implementation.

Regulators and securities exchanges have sought to surround corporate managements with individuals both inside and outside the corporation who are in a position to influence management's decisions and actions, but who are independent of management and in a position to act as a check on management.[1]

---

1. SOX and Dodd-Frank also attempt to ensure the independence of action by outside professionals such as auditors (SOX 201 et. seq.), attorneys (SOX 307), and compensation advisors (Dodd-Frank 952). As discussed in Chapter 1, regulation of outside advisers echoes some of the concerns the SEC has articulated from time to time in enforcement actions against corporate "gatekeepers"—individuals who, by virtue of their positions in the corporate decision-making and disclosure process, stand in a position to act on behalf of investors.

For securities law purposes, the definition of "independence" is derived in part from SOX, in part from Dodd-Frank, in part from SEC regulations, and substantially from the rules of the NYSE and NASDAQ.

Federal law requires that directors on the audit committee and most compensation committees be independent,[2] but does not dictate the independence of the rest of the board of directors or committees. NASDAQ and the NYSE require that publicly traded companies listed on those exchanges have independent directors review executive compensation and director nominations.[3] The SEC requires that companies identify their independent directors in the annual proxy statement, and set out the basis on which the independence was determined.[4] TARP recipients must establish a compensation committee comprised solely of independent directors.[5]

This chapter discusses the various factors that can influence whether a director is "independent" under the definitions used in SOX, Dodd-Frank, TARP and its successor statutes, the SEC rules, the NYSE and NASDAQ rules, or other applicable legal standards.

Federal law provides very limited guidance regarding the definition of an "independent" director. SOX required that, for purposes of participation in the audit committee, a director "may not, other than in his or her capacity as a member of the audit committee, the board of directors, or any other board committee (i) accept any consulting, advisory, or other compensatory fee from the issuer; or (ii) be an affiliated person of the issuer or any subsidiary thereof."[6] For most TARP recipients, the applicable exchange definition of independence will be used for compensation committee members.[7] Dodd-Frank specifies that the independence of compensation committee members shall be established according to relevant factors including "any consulting, advisory, or other compensatory fee" paid to

---

2. See SOX 301; Dodd-Frank 952.

3. See NYSE Rule 303A and NASDAQ Rule 5606.

4. SEC Regulation S-K, Item 407(a).

5. Interim Final Rule § 30.4 (Q-4) allows TARP recipients that have no securities registered pursuant to the Exchange Act and have received $25 million or less in financial assistance to either establish a compensation committee of independent directors or to delegate, as appropriate, to the board of directors the duties of the compensation committee. "Independent directors" are directors whose independence is determined in accordance with SEC Regulation S-K, Item 407(a).

6. SOX 301.

7. Interim Final Rule § 30.4 (Q-4). "Independent directors" are directors whose independence is determined in accordance with SEC Regulation S-K, Item 407(a).

a director and whether the director is an affiliate of the company or its related companies.[8]

Director independence definitions have largely been developed by the NYSE and NASDAQ rather than by the SEC. The SEC specifies minimum elements of the definition of independence for audit committee purposes.[9] The definitions of independence by each of the exchanges are substantially similar but vary in some details, as discussed in this chapter.

While it is not the primary arbiter of director independence, the SEC requires companies to make proxy statement disclosures regarding director independence. Companies must disclose:

- which directors and director nominees are determined to be "independent" using exchange listing standards (for companies whose shares are exchange traded) or other independence definitions;

- a description of transactions, relationships, and arrangements that the board considered in determining if the independence standards were met; and

- whether any audit, nominating, or compensation committee members are not independent.[10]

In addition to the definitions of "independence" for securities law purposes, directors must consider the related—but not identical— independence requirements that arise in the context of executive compensation transactions and special litigation committees, and the requirements for board approval of related party transactions aimed at preventing shareholders from being harmed by conflicts of interest.

2. Independence Factors

The statutory discussion of independence of directors under SOX and Dodd-Frank is limited to identifying whether the director is an "affiliate" of the company or has accepted any "consulting, advisory, or other compensatory fee." However, the consideration of independence is much more complex.

---

8.   Dodd-Frank 952.

9.   SEC Rule 10A-3.

10. SEC Regulation S-K, Item 407.

In adopting rules relating to the independence of directors, the NYSE and NASDAQ articulated basic principles relating to independence and require that the board determine the independence of its members.

Under the NYSE rules, "No director qualifies as 'independent' unless the board of directors affirmatively determines that the director has no material relationship with the listed company (either directly or as a partner, shareholder or officer of an organization that has a relationship with the company)." The NYSE requires that the board of directors affirmatively determine that an independent director has "no material relationship with the company (either directly or as a partner, shareholder or officer of an organization that has a relationship with the company)."[11]

The NYSE's general rule is that the board is responsible for determining the independence of a director based on the materiality of a relationship that could potentially pose a conflict of interest. The NYSE also sets out several specific rules on when a director cannot be considered independent. The NYSE guidance is that companies should "broadly consider all relevant facts and circumstances" in determining whether a director's relationship compromises independence, noting that it is "not possible to anticipate, or explicitly to provide for, all circumstances that might signal potential conflicts of interest, or that might bear on the materiality of a director's relationship" to a company.[12]

In considering the relevant facts and circumstances, the NYSE rules specify that "Material relationships can include commercial, industrial, banking, consulting, legal, accounting, charitable and familial relationships, among others." At the same time, the NYSE rules provide that "ownership of even a significant amount of stock, by itself, [is not] a bar to an independence finding." Although the NYSE rule on independence requires the board to determine the materiality of the director's relationships with the company, with respect to shareholding, the NYSE states that "the concern is independence from management."[13]

NASDAQ defines the term "independent director" to mean "a person other than an Executive Officer or employee of the Company or any other individual having a relationship which, in the opinion of the Company's board of directors, would interfere with the exercise of independent judgment in carrying out the responsibilities of a director."[14] For purposes of the

---

11. NYSE Rule 303A.02(a).
12. NYSE Rule 303A.02(a) Commentary.
13. NYSE Rule 303A.02(a) Commentary.
14. NASDAQ Rule 5605(a)(2).

NASDAQ rules, the term "Company" includes any parent or consolidated subsidiary.

If a director serves as an executive officer on an interim basis, the director will be nonindependent during the period of such service under both the NYSE and NASDAQ rules. As discussed below, the director would be able to resume independent status once the interim executive service ended (provided, in the case of NASDAQ, that the interim service did not last longer than one year).[15]

The commentary to the NASDAQ's independence rule states that the board has a responsibility to make an affirmative determination that no relationships exist that would impair a director's independence.[16]

While both NYSE and NASDAQ provide broader "subjective" determinations by a board regarding an individual director's independence, company's must be mindful of the specific nonindependence factors identified by each exchange (described below). For purposes of "proxy access" a shareholder nominee must meet any objective independence requirements of the company's exchange, as well as any state or federal eligibility requirements.[17]

A. Compensation or Employment by the Company

Both the NYSE and NASDAQ impose a three-year "look back" standard in reviewing whether an employment or compensation relationship with the company affects a director's independence.

The NYSE rules provide that a director who is an employee of the company, or whose immediate family member is an executive officer of the company, is not independent until three years after the end of such employment relationship.[18] However, the commentary to the NYSE rules notes that employment as interim chairman, CEO, or other executive officer does not operate automatically to disqualify a director from being considered independent following that employment.[19]

The NYSE also sets a $120,000 threshold for nonemployment compensation that renders a director not independent. This limitation is triggered if a director or an immediate family member receives more

---

15. See NYSE 303.02(b)(i) Commentary; NASDAQ IM-5605 –Definition of Independence –Rule 5605 (a)(2).
16. NASDAQ IM-5605 –Definition of Independence –Rule 5605 (a)(2).
17. SEC Rule 14a-11(c).
18. NYSE Rule 303A.02(b)(i).
19. NYSE Rule 303A.02(b)(i) Commentary.

than $120,000 per year in direct compensation from the company, other than director fees, pension, or other forms of deferred compensation for prior service (provided the compensation is not contingent on continued service). This rule also has a three-year "look back" for the director personally, and looks only to the most current year with respect to the director's family members. In addition, the limitation will not be triggered if a director's family member is an employee of the company, but not an executive officer.[20]

The NASDAQ rules provide that a director who is, or at any time during the past three years was, employed by the company or by any parent or subsidiary of the company is not independent,[21] nor will a director be independent if a family member served as an executive officer of the company or any parent or subsidiary.[22] NASDAQ does not automatically disqualify a director from being independent as a result of prior service as an interim executive, provided the interim position does not exceed one year. However, in those circumstances the board is still required to consider whether compensation or other factors arising from the interim employment would interfere with the director's exercise of independent judgment.[23]

NASDAQ sets a $120,000 threshold for nonemployment compensation to a director or family member that disqualifies a director from being independent, with a three-year "look back." However, NASDAQ excludes the following payments from that calculation:

- director fees;

- compensation paid to a family member who is a nonexecutive employee of the company or a parent or subsidiary; and

- benefits under a tax-qualified retirement plan, or nondiscretionary compensation.[24]

B. Relationship to Auditor

The NYSE rules prohibit a director from being independent based on relationships to the company's internal or external auditor (a "company

---

20. NYSE Rule 303A.02(b)(ii).
21. NASDAQ Rule 5605(a)(2)(A).
22. NASDAQ Rule 5605(a)(2)(C).
23. NASDAQ IM-5605 – Definition of Independence – Rule 5605(a)(2).
24. NASDAQ Rule 5605(a)(2)(B)(i)-(iii).

auditor"). A director will not be independent if the director is a current partner or employee of a company auditor, or has an immediate family member who is a current partner of a company auditor or who is a current employee of a company auditor and personally works on the company's audit. In addition, a director will not be independent if the director or an immediate family member was, within the last three years, a partner or employee of a company auditor and personally worked on the listed company's audit during that period.[25]

NASDAQ provides that a director (or family member) who is a current partner of the company's outside auditor is not independent. In addition, if a director (or family member) was a partner or employee in the company's outside audit firm and worked on the company's audit in the prior three years, that director will not be independent until the end of the three-year "look back" period.[26]

C. Compensation Committee Interlocks

Under the NYSE and NASDAQ rules, a director is not independent if that director, or an immediate family member, is employed as an executive officer of another company where any of the company's present executives serve on the other company's compensation committee until three years after the end of such service or the employment relationship.[27]

The SEC requires that a public company must disclose in its proxy statements whether any of its executives serves as a director for another company, if (i) that company in turn has an executive who serves on the public company's board, and (ii) any of those individuals sits on either company's compensation committee.[28]

D. Family Relationships

Many of the NASDAQ and NYSE independence disqualifications apply if either the director or a family member of the director has the disqualifying relationship. The NYSE and NASDAQ definitions of family both cover essentially the same group of persons, although not with identical definitional language.

---

25. NYSE Rule 303A.02(b)(iii)(A).
26. NASDAQ Rule 5605(a)(2)(F).
27. NYSE Rule 303A.02(b)(iv); NASDAQ Rule 5605(a)(2)(E).
28. SEC Regulation S-K, Item 407(e)(4).

The NYSE rules use the term "immediate family member," which "includes a person's spouse, parents, children, siblings, mothers and fathers-in-law, sons and daughters-in-law, brothers and sisters-in-law, and anyone (other than domestic employees) who shares such person's home." For purposes of applying the "look back" provisions of the NYSE rules, the family relationship will not be attributed to individuals who have died or become incapacitated, or ceased to be family members for legal purposes as a result of legal separation or divorce.[29]

NASDAQ rules use the term "family member," which is defined to mean a person's "spouse, parents, children and siblings, whether by blood, marriage or adoption, or anyone residing in such person's home."[30]

E. Significant Business Relationship

A business relationship between a director and the company, or between the company and another company for which the director is an executive or director, can trigger an independence disqualification under the NYSE and NASDAQ rules.

Under the NYSE rules, a corporate director is not independent if that director (or an immediate family member) is an executive officer of, or if the director is a current employee of, a company that pays, or is paid by, the corporation above a threshold amount. The restriction is triggered by payments for property or services in an amount which, in any single fiscal year, exceeds the greater of $1 million, or 2% of the other company's consolidated gross revenues. This rule also has a three-year "look back" period.[31]

NASDAQ provides that a director will not be independent if that director is a partner in, a controlling shareholder of, or an executive officer of, any organization that either received or made payments for property or services to the corporation, if those payments during any of the past three fiscal years exceed 5% of the recipient's consolidated gross revenues for that year, or $200,000, whichever is more. The rule excludes from that calculation:

- payments arising solely from investments in the company's securities or

---

29. NYSE Rule 303A.02(b) Commentary.
30. NASDAQ Rule 5605(a)(2).
31. NYSE Rule 303A.02(b)(v).

- payments under nondiscretionary charitable contribution matching programs.[32]

NASDAQ also notes that when an attorney acts as a director, any partner in a law firm that receives payments from the company would be ineligible to serve on the audit committee. An attorney could serve as counsel to the company and as an independent director, if the legal fees paid by the company do not exceed $120,000 for an attorney in a sole proprietorship or the "5% of gross revenues/$200,000" test if the attorney was in a law firm.[33]

F. Charity Relationship

Both the NYSE and NASDAQ recognize that charitable and nonprofit relationships, like significant business relationships, have the potential to affect the independence of a director, but the two exchanges provide different approaches to determining independence in the charity context.

NYSE expressly does not apply the same test to charitable relationships as it does to business relationships for purposes of determining director independence. "Contributions to tax exempt organizations shall not be considered payments for purposes [of the rules on payment relationships]" but the company is required to disclose such contributions through its website or proxy statement, if "within the preceding three years, contributions in any single fiscal year from the listed company to the organization exceeded the greater of $1 million, or 2% of such tax exempt organization's consolidated gross revenues" and an independent director of the company served as an executive officer of that organization.[34]

While there is not an automatic disqualification from independence under the NYSE rules for a director whose charity receives a contribution from the company, there is still a requirement that the board consider the materiality of any such relationship according to the NYSE's mandate that the board evaluate a director's independence.[35]

NASDAQ provides for an automatic disqualification from independence in the context of a charitable organization "if the company makes payments to the charity in excess of the greater of 5% of the charity's revenues or $200,000" and further recommends that companies consider

---

32. NASDAQ Rule 5605(a)(2)(D)(i)-(ii).
33. NASDAQ IM-5605 –Definition of Independence –Rule 5605 (a)(2)(B).
34. NYSE Rule 303A.02(b)(v) Commentary.
35. NYSE Rule 303A.02(b)(v) Commentary.

other situations where a director [or family member] and the company each have a relationship with the same charity when assessing director independence.[36]

G. Affiliated Person

Under the SOX 301 definition of independence, an "affiliated person" of the company or its subsidiaries is not independent.[37] Dodd-Frank requires that independence be evaluated based on whether a director is "affiliated with an issuer, a subsidiary of an issuer, or an affiliate of a subsidiary of an issuer."[38]

In its rulemaking to implement SOX 301, the SEC defined "affiliate" consistently with the affiliation definition used by the SEC for other purposes under the securities laws,[39] focusing on the control relationship of the parties involved: "The term 'affiliate' of, or a person 'affiliated' with, a specific person, means a person that directly, or indirectly through one or more intermediaries, controls, or is controlled by, or is under common control with, the person specified."[40]

The SEC further provided guidance on how to determine what constitutes control for purposes of the definition. "The term 'control' (including the terms 'controlling,' 'controlled by' and under 'common control with') means the possession, direct or indirect, of the power to direct or cause the direction of the management and policies of a person, whether through the ownership of voting securities, by contract, or otherwise."[41]

Control is not presumed on the basis of the size of shareholdings alone.

> .....A person will be deemed not to be in control of a specified person . . . if the person (1) Is not the beneficial owner, directly or indirectly, of more than 10% of any class of voting equity securities of the specified person; and (2) Is not an executive officer of the specified person.[42]

---

36. NASDAQ IM-5605 –Definition of Independence –Rule 5605 (a)(2).
37. SOX 301.
38. Dodd-Frank 952.
39. See, e.g., SEC Rule 144.
40. SEC Rule 10A-3(e)(1)(i).
41. SEC Rule 10A-3(e)(4).
42. SEC Rule 10A-3(e)(1)(ii)(A)(1)-(2).

The SEC noted that its creation of the 10% "safe harbor" definition for affiliate status "does not create a presumption in any way that a person exceeding [the 10 %] ownership requirement . . . controls or is otherwise an affiliate," so a party could hold more than a 10% ownership stake and, depending upon the facts and circumstances, nonetheless be deemed not to be an affiliate.[43]

This approach is consistent with the approach taken by both the NYSE and NASDAQ, which take the position that ownership of a significant amount of stock is not, by itself, enough to disqualify a director from being independent.[44]

The SEC sets out specific additions to the definition of "affiliate" to include those cases in which a person is:

- an executive officer of an affiliate;
- a director who also is an employee of an affiliate;
- a general partner of an affiliate; and
- a managing member of an affiliate.[45]

The question of the independence of those directors who represent significant shareholders is a particularly critical question for the venture capital ("VC") investors whose portfolio companies conduct a public offering. The VC investors will have typically accumulated a significant percentage of ownership stake in a corporation by supplying necessary development capital in the early stages of the business, and may retain significant share ownership after the corporation becomes publicly traded.

3. Other Independence Issues

A. Audit Committee Qualifications

The SEC independence requirements for members of the audit committee (the "SEC Rule 10A-3 requirements") are that a director not be an affiliate of the company, and that the director not accept "directly or indirectly any consulting, advisory, or other compensatory fee...[other than] fixed

---

43. SEC Rule 10A-3(e)(1)(ii)(B).
44. NYSE Rule 303A.02(a) Commentary; NASDAQ IM-5605 –Definition of Independence –Rule 5605 (a)(2).
45. SEC Rule 10A-3(e)(1)(iii)(A)-(D).

amounts of compensation under a retirement plan (including deferred compensation) for prior service" with the company. If retirement plan or deferred compensation amounts are contingent on continued service, a director will not be independent.[46]

The NYSE requires that a director serving on an audit committee meet all of the NYSE independence requirements[47] and also the SEC Rule 10A-3 requirements.[48]

In addition, under the NYSE rules, the board must make a determination that a director's ability to serve effectively on the audit committee is not impaired if that individual is serving as a member of more than three public company audit committees. Disclosure of that determination must be made on the company's website or in the proxy statement.[49]

NASDAQ requires that a director serving on an audit committee meet all NASDAQ independence requirements, the SEC Rule 10A-3 requirements, and must not have participated in preparing the company's financial statements in any of the prior three years.[50] In addition, the audit committee member must disclose in the proxy statement if the director is a more than 10% shareholder.[51]

NASDAQ also permits a director who might otherwise fail the NASDAQ independence standards, but who meets the SEC Rule 10A-3 requirements, to be appointed to the audit committee if that director (or a family member) is not a current officer or employee of the company and "if the board, under exceptional and limited circumstances, determines that membership on the committee by the individual is required by the best interests of the company and its shareholders, and the board discloses, in the next annual proxy statement ... the nature of the relationship and the reasons for that determination. A member appointed under this exception may not serve longer than two years and may not chair the audit committee."[52]

---

46. SEC Rule 10A-3(b)(ii).
47. NYSE Rule 303A.07.
48. NYSE Rule 303A.06.
49. NYSE Rule 303A.07 Commentary.
50. NASDAQ Rule 5605(c)(2)(A).
51. NASDAQ IM-5605 –Definition of Independence –Rule 5605 (a)(2).
52. NASDAQ Rule 5605(c)(2)(B).

B. Compensation Committee Qualifications

Under Dodd-Frank, the securities exchanges and NASDAQ must require companies to have an independent compensation committee established in accordance with SEC rules, as a condition of listing securities for trading.[53] TARP recipients and NYSE-listed companies must have compensation committees and NASDAQ requires that independent directors oversee executive compensation.

The NYSE requires its listed companies to conduct executive compensation review through a compensation committee comprised entirely of independent directors.[54] Prior to passage of Dodd-Frank, NASDAQ did not require formation of a separate compensation committee, but required that executive compensation decisions be made only by independent directors.[55] The SEC requires that any company that does not have a compensation committee make disclosures in its proxy statement respecting the basis of the decision not to handle executive compensation through a separate committee of the board.[56]

Neither NYSE nor NASDAQ imposes additional or different independence requirements on directors who serve on compensation committees. However, there are two types of transactions typically handled by compensation committees—the provision of share-based compensation (such as stock options) to officers and directors, and the tax deductibility of executive compensation in excess of $1 million—for which director independence is determined using standards not set by NYSE or NASDAQ. For TARP recipients, share-based compensation and tax-deductible executive compensation are subject to special, more stringent rules than those applied to other companies.[57]

Because these requirements are not quite the same as the other independence requirements, companies should not assume that an independent director automatically will meet them.

Under SEC rules relating to share-based compensation, the company and the officers and directors can avoid the "short swing" profits liability imposed under Section 16 of the Exchange Act (See Chapter III.3) if the

---

53. Dodd-Frank 952.
54. NYSE Rule 303A.05(a).
55. NASDAQ Rule 5605(d).
56. SEC Regulation S-K, Item 407(e).
57. See discussion in Chapter III.3 regarding TARP recipient compensation limitations, and Interim Final Rule.

transactions are approved by "non-employee directors" under Exchange Act Rule 16b-3(b)(3).

To be a "non-employee director" the director must not:

• currently be an officer or employee of the company;

• receive $120,000 or more in any year in a transaction or relationship with the company[58]

The exemptions under Rule 16b-3 also could be obtained by having the transaction approved by the full board of directors or a majority of the shareholders.

In order for executive compensation in excess of $1 million per year to be deducible for tax purposes, the compensation must be established by a compensation committee consisting of "outside directors." In most circumstances, an NYSE or NASDAQ "independent director" also will qualify as an "outside director" for purposes of the tax laws. However, for purposes of the tax laws, an "outside director" must never have served as an officer of the corporation.[59]

C. Nominating Committees

As with compensation committees, the federal securities laws do not require a public company to have a nominating committee, but NYSE and NASDAQ require that independent directors oversee the director nomination process.

The NYSE requires its listed companies to conduct nominations through a nomination committee consisting entirely of independent directors.[60] NASDAQ does not require formation of a separate nominating committee, but requires that the nominating decisions be made only by independent directors.[61] The SEC requires that any company that does not have a nominating committee make disclosures in its proxy statement respecting the basis of the decision not to handle nominations through a separate committee of the board.[62]

There are no additional or different independence requirements under the NYSE or NASDAQ rules for directors who serve on a nominating committee or serve the nominating function on the board. However, even

---

58. SEC Rule 16b-3; See SEC Regulation S-K Item 404(a).
59. Internal Revenue Code Sec. 162(m).
60. NYSE Rule 303A.04(a).
61. NASDAQ Rule 5605(e).
62. SEC Regulation S-K, Item 407(c)(2).

though NYSE and NASDAQ permit a board to determine that a director with ties to a significant shareholder is independent, a board dealing with a shareholder that controls significant voting power in an election of directors should weigh that factor in its independence decision.

D. Related Party Transactions

As discussed in greater detail in Chapter II.2, a director who has a direct or indirect financial or personal interest in a matter relating to the corporation or its assets has a potential conflict of interest. In those circumstances, the fiduciary duties of the "interested director" require that director to disclose the material facts of the transaction and the director's interest in such transaction to the board, and obtain approval from either "disinterested" directors or the shareholders.

A "disinterested" director for purposes of a particular transaction would not necessarily be the same as an "independent" director. A transaction involving a nonemployee director, for example, could require approval by "disinterested" directors, including the company's CEO, who would not be an independent director.

In addition to considerations of the impact on director independence, such transactions also may trigger reporting requirements under the securities laws or waivers of the corporate code of ethics. The board will also have to consider its fiduciary duties in dealing with such issues. These matters are addressed in Chapter II.2.

Under the SEC proxy rules, companies must disclose their policies and procedures regarding approval of related party transactions. Such descriptions must address the types of transactions covered by the policies, the standards the company uses to review such transactions, whether the policies are written (or if not, how they are evidenced), and which members of the board are responsible for review of the transaction.[63]

The company's auditors may also subject related party transactions to additional scrutiny, inasmuch as transactions "involving related parties cannot be presumed to be carried out on an arm's-length basis, as the requisite conditions of competitive, free-market dealings may not exist."[64]

---

63. SEC Regulation S-K, Item 404(b)(1).
64. Statement of Financial Accounting Standards No. 57 (1982).

E. Social Relationships

In recent years, Delaware courts have been asked to consider cases in which the independence of directors as a state fiduciary law matter was challenged on the grounds that social relationships among directors and executives impaired independence of judgment.

One such case, involving Martha Stewart and her company, involved claims that certain nonmanagement directors of the company were "beholden" to Ms. Stewart because of their personal friendships with her and because she could, as controlling shareholder of the company, remove them from office.

While a set of facts could conceivably exist in which social relationships impaired director independence, the court noted: "Allegations of a mere personal friendship or a mere outside business relationship, standing alone, are insufficient to raise a reasonable doubt about a director's independence."[65]

F. Special Litigation Committee

The role of a special litigation committee in obtaining control over so-called derivative litigation is discussed in Chapter III.1. Key to the creation of such a committee is a requirement that the committee's actions and membership withstand judicial review of its independence.

Whether a court will determine that a director is independent in such matters will always be highly dependent on the facts that are peculiar to the individual circumstance. While there is not a higher "independence" standard for a special litigation committee, independence in the special litigation committee context is considered not only on a financial basis, but also on whether a director is potentially "beholden" to an interested party.[66]

For example, social and economic relationships among directors in a special litigation committee formed by Oracle Corporation were sufficient to cause independence problems.[67] In the Oracle case, the committee members and the parties involved in the litigation had close ties to Stanford University—two Stanford professors (one of them a former SEC commissioner) were asked to review the allegations regarding another Stanford professor, a key Stanford donor, and a potential Stanford donor.

---

65. *Beam v. Martha Stewart*, 833 A.2d 961, 976, Del. Supr., March 31, 2004.
66. Oracle II at 939-39.
67. *In re Oracle Derivative Litigation*, 824 A.2d 917 (Del. Ch. 2003).

The court held "this was a social atmosphere painted in too much vivid Stanford Cardinal red" for the committee to be deemed independent.[68]

G. Extended Tenures of Management and Directors

Both NYSE and NASDAQ provide for boards to make determinations as to the independence of directors. In addition to the circumstances enumerated above, a board might also consider, as part of its board evaluation process, whether having a long-standing management and board structure works against independence in thinking by directors.

It is valuable for boards and managers to have a working history and common set of experiences, knowledge, and frame of reference regarding the company. It can be difficult for an incoming director just joining a board to be effective or efficient until that director has built up knowledge about the company and the other board members.

At the same time, a group that has worked together for a long period can encounter decision-making failures as a result of "groupthink" or failing to challenge or review important assumptions that underlie decisions.

4. Further Independence Recommendations

In addition to the director independence elements that are required by state and federal law, and under the listing agreements with the NYSE or NASDAQ, independent organizations with an interest in governance matters also provide recommendations on how independence should be addressed.

The recommendations of parties such as RiskMetrics or the Council of Institutional Investors ("CII") do not represent a legal requirement. For corporate boards, the immediate practical impact of their recommendations is that institutional investors that follow the RiskMetrics recommendations or CII guidelines might elect to "withhold" votes for election of directors who fall short of such standards, rather than voting to elect them.

Also, to the extent that RiskMetrics or CII represent forward-looking thinking on matters of corporate governance or investor sentiment, their standards may become de facto standards for some companies.

Generally, the RiskMetrics and CII standards track those set by NYSE and NASDAQ, although CII favors a five-year "look back" for relationships

---

68. *Id.* (page 69 of slip opinion).

between directors and companies rather than the three-year "look back" used by the NYSE and NASDAQ.

Their recommendations detail broader categories of exclusions from independence than do the NYSE and NASDAQ (excluding former executives of a company acquired by the corporation, for example) and additional detail on affiliate relationships that would disqualify directors from being independent.[69]

In addition, the CII definition of independence is more draconian than that of the NYSE or NASADAQ: "An independent director is someone whose only nontrivial professional, familial or financial connection to the corporation, its chairman, CEO or any other executive officer is his or her directorship. Stated most simply, an independent director is a person whose directorship constitutes his or her only connection to the corporation."[70]

5. Conclusion

Depending on the individual situation, a board's determination that its directors are independent can require a complex set of decisions.

A director's independence can be measured not only by direct financial relations with the company but also by the relationship of the company and the businesses, charities, and family members affiliated with the director. The definitions of independence derive from multiple sources, including SOX, SEC regulation, and the rules of the NYSE and NASDAQ.

However, when a director considers related party transactions in meeting state laws on fiduciary duty, "independence" is not always the same as "disinterestedness," even though there is substantial overlap. Also, when the board needs to consider specific situations, such as a special litigation committee, executive compensation over $1 million, or stock option grants, different standards for defining the director's independence from the company can apply.

---

69. *See* RiskMetrics Group 2010 U.S. Proxy Voting Guidelines Summary, Risk MetricsGroup (2009); The Council of Institutional Investors Corporate Governance Policies, Council of Institutional Investors (updated May 1, 2009).

70. The Council of Institutional Investors Corporate Governance Policies, Council of Institutional Investors (updated May 1, 2009), Section 7.2

Fiduciary Duties and Director Liability

1. Introduction

In directing the activities of a corporation, the board of directors is obligated to act in good faith and in the reasonable belief that its actions are in the best interests of the corporation's shareholders. A director who violates those duties could be personally liable to the corporation or its shareholders.

The basic fiduciary duties of directors are generally described as duties of loyalty and of due care. In addition, boards can face subsets of these general duties in certain situations, such as a "duty of disclosure" when presenting information in a request for shareholder action, or the so-called "Revlon" duty, which is the legal obligation to seek the best sale terms for shareholders when a public company has determined to put itself up for sale.

As a result of SOX and Dodd-Frank, public company directors face specific additional statutory and regulatory obligations. Independent directors are not held to a higher standard or different standard for fiduciary duties than the standard applied to directors who are not independent. It is possible, however, that a grossly negligent or bad faith violation of a specific federal requirement by an independent director might in some circumstances constitute a breach of that director's fiduciary duties.[1]

Often, fiduciary duty issues arise in the context of the board making a decision on a transaction in which one or more directors has a personal or financial interest. The analysis of whether a director is an "interested director" with respect to a particular transaction or arrangement is similar to, but not identical to, the analysis of whether a director is "independent."

For example, the CEO would not be an independent director, but for purposes of voting on a transaction in which another director had a financial interest, the CEO might be a "disinterested director."

When breaches of a director's duty are alleged, courts offer directors the benefit of a legal presumption called the "business judgment rule." Under the business judgment rule, directors are presumed to have acted in what they understand to be the best interests of the corporation and its shareholders. The rule is intended to prevent the court from second-guessing board decisions with the benefit of hindsight.

Corporations generally are empowered to indemnify their directors for losses incurred if directors are found liable for breach of a fiduciary duty, and corporations often provide insurance coverage for such claims. However, such indemnification and insurance coverage typically will not be available if a director has not acted in good faith.

Directors also face potential liability under the securities laws, either in class action shareholder litigation claiming omissions or misstatements of material facts by the corporation or in connection with individual actions by a director.

Examples of actions that could lead to individual director liability are:

- violations of the "short-swing" profits rule of Section 16 of the Exchange Act;

---

1. Dodd-Frank 951expressly provides that no changes in board fiduciary duties are to be implied from the requirements of nonbinding shareholder approval of executive compensation. SEC Regulation S-K, Item 407 provides that an audit committee's "financial expert" is not held to a higher standard than other directors for fiduciary or securities law purposes.

- trading or tipping others to trade on the basis of material nonpublic information; or

- engaging in misconduct that causes the individual to be determined to be "unfit" for public company board or officer service and therefore subject to a lifetime ban on such service by the SEC.

This chapter will review the fiduciary duty standards for directors and how the specific application of those standards is affected by a continuously evolving body of corporate governance rules and principles.

Individual board member liabilities for illegal stock trading activities are discussed in Chapter IV.2, and SEC sanctions are discussed in Chapter IV.1.

2. Fiduciary Duties of Directors

Control of the assets of a corporation resides with an elected board of directors and the officers of the corporation who are appointed by the board of directors to act for the benefit of shareholders.

The core fiduciary duties of corporate directors (duty of care, duty of loyalty) are aimed at providing shareholders assurance that the company's officers and directors will not use their control over the company's assets to benefit themselves at the expense of the shareholders or be lax and inattentive in their control and use of the company's assets.

The duty of loyalty is aimed at preventing inappropriate self-dealing; the duty of care is aimed at ensuring directors pay appropriate attention to the corporation's activities.

Boards are sometimes described as having additional duties, such as a duty of disclosure in connection with presenting matters to shareholders, or a duty of good faith. In specific situations, such as a change of control or insolvency of the corporation, the focus of the directors' duties may shift to parties such as minority shareholders or creditors rather than to the corporation's shareholders as a whole.

Change of corporate control situations are particularly susceptible to challenge and to careful after-the-fact judicial scrutiny of the board's performance.

The discussions of fiduciary duty in this chapter are based on Delaware law, which is well developed, well articulated, and well known in the corporate community. Individual state laws will vary in particular details and procedures, but the policy considerations and principles relating to fiduciary duties tend to be similar from state to state.

A. The Duty of Loyalty

The Delaware judiciary has a long-established description of the principles underlying the fiduciary duty of loyalty:

> Corporate officers and directors are not permitted to use their position of trust and confidence to further their private interests. . . . [A] corporate officer or director [must act] affirmatively to protect the interests of the corporation committed to his charge [and] refrain from doing anything that would work injury to the corporation.... The rule that requires an undivided and unselfish loyalty to the corporation demands that there be no conflict between duty and self-interest.[2]

Requirements of director independence are, at their core, a mechanism for ensuring that the board includes members who do not inherently face conflicts between their financial self-interest and their duties to shareholders. In addition, independent directors theoretically are less subject to direct or implicit pressure to support, or ignore, management actions that might be disadvantageous to the corporation.

Executives of a corporation who also sit on its board ("management directors") are not considered independent directors for purposes of considering their own compensation or other purposes. However, for purposes of considering a given transaction involving another director who has a financial or personal interest in the proposed transaction (an "interested director"), a management director could be considered "disinterested."

Directors must evaluate real and potential conflicts of interest in fulfilling their fiduciary duties regarding transactions between the company and an interested director. Under the proxy rules, public companies must disclose the policies and procedures they use in dealing with interested party transactions.[3]

In determining the independence of directors for corporate governance purposes, the NYSE and NASDAQ require boards to consider not only whether the director has a direct financial relationship with the company

---

2.   *Guth v. Loft, Inc.,* 5 A.2d 503, 510 (Del. 1939).

3.   SEC Regulation S-K, Item 404(b)(i).

(such as vendor, consultant, etc.) but also whether the family members of the director or organizations with which the director is associated might benefit financially from the director's participation on a corporation's board.[4]

(1) Examples of Situations That Raise Duty of Loyalty Questions

Even if a director is generally considered to be an independent director, a director who has an interest in a particular transaction will not be considered to be independent for purposes of that transaction. A director's duty of loyalty can be at issue in a number of different circumstances. The situations listed below represent common examples of circumstances implicating duty of loyalty issues.

(a) Conflicts of Interest

When a director has a direct or indirect financial or personal interest in a matter relating to the corporation or its assets, there is a potential conflict of interest.[5] Examples of such direct or indirect financial interests would include situations in which the director or a company or organization with which the director is affiliated:

- enters into an agreement with the corporation;
- provides goods or services to the corporation;
- acquires goods or services from the corporation; or
- competes with the corporation.

For purposes of such a transaction, the duties of the "interested director" and the other directors diverge. The interested director must disclose the material facts of the transaction and the director's interest in such transaction to the board, and obtain approval from either disinterested directors or the shareholders.[6] The disinterested directors must exercise their duties of loyalty and due care in evaluating whether to approve the transaction. The interested director will abstain from voting on the matter and typically should leave the meeting while the disinterested directors consider the matter.[7]

---

4. NYSE Rule 303A.01-.02; NASDAQ Rule 4200.
5. Model Bus. Corp. Act. § 8.60(1)(i)-(ii).
6. Delaware General Corporation Law, Sec. 144(a)(1)-(2).
7. See Corporate Director's Guidebook-1994 Ed., 49 Bus. Law 1243, 1255 (1994).

The law of the corporation's state of incorporation will provide specific procedures regarding approval of interested director transactions including any required threshold vote for director and shareholder approval.

(b) Corporate Opportunity

If a director has access to a business opportunity that is related to the business of the corporation (or its subsidiaries or affiliates), the director should inform the corporation of the opportunity and make the opportunity available to the corporation.[8] The director should not pursue the opportunity personally without first offering it to the corporation.

The evaluation of whether the business opportunity is one that must be offered to the corporation may not be simple. The outcome depends on such factors as the similarity of the opportunity to the corporation's present or planned business, the circumstances in which the opportunity arose, the materiality of the opportunity to the corporation, and whether the corporation wants to pursue the opportunity.[9]

As with a conflict of interest, the director who is involved in the potential corporate opportunity must disclose the material facts of the transaction and the director's interest in the transaction to the board and obtain approval from the disinterested directors or the shareholders before pursuing the opportunity personally.

(c) Executive and Director Compensation

The CEO generally will be a member of the board, and other senior officers of the corporation also may hold board positions. Even prior to the passage of Dodd-Frank, NYSE and NASDAQ rules provided that executives and other nonindependent directors could not be part of the compensation committee or board process approving CEO compensation, including bonuses, equity compensation such as stock options or stock grants, perquisites, or severance agreements.[10] Under Dodd-Frank, compensation committees are required to consist of independent directors only.

---

8. *Guth v. Loft, Inc.,* 5 A.2d at 510-511.

9. *Science Accessories Corp. v. Summagraphics Corp.,* 425 A.2d 957, 963-964 (Del. 1980).

10. Under Delaware General Corporation Law, Sec. 141(h), the board of directors has the authority to fix the compensation of directors, but independent review of compensation provides legal protection as seen in *Beard v. Elster,* 160 A.2d 731 (Del. 1960) (the fact that disinterested board of directors approved stock options is entitled to "utmost consideration").

As a practical matter in the compensation process, the board and the compensation committee should obtain the input of such management directors as part of their discussions regarding compensation matters, but the management directors cannot otherwise be active participants in the determination of their own pay.[11]

The board is the only party that can determine compensation of directors, creating an inherent potential conflict. Under the proxy rules, board policies on director compensation must be disclosed in public company proxy statements.[12]

(d) Purchase of Control

In some circumstances, the board may be asked to consider a transaction proposed by management to buy the company from the other shareholders, such as in a leveraged buy-out ("LBO") or a proposal by founding shareholders to sell the company to management or an employee stock ownership plan ("ESOP").

Such transactions can involve complex analyses of the duties of parties on multiple sides of the transaction. In such transactions, a key issue is often whether the price and terms are fair to the corporation and minority shareholders.[13]

In considering such transactions, directors typically will want to have an independent appraiser or an investment banker perform a valuation analysis, rather than relying solely on their own judgment as to valuation. Such outside valuations help ensure that the directors have met their duty of loyalty and provide evidence of the "total fairness" of the transaction.[14]

(e) Majority Shareholders/Controlling Shareholders

A director may personally hold a majority or significant block of shares in the corporation, or serve as the representative of a shareholder owning a significant block of shares (a "shareholder director"). In some circumstances, a shareholder director still may be considered an independent director, but

---

11. *See* TIAA-CREF Policy Statement on Corporate Governance, Executive Compensation, available at http://www.tiaa-cref.org/pubs/pdf/governance_policy. pdf.
12. SEC Regulation S-K, Item 407(e). See footnote 8.
13. *Weinberger v. UOP, Inc.*, 457 A.2d 701, 711 (Del. 1983).
14. *See, e.g. Weinberger v. UOP, Inc.*, 457 A.2d at 709 n.7.

will owe a duty of loyalty to all shareholders regardless of whether the director is considered independent or not.[15]

A shareholder director may have interests that are not shared by other directors. Initiatives proposed by a shareholder director, such as a sale of corporate divisions or assets or pursuing new corporate strategies, may be inconsistent with the interests of minority shareholders or may be opposed by the other members of the board of directors or management on conflict of interest grounds.

In recent years, hedge funds have amassed increasing amounts of capital and influence. In some cases, hedge funds will take significant investment positions in a company and thereafter seek to influence corporate strategy. For example, such investors might target a company with lagging performance, a large cash position, and a history of rejecting takeover advances, with the goal of spurring the board to accept a takeover bid. In so doing, the investor obtains a return based not on business development but on the ability to affect corporate strategy.[16]

As with other interested director transactions, transactions involving a shareholder director need full disclosure of the director's personal or financial interest and approval by disinterested directors.

(f) Corporate Defenses

A board of directors is entitled to determine that the corporation's continued independence and ability to execute a business strategy over time requires the corporation to adopt defensive measures against unwanted acquirers.[17]

Accordingly, notwithstanding that corporate defenses such as "poison pill" plans or other mechanisms to prevent an unwanted acquisition bid for the corporation are sometimes considered to be methods to "entrench"[18] the existing management of a corporation, such mechanisms have been

---

15. *Unocal Corp. v. Mesa Petroleum Co.*, 493 A.2d 946, 958 (Del. 1985); citing *Allied Chemical & Dye Corp. v. Steel & Tube Co. of America*, 120 A. 486, 491 (Del. Ch. 1923) ("majority shareholder owes a fiduciary duty to the minority shareholders").

16. *See, e.g.*, Stephen Davis, Jon Lukomnik, and David Pitt-Watson, "The New Capitalists," (Harvard Business School Press, 2006) at 89-92.

17. *See, e.g. Unocal Corp. v. Mesa Petroleum Co.,* 493 A.2d 946.

18. Id. at 954 ("Delaware corporation may deal selectively with its stockholders, provided the directors have not acted out of a sole or primary purpose to entrench themselves in office.").

upheld as being valid corporate actions undertaken to defend a corporate strategy, when done appropriately.[19]

In recent years, accompanied by changing perceptions of governance matters and advocacy by institutional investors, a number of companies have abandoned "poison pill" defenses. However, poison pills still exist, and as recently as 2010 a challenged poison pill plan has been upheld by the Delaware courts.[20]

When a board can no longer reasonably defend the continued independence of a publicly traded corporation, the board's duty to shareholders shifts to a duty to obtain the best price and terms in the circumstances (the so-called "Revlon" duty, named after the case in which the duty was first articulated).[21]

As with any other change of control situation, such as a tender offer, merger, or proxy contest, the board will need to consider multiple factors in discharging its duties, such as the nature of the proposal, whether the corporation's management is participating in the proposal transaction, and who will own the corporation at the end of the transaction.[22]

(2) Fairness of the Transaction

In reviewing a transaction involving an interested director, the disinterested directors must determine whether the terms of the proposed transaction are comparable to the terms the corporation would receive from other noninterested parties and whether the transaction is in furtherance of the corporation's business objectives.[23]

In addition to reviewing the fairness of the terms of a proposed transaction, the directors are responsible for ensuring that the decision-

---

19. *Moran v. Household International, Inc.*, 500 A.2d 1346, 1348 (Del. 1985) (the Supreme Court of Delaware affirmed the lower court's ruling that validated a preferred share purchase rights plan).

20. *Selectica v. Versata Enterprises*, Del. Court of Chancery, Feb. 26, 2010. WL 703062.

21. *Revlon, Inc. v. MacAndrews and Forbes Holdings, Inc.*, 506 A.2d 173, 182 (Del. 1986).

22. *Unocal Corp. v. Mesa Petroleum Co.*, 493 A.2d at 955-956.

23. *Pepper v. Litton*, 308 U.S. 295, 306-307 (1939) ("A director is a fiduciary. Their dealings with the corporation are subjected to rigorous scrutiny and where any of their contracts or engagements with the corporation is challenged the burden is on the director or stockholder not only to prove the good faith of the transaction but also to show its inherent fairness from the viewpoint of the corporation and those interested therein. The essence of the test is whether or not under all the circumstances the transaction carries the earmarks of an arm's length bargain.").

making process is fair to the corporation, and to its minority shareholders, if the interests of the corporation's minority shareholders might be adversely affected by the transaction. Transactions should be proposed and approved in a manner consistent with the corporation's code of ethics and other policies relating to conflicts of interest.

In the event of a legal challenge to a transaction involving an interested director, the transaction may be upheld, notwithstanding failures in the decision-making process or breaches of the duty of loyalty, if the transaction is entirely fair to the corporation or if it has been approved by the corporation's shareholders with full disclosure to them of all material facts.[24]

As discussed below, the directors may seek the advice of outside parties, such as investment bankers or appraisers, in considering the fairness of an interested director transaction and may rely on such advice where such reliance is reasonable.

B. Duty of Care

The duty of care is the obligation of a director to be adequately informed and diligent when making corporate decisions and overseeing the management of the corporation.[25] Each director has the responsibility to ensure that he or she:

- devotes adequate time to board and committee activities;

- reviews materials prepared for board and committee meetings in advance of the meetings;

- informs fellow directors of relevant information known to the director; and

- candidly discusses matters brought before the board or committee.[26]

---

24. Delaware General Corporation Law, Sec. 144(a) (2005-2006); *See also Marciano v. Nakash*, 535 A.2d 400 (Del. 1987) (where the Supreme Court of Delaware affirmed a lower court ruling validating an interested director transaction that passed the intrinsic fairness test).

25. *Paramount Communications v. QVC Network*, 637 A.2d 34, 44 (Del. 1994).

26. See Manning, The Business Judgment Rule & the Director's Duty of Attention: Time for Reality, 39 Bus. Law 1477, 1499-1500 (1984).

(1) Sources of Information; Right to Rely on Others

Directors can obtain information from a number of sources in order to fulfill the duty of care. A director is entitled to rely on information and financial data presented by the corporation's officers or employees, by the corporation's outside professional advisors, such as attorneys, accountants, appraisers, or financial advisors, and by committees of the board. However, a director is not entitled to rely on such information if the director has other knowledge that would make reliance unreasonable.[27]

(2) Information Prepared by Management

Management typically will prepare materials for the board to review. Management inherently will possess more information about the corporation than does the board and must select the most relevant and important information regarding any issue under consideration by the board for the board to use in its deliberations.

Management's selection process will necessarily require it to make judgments about the nature, quality, and quantity of the data it presents to the board. The board is obligated to ensure that it is comfortable with the data that it has in hand in connection with its deliberations and should make inquiries of management regarding the completeness of the data provided and whether there are alternative possible analyses of the data.

If the board repeatedly determines that the data presented by management is insufficient, the board should proactively ensure that management provides the data the board needs.[28] If management refuses or is unable to provide the data required by the board, the board may consider replacing management, and individual directors should consider whether to continue on the board in such circumstances.

(3) Inquiry

If a director becomes aware of a potential problem or issue, such as information that the director considers to be inaccurate or inadequate or information that indicates the existence of a legal or business problem, the director should inquire into whether additional board attention to such

---

27. Delaware General Corporation Law, Sec. 141(e).
28. See *Graham v. Allis-Chalmers Mfg. Co.*, 188 A.2d 125, 130 (Del. 1963) (where liability for directors ensues if failed to install proper control when there was notice of wrongdoing).

matter is needed.[29] In such circumstances, the director must ensure that he or she is satisfied that the questions are resolved satisfactorily and that management is adequately dealing with the situation.

(4) Disclosure among Directors

Directors must inform one another and management of material information bearing on corporate decisions. The strength of a board depends upon the individual contributions of each of its directors.

(5) Time Commitment; Timeliness of Data

Directors must devote adequate time to their duties on the board and on board committees to ensure that they are discharging their duty of care. The minimum time requirement is not merely the time involved in consistent attendance of board and committee meetings. Directors also should devote time to reviewing material provided prior to board meetings, and to the adequate consideration of the decisions made at meetings.[30]

Management should facilitate the board's effective use of time by preparing and distributing board materials in advance of the meetings with sufficient time for review. In emergency circumstances, there may be a limited ability for management to prepare and circulate materials or for the board to review materials in advance but such situations should be rare.

(6) Evidence of Due Care

Directors must evidence their use of due care in deliberation by ensuring that board and committee minutes are prepared and adopted so as to reflect the existence of adequate review of available information and necessary deliberation.

Minutes currently tend to be somewhat more comprehensive than in the past, but they should consist of summaries, not transcripts, of the meetings. Generally, a board should want the minutes to reflect the existence of a discussion of a matter, refer to the nature of the information presented to the board, and refer to key discussion topics, as well as the outcome of the vote.

---

29. *Id.* (a duty exists if there is cause for suspicion).
30. See *Smith v. Van Gorkom*, 488 A.2d 858 (Del. 1985) (where directors were found grossly negligent for approving a sale of the company upon two hours of consideration, relying solely on a 20-minute oral presentation, and without any prior notice of the subject of the meeting).

C. Duty of Disclosure

The duty of disclosure is a duty to make material facts known to shareholders in connection with actions presented to the shareholders for vote.[31] Federal proxy solicitation law makes it illegal, and a species of fraud, to misstate or omit material facts in connection with a proxy solicitation.[32] The duty of disclosure is aimed at preventing shareholder consent to a corporate action from having been obtained on false pretenses.

D. Good Faith

Under Section 102(b)(7) of the Delaware General Corporation Law, corporations may "exculpate" directors from monetary liability for breach of the duty of care.[33] Such exculpatory provisions are common, and corporations often enter into indemnity agreements with directors and officers to provide not only a contractual right to recover any such damages but also to provide a means by which the corporation is obligated to advance the expenses of a legal defense to the director or officers. However, Section 102(b)(7) expressly provides that corporate charters may not eliminate or limit director liability for "acts or omissions not in good faith."[34]

Under Delaware law, the good faith required of a corporate fiduciary

> includes not simply the duties of care and loyalty, ... but all actions required by a true faithfulness and devotion to the interests of the corporation and its shareholders. A failure to act in good faith may be shown, for instance, where the fiduciary intentionally acts with a purpose other than that of advancing the best interests of the corporation, where the fiduciary acts with the intent to violate applicable positive law, or where the fiduciary intentionally fails to act in the face of a known duty to act, demonstrating a conscious disregard for his duties.[35]

---

31. *Stroud v. Grace,* 606 A.2d 75, 84 (Del. 1992).
32. SEC Rule 14a-9a.
33. Delaware General Corporation Law, Sec. 102(b)(7).
34. *Id.*
35. *In re Walt Disney Co. Derivative Litigation,* 2005 Del. Ch. LEXIS 113, 176-177; *aff'd, Brehm v. Eisner (In re Walt Disney Co. Derivative Litig.), 2006 Del. LEXIS 307.*

Corporation laws in other states contain similar "exculpatory" provisions. Whether such laws create a separate duty of good faith distinct from the duty of care and the duty of loyalty may depend on the specific statutory provisions in those states.

E. Other Duties

In making business decisions about the corporation's best interest, corporations are typically not required to take into account the concerns of nonshareholders. The corporation is not prevented, however, from considering the impact on other constituencies, such as local communities, employees, or the environment, if the board believes that the corporation's best interests are served by considering them.

However, the board is obligated to consider one nonshareholder group—creditors—in some circumstances. If a corporation is insolvent or near insolvency, directors may have duties to creditors as well as to shareholders.[36] In such situations, insolvency counsel should be consulted prior to the approval of any significant corporate transactions, including recapitalizations or reorganizations.

F. The Business Judgment Rule

If a board's decisions are challenged in litigation, the court typically will evaluate the case using the business judgment rule.[37] The business judgment rule is the name given to the judicial method used to analyze director conduct. Under this rule, a disinterested director can avoid personal liability to the corporation or its shareholders, even if a corporate decision the director has approved turns out unfavorably.[38]

The rule provides that directors are presumed to have acted in accordance with their fiduciary duties.[39] The presumption can be rebutted

---

36. *Official Comm. of Unsecured Creditors v. Fleet Retail Fin. Group*, 280 B.R. 90, 92 (2002) ("…it is well-established that creditors are owed fiduciary duties in the zone of insolvency…"); *See also* Laura Lin, Shift of Fiduciary Duty Upon Corporate Insolvency: Proper Scope of Directors' Duty to Creditors, 46 Vand. L. Rev. 1485, 1492 (1993).

37. *Moran v. Household International, Inc.,* 490 A.2d 1059, 1076 (Del. Ch. 1985).

38. *Unocal Corp. v. Mesa Petroleum Co.*, 493 A.2d at 1074 ("[I]n the absence of fraud or bad faith, directors will not be held liable for mistakes of judgment in actions arguably taken for the benefit of the corporation.").

39. *Aronson v. Lewis*, 473 A.2d 805, 812 (Del. 1984) ("It is a presumption that in making a business decision the directors of a corporation acted on an informed

by showing that the board violated a fiduciary duty. In such cases, the burden then shifts to the directors to prove that the transaction is "entirely fair" to the corporation and shareholders.

Where directors have not exercised judgment (i.e., have taken no action), the protections of the business judgment rule do not apply.[40]

The legal standard for imposing liability on directors is gross negligence, which means reckless indifference to or a deliberate disregard for stockholders or actions "outside the bounds of reason."[41]

3. Indemnification and D&O Insurance

If a director is sued, even in a case that has no chance of winning, the director is still going to incur costs in time, aggravation, and money.

Corporation laws permit companies to indemnify directors for the monetary costs of litigation they encounter in their capacities as directors,[42] and corporations routinely provide in their organizational documents that they will provide indemnification for directors to the fullest extent of the law.

The ability to indemnify directors is critical to the ability of corporations to recruit and retain directors, since few individuals would desire to serve on a board of directors if the exposure to litigation risk could not be mitigated.

A director will want to have the corporation enter into an indemnity agreement. Rather than having the director present a bill at the end of litigation and request indemnification, the indemnity agreement will provide the director with clearly understood and enforceable rights to obtain indemnification from the corporation and typically provides for advancement of legal costs as well.

Corporations generally obtain directors and officers insurance ("D&O insurance") to help fund indemnity obligations and provide coverage in the event of litigation. Terms of D&O insurance can vary, and directors should take steps to be certain that the coverage they believe that they have is in fact in place.

---

basis, in good faith and in the honest belief that the action taken was in the best interests of the company.").

40. *Id.* at 813.
41. *Smith v. Van Gorkom*, 488 A.2d at 873.
42. Delaware General Corporation Law Sec. 145(a).

In some circumstances, such as bankruptcy, the director might not be able to obtain indemnification from the corporation, but might be protected by a D&O policy.

A. Indemnity Agreements

An indemnity agreement is an agreement between the corporation and the individual director. The agreement will typically apply if the director is made a party, or is threatened to be made a party, to any sort of civil, criminal, or administrative litigation or investigation.

The agreement would cover the director's legal and other expenses, fines, and payments made in judgments or settlements.

An indemnity agreement typically will require that to qualify for the indemnification, the director must have acted in good faith, in a manner that the director reasonably believed to be in (or not opposed to) the best interests of the corporation, and (if the matter is criminal) that the director had no reasonable cause to believe the conduct was unlawful.

There will be some exceptions to the indemnification obligation, such as violations of Section 16(b) of the Exchange Act or situations in which the director has been determined to be liable to the company, and a majority of disinterested directors or disinterested shareholders, independent counsel, or a court with jurisdiction over the matter determines that in the circumstances indemnification should not be available.

The agreement would provide the director with assurance that settlement of a matter, or termination of a matter by a plea of no contest, will not act as a presumption that the director had not been acting in good faith or in the corporation's best interests. In situations in which the director was determined to be partially at fault, the agreement also would provide indemnification with respect to those matters for which no fault was found.

One critical component of an indemnity agreement is the requirement that the corporation advance expenses, including legal fees. The ongoing litigation costs can be significant, and litigation can last for years. Indemnification would lose much of its value if a director was forced to wait until the end of the litigation before those costs were repaid.

The advancement of expenses is accompanied by a requirement that if the director ultimately is determined not to be eligible for indemnification, the director would be obligated to repay the advanced funds.

Indemnity agreements will also typically provide for certain procedures to be followed in connection with a director obtaining indemnification or expense advances, and may also require that the director turn over defense of the matter to the corporation.

If D&O insurance is in place, the indemnity agreement also may include provisions for the use of the insurance proceeds for indemnification purposes or subrogation of the corporation to the director with respect to the rights under the policy.

B. D&O Insurance

Directors and officers liability insurance is intended to provide coverage to the corporation and to the individual directors and officers in the event of claims against them.

The corporation could rely solely on its own resources to indemnify a director. However, insurance can expand the capabilities of a corporation to offer protection to its directors in situations in which the company is legally or practically prevented from providing indemnification.

D&O insurance policies will not be simple arrangements. The policies will contain multiple conditions to coverage and exclusions from coverage. Moreover, the way terms are defined (such as describing what kinds of losses would be covered) can effectively represent limitations on coverage.

One typical exclusion will prevent payment of proceeds in the event a director has acted in a deliberately dishonest way. The definition of such an exclusion could have significant impact on the ability of a director to receive coverage.

Directors should be particularly interested in the portion of the policy that covers directors personally ("Side A coverage"). The advantage to a director of Side A coverage is that it can provide protection to the director when the corporation cannot provide indemnity, as in bankruptcy situations.

Side A coverage may be part of the overall D&O insurance policy or it may be purchased in some cases as a stand-alone policy. Directors should understand the nature and the extent of the coverage. Some terms, for example, may not be effective until the company has exhausted other resources.

Directors also will want to be aware of the D&O policy application process, and aware of whether they can have their coverage terminated if management erred or lied in preparing the application. Some policies permit the parties who were not responsible for the misrepresentation to retain coverage, but others do not.

C. Enforcement Issues

For a company facing SEC or Department of Justice enforcement actions, the issues surrounding indemnification have the potential to affect the enforcement outcome.

The SEC and the Department of Justice have opposed indemnification and the advancement of legal expenses on the grounds the laws do not have their full deterrent effect against parties who are indemnified from personal liability.[43]

The Department of Justice has stated that in determining whether it considers a corporate defendant to be cooperative, a factor to be considered is

> "whether the corporation appears to be protecting its culpable employees and agents…through the advancing of attorneys fees, through retaining the employees without sanction for their misconduct, or through providing information to the employees about the government's investigation pursuant to a joint defense agreement."[44]

However, in a 2006 federal district court case, the Department of Justice's efforts to dissuade the KPMG accounting firm from offering legal fee advancement was held to be an unconstitutional violation of the right to counsel.[45]

4. Conclusion

Potential personal liability is a concern for every person who is asked to serve on a board of directors. Because independent directors are not involved in the day-to-day operation of the company, they must rely on managers for information on key performance metrics. Ensuring the

---

43. SEC Speech, Stephen M. Cutler, Director, SEC Division of Enforcement, Chicago, Ill, April 29, 2004 ("Cutler 2004 Chicago").

44. January 20, 2003, Memorandum, Larry D. Thompson, U.S. Deputy Attorney General, "Principles of Federal Prosecution of Business Organizations" ("Thompson memo").

45. *U.S. v. Stein* (S.D.N.Y., June 27, 2006) 435 F. Supp. 2d 330.

accuracy of that information is paramount to the independent director's avoidance of personal liability.

The complexity and volume of rules in corporate governance can provide traps for the unwary, but they also provide a road map to the avoidance of liability for directors. In particular, the emphasis under Delaware law on appropriate process means that directors who act on an informed basis in good faith in the best interests of the company and its shareholders should feel comfortable that their business judgments will not be second guessed by courts.

Corporate Laws, Rules, and Recommendations

1. Introduction

Corporate governance questions were not ignored prior to the corporate scandals in the early 2000s, but the collapses of Enron, WorldCom, and other public corporations provided a sense of urgency that led to the adoption of SOX in 2002. While SOX represented a significant development in legally mandated corporate governance standards, it was not the first word, nor the final word, on corporate governance; it was a continuation of an evolutionary process that continues in the wake of the financial crisis of the later 2000s.

In the case of *In re Disney Corporation Derivative Litigation* ("Disney"), the Delaware Chancery Court undertook an articulate and thorough review of the state of Delaware corporate fiduciary duties law as it stood in 2005 (and as applied to a case that grew out of transactions that took place in 1995).

The *Disney* court articulated the distinction between corporate governance practices that are desirable and those that give rise to a successful cause of action for breach of fiduciary duty as a matter of Delaware corporate law:

> All good corporate governance practices include compliance with statutory law and case law establishing fiduciary duties. But the law of corporate fiduciary duties and remedies for violation of those duties are distinct from the aspirational goals of ideal corporate governance practices. Aspirational ideals of good corporate governance practices for boards of directors that go beyond the minimal legal requirements of the corporation law are highly desirable, often tend to benefit stockholders, sometimes reduce litigation and can usually help directors avoid liability[1]...... But Delaware law does not—indeed, the common law cannot—hold fiduciaries liable for a failure to comply with the aspirational ideal of best practices.[2]

The Disney court concluded that fiduciary duties of directors, whether characterized as the general duties of loyalty and care or as a duty of good faith or as duties in specific situations, such as the "Revlon" duties in a sale of the corporation, were in essence variations on a single duty of a director to act so that the director's interests were not placed ahead of those of the corporation and its shareholders.[3]

Disney involved a dispute over a 1995 executive termination payment of $140 million.[4] The dispute was resolved in the board's favor 10 years after the board's decision was made.[5] While the legal definition of the fiduciary duties did not change over that time, the court's scathing comments concerning management and the board suggested that the 1995 conduct by

---

1.　*In re Walt Disney Co. Derivative Litigation.*, 2005 Del. Ch. LEXIS at 147 n.399.

2.　*Id. at 117.*

3.　*Id. at 148.*

4.　*Id. at 116-118 n.315.*

5.　*Id. at 116.*

the Disney board fell far short of what would be considered appropriate for a board in 2005.[6]

Disney implicitly recognized that investor expectations regarding appropriate board conduct had changed between 1995 and 2005. Similarly, Congress and the SEC were not writing on a blank slate when SOX and its related rulemaking were crafted in response to the 2001-2002 corporate scandals. Many SOX elements were adopted from then-existing critiques of corporate governance by academics,[7] institutional shareholders,[8] and regulators.[9]

These critiques reflected concerns that company performance could go awry as a result of operational and oversight problems, even where as a matter of law the corporate directors were fulfilling their fiduciary duties. Such concerns are not fanciful: In 2009, the directors of Citigroup, which lost hundreds of billions of dollars in shareholder wealth and required hundreds of billions of dollars of taxpayer guarantees and capital infusions in the immediate aftermath of the 2008 financial crisis, were the target of a Delaware shareholder suit alleging breach of fiduciary duty, and the suit was dismissed.[10]

Congress adopted SOX to restructure specific corporate behavior, primarily relating to the preparation and presentation of financial statements. No law could cover all aspects of good corporate governance for all companies and all situations, and SOX did not attempt to do so. SOX did establish certain key legal requirements for governance relating to such matters as the establishment and operation of audit committees,[11]

---

6. *Id.*

7. *See, e.g.*, Margaret Blair, *Ownership and Control* (The Brookings Institute Press, 1995); Jay Lorsch, *Empowering the Board, Harvard Business Review*, 1995; Testimony of Professor John C. Coffee, Jr. Before the Senate Committee on Commerce, Science and Transportation, December 18, 2001, "The Enron Debacle and Gatekeeper Liability: Why Would the Gatekeepers Remain Silent?"; "The Acquiescent Gatekeeper: Reputational Intermediaries, Auditor Independence and the Governance of Accounting," John C. Coffee, Jr., May 21, 2001.

8. *See, e.g.*, Calpers Governance Standards, available at http://www.calpers-governance.org; TIAA-CREF Policy Statement on Corporate Governance, available at http://www.tiaa-cref.org/pubs/pdf/governance_policy.pdf.

9. *See, e.g.*, SEC Release 33-7606 (November 3, 1998) as amended by Release No. 33-7606A (November 13, 1998) ("Aircraft Carrier Release").

10. *In re Citigroup Shareholder Derivative Litigation*, Civ. A. No. 3338-CC (Del. Ch. Feb. 24, 2009).

11. SOX 201-301.

the independence of directors, and the need for disclosure controls[12] and internal financial controls.[13] In the intervening years, those requirements have become the present-day baseline from which public companies work.

Following the 2008 financial crisis, Congress adopted legislation to implement the Troubled Asset Relief Program ("TARP") for financial institutions.[14] TARP, and subsequent rulemaking by the U.S. Treasury and the SEC, focused on restructuring executive compensation to remove the incentive of executives to take excessive risks with corporate assets.[15] Dodd-Frank, adopted in 2010, addresses executive compensation processes and disclosures, and mandates risk committees for financial institutions.[16]

In the early 2000s, SOX mandated that companies and outside professionals adopt policies designed to proactively promote honest performance by companies and their managers. Requirements for codes of ethics, whistleblower policies, and "up the ladder" reporting of critical legal issues by counsel were aimed at ensuring that companies had compliance mechanisms in place to prevent or detect corporate misbehavior, without specifying each element of such mechanisms.[17] Such policies are required by law but are not themselves laws.

In addition, companies whose shares trade either on the NYSE or through NASDAQ are obligated to adopt certain governance practices contained in the rules governing companies whose shares trade in those markets.[18] Failure to comply with those rules would violate the listing agreement between the company and the market, and the company would face the penalty of having its shares "de-listed" and being unable to trade on the market.[19]

---

12. SOX 401-409.

13. SOX 302.

14. Emergency Economic Stabilization Act of 2008 (EESA), as amended by the American Recovery and Reinvestment Act of 2009 (ARRA), provides guidance on the executive compensation and corporate governance provisions of EESA that apply to entities that receive financial assistance under the Troubled Asset Relief Program (TARP). Section 111 of EESA requires entities receiving financial assistance (TARP recipients) from the Department of the Treasury (Treasury) to meet appropriate standards for executive compensation and corporate governance.

15. *See* SK 404 s, Interim Final rule at § 30.5 (Q-5).

16. Dodd-Frank 165, 952.

17. SOX 307, 406, and 1107.

18. NYSE Rule 303A (2003), NASDAQ Rules 4200 et seq.

19. *Id.*

Beyond what is required by law or by contract, companies are also exposed, through the activism of institutional shareholders and professional organizations, to demands for the adoption of various "best practices" for governance and of mechanisms for receiving shareholder input into the corporate decision-making process.

As a result, corporate governance considerations cover a spectrum from the direct regulation of board and corporate behavior as matters of fiduciary duty and compliance with SOX, Dodd-Frank, EESA, and ARRA, together with SEC and U.S. Treasury regulations, to the indirect regulation through compliance with legally required codes of ethics or SEC proxy disclosures, to the voluntary agreement to follow the rules of the NYSE or NASDAQ, and finally to the best practices prescriptions of various institutional investors or other institutions.

2. The Governance Spectrum, from Law to "Best Practices"

A. Legal Requirements

The legal standards governing board activities are found in state and federal statutes and regulations, the laws respecting fiduciary duties, and the corporate charter and bylaws. Directors must ensure, through oversight or direction of management, that the corporation and corporate management comply with the law.

Violations of legal standards of director conduct could subject a director to claims of breach of fiduciary duty or to civil or criminal penalties under the securities laws,[20] including a lifetime ban on serving as a public company officer or director.[21]

Directors, companies, and managers are subject to different legal requirements, with distinct but overlapping elements and consequences. For example, if failure of an oversight program results in a violation of law by the corporation, the corporation could face legal consequences for the violation of law, while the directors and management might face separate legal consequences for failing to exercise proper oversight of the corporate activities that led to the violation.

---

20. SOX 801-905.
21. SOX 1105.

(1) Committees

Audit committees of public companies received detailed directions under SOX and the related rulemaking by the SEC. These directions included requirements as to:

- the nature of the membership of the committee (independent directors only);

- the need for at least one committee member to be a financial expert;

- specific obligations relating to the relations between the committee and the company's outside auditors;

- obligations to review corporate securities disclosures; and

- obligations to establish whistleblower policies to facilitate the detection of fraud.[22]

Dodd-Frank mandates that compensation committees be independent, and that SEC rulemaking and exchange listing requirements provide details on the implementation of the independence requirements of the members of the committee and any compensation consultants, legal counsel, or other advisors engaged by the compensation committee.[23]

The structure and activities of the nominating committee (sometimes joined with a governance committee) are not directly regulated, but effectively are governed by the SEC's disclosure requirements. Under SEC rules, a corporation must explain to shareholders if the existence, membership, or activities of the nominating committee does not meet minimum SEC requirements. This disclosure rule makes those substantive committee operations desirable, even if they are not mandatory.

In addition, even prior to adoption of Dodd-Frank, the NASDAQ and NYSE listing rules required that independent directors conduct the compensation and nominating functions for the board, with NYSE requiring the formation of separate committees.[24]

---

22. SOX 201-301, 407.
23. Dodd-Frank 952.
24. NYSE Rule 303A.05, NASDAQ Rule 4350(b)(1)(B).

(2) Oversight of Corporate Legal Compliance

(a) Fiduciary Duty

Corporations must obey wage and hour laws, environmental laws, tax laws, antitrust laws, and myriad other laws respecting the specific industry in which the corporation competes, as well as the requirements of corporate and securities laws.

In their capacities as fiduciaries, directors could face liability for failure to make certain that a company has adopted polices to ensure compliance with applicable laws, although the degree of failure by the directors must be high for liability to be found, as noted by the court in the case of *In re Caremark International Derivative Litigation* ("Caremark").

> [D]irectors have "a duty to attempt in good faith to assure that a corporate information and reporting system, which the board concludes is adequate, exists...."[25] [However,] only a sustained or systematic failure of the board to exercise oversight—such as an utter failure to attempt to assure a reasonable information and reporting system exists—will establish the lack of good faith that is a necessary condition to liability. Such a test of liability—lack of good faith as evidenced by sustained or systematic failure of a director to exercise reasonable oversight—is quite high.[26]

SOX established requirements that companies adopt whistleblower policies and codes of ethics, and that the CEO and CFO certify as to specific disclosure matters in quarterly and annual SEC filings.[27] SOX also required revisions to the federal Organizational Sentencing Guidelines, which include standards for the corporate adoption of policies to detect and prevent violations of law.[28]

Failure by directors to oversee those various policies and processes could lead to legal consequences for directors if the failure of oversight was significant.

---

25. *In re Caremark Int'l Inc. Derivative Litigation*, 698 A.2d 959, 970 (Del. 1996).
26. *Id.* at 971.
27. SOX 301-302, 406.
28. SOX 1104.

(b) Federal Sentencing Guidelines

SOX mandated an update of federal sentencing guidelines relating to white collar crime, securities fraud, and institutional sentencing.[29] The U.S. Sentencing Commission amended the Organizational Sentencing Guidelines, effective November 1, 2004 (the "Guidelines"), including descriptions of the elements of an effective corporate legal compliance program.[30] The amended Guidelines emphasize the obligations of directors in effective corporate governance.

Taken together with the Caremark line of cases, the Guidelines have generated concern in the securities bar that failure to adopt programs demonstrating the board's intent to prevent fraud could permit plaintiffs to sue for breach of the duties described in Caremark.

The amended Guidelines impose three obligations on directors for corporate compliance programs:

1. directors must be knowledgeable about the "content and operation" of the corporation's compliance and ethics program;

2. directors must receive training appropriate to their roles and responsibilities, and

3. directors need to oversee the "implementation and effectiveness" of the corporation's compliance program, which must be "generally effective in preventing and detecting criminal conduct.[31]

(c) Corporate Disclosure/Management Certifications

Public company corporate officers are required to make two certifications under SOX when quarterly and annual reports are made to the SEC. SOX Section 306 requires that:

• the CEO and the CFO must each individually certify that they have reviewed the report;

• the report does not misstate or omit any material fact;

• the financial statements are accurate;

• the officers are responsible for establishing and maintaining internal controls; and

---

29. SOX 801-906, 1104.

30. U.S. Sentencing Commission, Organizational Guidelines, Chapter 8 Sentencing of Organizations, http://www.ussc.gov/orgguide.htm.

31. *Id.*

- the controls are adequate to generate accurate and timely disclosure, including with respect to financial matters and fraud.[32]

The second certification, under SOX Section 906, requires signing officers to attest that the report fully complies with the SEC's reporting requirements and that the information contained in the report fairly presents, in all material respects, the financial condition and results of operations of the company.[33]

An officer who "knowingly" makes a false Section 906 certification "shall" be fined up to $1 million and imprisoned for up to 10 years; an officer who "willfully" makes a false Section 906 certification "shall" be fined up to $5 million and imprisoned for up to 20 years.[34]

In order for an officer to make such certifications without making a knowing or willful false statement, the officers must have in place internal systems that permit the capture of relevant information and adequate reporting.[35]

Although the certification obligation belongs to the CEO and CFO, the audit committee must review and approve the company's SEC disclosures and the audit committee must recommend the inclusion of the financial statements in the Form 10-K. In the case of the annual report on Form 10-K, directors are obligated to sign the report. Directors need to assure themselves that they have a basis for believing that the company's disclosures are proper.

To develop such assurance, management should prepare, and the board should review, documentation describing how corporate information is gathered and recorded, processed, summarized, and reported to the SEC. Directors should be comfortable that the documentation appropriately identifies the employees who will gather information for periodic reports, sets out the process whereby the information is communicated and evaluated internally for preparation of reports, and ensures that the reports are prepared on an accurate and timely basis, including making time for the audit committee's review of financial statements and press releases of financial results.

SOX Section 404 requires that management make an assessment of the effectiveness of the internal control structure and procedures of the company

---

32. SOX 302(1)-(5).
33. SOX 906.
34. *Id.*
35. SOX 302.

for financial reporting.[36] The requirement relating to the certification concerning internal financial controls has been of particular complexity and has required the corporations to make significant expenditures of capital and effort.

For many companies, meeting the Section 404 requirements has required the addition of personnel, adoption of new procedures to process and record transactions, and the acquisition of additional equipment and software for these purposes. Even if directors are not directly knowledgeable about the implementation specifics of Section 404, they should require management to report on the status of such programs. In addition, the auditors will report to the board and the audit committee on any material weaknesses in financial controls,[37] and directors should take any necessary actions to correct deficiencies identified in such reports. Under Dodd-Frank, some public companies with smaller market capitalizations will be relieved of SOX Section 404 compliance requirements.[38]

(3) Oversight of Risk

Boards are responsible for the strategic direction of the company and for overseeing the risks that the company faces. As demonstrated in the financial crisis of the 2000s, the risk function is critical to corporate well being. EESA, ARRA, and related SEC and U.S. Treasury rulemaking established new requirements relating to the oversight of risk in response to problems that were identified as a result of the crisis. Dodd-Frank mandates the formation of risk committees for financial institutions.[39]

The rules for TARP recipients specifically limit executive compensation and prescribe compensation and risk evaluation activities that directors of TARP recipients must take.[40] Those requirements are extended for financial services companies in Dodd-Frank.[41]

---

36. SOX 404(a),(b).
37. SOX 103(A)(iii)(III).
38. Dodd-Frank 989 G.
39. Dodd-Frank 165.
40. Not all companies that received benefits as a result of EESA or ARRA are covered by the Treasury regulations. Entities that post collateral to and receive loans from the Federal Reserve Term Asset-Backed Securities Loan Facility (TALF) are not receiving "financial assistance provided under the TARP" and, therefore, are not TARP recipients under the Interim Final Rule.
41. Dodd-Frank 956.

The SEC adopted proxy rules that have the impact of requiring the boards of publicly traded companies in all industries, not only the financial services industry, to analyze whether the company's executive compensation policies foster undue risk. A company is required to disclose in its proxy statements that, upon review of its compensation policies, it has identified areas of risk. The board must make a determination whether such undue risk exists, and silence in the proxy statement on risk and compensation is permitted only if the board has affirmatively determined that its compensation programs do not foster such risk.[42]

(4) Shareholder "Say on Pay"

Beginning in 2011, Dodd-Frank mandates that public companies must provide shareholders the opportunity to vote on whether they approve of the compensation packages provided to the corporation's executives at least once every three years. The "say on pay" votes are advisory, and not binding.[43]

The legislation specifies that the shareholder vote on compensation shall not overrule a compensation decision by a company or its board, shall not be construed as changing or increasing the fiduciary duty of the company or its board of directors, and shall not restrict the ability of shareholders to make proposals for inclusion in proxy materials relating to executive compensation.

Nonetheless, a negative vote by shareholders against an executive compensation arrangement would be information that the board and compensation committee would want to consider as it makes compensation decisions on an ongoing basis.

The company's shareholders also must vote at least every six years on how frequently the "say on pay" vote will be taken. The shareholders may chose whether the "say on pay" vote will be conducted annually, every two years, or every three years.

Prior to enactment of Dodd-Frank, a number of companies had voluntarily adopted a "say on pay" vote, with some conducting annual votes, and other companies conducting votes every two years or every three years. During 2010, prior to adoption of Dodd-Frank, most companies that

---

42. SEC 404.

43. Dodd-Frank 951. Prior to adoption of Dodd-Frank, TARP recipients were subject to "say on pay" requirements under the American Recovery and Reinvestment Act of 2009 (ARRA) Feb. 17, 2009; Interim Rule § 14a-20.

conducted "say on pay" votes received shareholder approval, with notable exceptions being Motorola, Occidental Petroleum, and KeyCorp.[44]

If a company conducts a merger or acquisition for which shareholder approval is acquired, there is a separate, nonbinding "say on pay" shareholder approval required under Dodd-Frank for executive compensation that is related to the transaction.[45] The shareholder vote on "golden parachute" compensation is to be a separate vote from the vote to approve the transaction.

Other elements of Dodd-Frank may affect how "say on pay" voting works in practice. Under Dodd-Frank, the SEC must require securities exchanges to prohibit brokers from voting customer shares without receiving voting instructions from the beneficial holders, when the vote relates to election of directors, executive compensation, or "significant matters."[46] As a result, a company cannot expect automatic votes by brokers in favor of compensation resolutions.

In addition, Dodd-Frank requires that the investment managers of certain major institutional investors disclose at least annually how they voted on "say on pay" and "golden parachute" votes for companies in which they have investments.[47]

(5) Shareholder Nominations of Directors

Another significant issue relating to director nomination and elections is the question of shareholder nomination of directors, and the ability of a shareholder nominee to be included in the corporation's proxy materials (typically called "proxy access"). Section 971 of Dodd-Frank provided the SEC with express authority to adopt rules regarding inclusion of shareholder nominees in company proxy materials.

Prior to receiving the express authority under Dodd-Frank, the SEC had proposed, but not adopted, proxy access rules.[48] As finally adopted (subject to pending litigation), the proxy access rules require that director nominations from shareholders that have certain shareholding size and longevity profiles would be required to be included in company proxy materials.[49]

---

44. See reports at the CorporateCounsel.net (payment required).
45. Dodd-Frank 951.
46. Dodd-Frank 957.
47. Dodd-Frank 951.
48. SEC Release No. 33-9046 ("Proxy Access Proposal").
49. SEC Release No. 33-9136 ("Proxy Access Adopting Release").

The practical effect of proxy access is that a shareholder that might previously have been dissuaded from incurring the expense of preparing and distributing proxy materials to offer its own nominee for director may be able to use the company's proxy materials for that candidate. The proxy access rules are not the exclusive method by which shareholders can nominate directors. Traditional proxy contests remain available to shareholders.

The proxy access rules are discussed in greater detail in Chapter II.4.

B. *Internal Governance Policies and Indirect Regulation through SEC Disclosure and Exchange Listing Requirements*

SOX mandated that public companies adopt codes of ethics for senior officers[50] and a policy for the confidential receipt of information about potential fraud ("whistleblower policy").[51] Once adopted by a company, these and other policies adopted by the company do not themselves have the force of law, but they can have a legal impact on the company and its directors and management.

For example, a waiver of the company's code of ethics, including an implied waiver, gives rise to a reporting obligation under Form 8-K; failure to make accurate and timely disclosure would be a violation of the securities laws.[52] Similarly, under the Caremark line of cases, directors could conceivably find themselves personally liable if they did not oversee the development of legal compliance policies within the corporation that take into account the requirements of the federal sentencing guidelines relating to white collar crime.[53]

While the board has responsibility for establishing that the company acts in compliance with law, such an obligation is broad. The task of mastering compliance details, such as the appropriate methods of filing specific forms, typically falls not on the board nor on senior management but on line personnel or managers. In some cases, such as implementation of whistleblower policies, the directors may decide to remove the function from the company entirely and place it into the hands of third parties.

---

50. SOX 406(a).
51. SOX 301.
52. Form 8-K, Item 5.05.
53. *See, generally, In re Caremark Int'l Inc. Derivative Litigation*, 698 A.2d at 969-970 (Del. 1996).

In each situation, however, the board should oversee whether the policies are in fact being implemented. In litigation, a company that has adopted a policy and then failed to follow through will not be able to claim a lack of knowledge about what was required of it.

Set out below is a discussion concerning specific areas for which corporate policies must be adopted. Because each corporation's needs are unique, a corporation may require additional policies to address its particular circumstances.

In addition to the statutory or fiduciary obligations to create corporate policies, public companies are contractually bound to meet the listing standards of the market on which their securities are traded.[54] Breach of those standards could give the NYSE or NASDAQ the right to suspend or delist a company.[55] These standards are often reflected in corporate policies and committee charters, including with respect to determining the qualifications for a director's "independence." Under Dodd-Frank, the SEC was directed to use its control over listing standards to implement the statute's mandates respecting compensation committee independence, "clawbacks" of incentive compensation, and broker voting.[56]

As well, Dodd-Frank and the SEC have certain disclosure requirements regarding the operation of a corporation's compensation and nomination committees, which do not mandate specific committee actions but mandate additional disclosure regarding the committees' justifications for not taking those actions, which acts to a significant degree as substantive regulation through the disclosure requirement.[57] As with listing standards, the disclosure requirements may be reflected in corporate policies and committee charters.

(1) Code of Ethics

A code of ethics represents a set of standards that, adopted as company policy, commits the company to take actions beyond those that are merely sufficient to fit within the boundaries of the law.

SOX Section 406 mandated that each public company "disclose whether or not, and if not, the reason therefor, [it] has adopted a code of ethics for senior financial officers, applicable to its principal financial officer

---

54. NYSE Rule 303A(12)(A)(2003), NASDAQ Rule 4200 et seq.

55. *Id.* at 303(A)(13) commentary.

56. *See* Dodd-Frank 952, 954, and 957.

57. *See generally,* Dodd-Frank 953; SEC Regulation S-K Item 402(k), and SEC Schedule 14A, Item 7(d).

and comptroller or principal accounting officer, or persons performing similar functions."[58]

In its implementing regulations, the SEC defined the term "code of ethics" to mean written standards that are reasonably designed to deter wrongdoing and to promote honest and ethical conduct, avoid conflicts of interest, and promote full disclosure to investors and compliance with law.[59]

Both NASDAQ and the NYSE have adopted a requirement that companies listed for trading with them must adopt a code of conduct or code of ethics that would promote honest and fair operations of such company.[60]

The commentary by the NYSE relating to the code of ethics standards it adopted for companies listed on the NYSE aptly summarizes the value of, and the limitations of, a corporate code of ethics.

> No code of business conduct and ethics can replace the thoughtful behavior of an ethical director, officer or employee. However, such a code can focus the board and management on areas of ethical risk, provide guidance to personnel to help them recognize and deal with ethical issues, provide mechanisms to report unethical conduct, and help to foster a culture of honesty and accountability.[61]

The mere existence of a code of ethics is insufficient to prevent fraud or unethical conduct. As with many other failures of corporate governance, Enron provides a cautionary example—Enron had a code of ethics, which its board waived to permit its CFO to establish the many special purpose entities that were used to perpetrate the financial frauds that ultimately undid the company.[62]

Accordingly, waivers of the code of ethics must be disclosed in a current report on Form 8-K.[63] If there has been a breach or a waiver, including an

---

58. SOX 406(c).
59. SEC Regulation S-K, Item 406(c).
60. NYSE Rule 303A(10) (2003), NASDAQ Rule 4350(n).
61. NYSE Rule 303A(10) commentary, (2003).
62. *See, generally,* Ronald E. Berenbeim, *The Enron Ethics Breakdown*, Executive Action No. 15 (Feb. 2002), at http://www.infoedge.com/samples/CB-EA15free.pdf.
63. Form 8-K, Item 5.05.

implicit waiver of the company's code of ethics, Form 8-K requires that the company must report it within four business days of the event.

Failure of an officer to abide by the terms of the code of ethics would not necessarily be a violation of law. Failure of the company to discipline an officer who violated the code of ethics would not necessarily be a violation of law. However, failing to disclose any breaches or waivers of the code of ethics could be a violation of the disclosure requirements of the Exchange Act, which would be a violation of law. The penalty, depending upon the circumstances, could include sanctions under Section 21C of the Exchange Act[64] or Section 8A of the Securities Act for "causing a violation" of law[65] or a SEC-imposed ban on serving as an officer or director[66] or, depending upon the circumstances, give rise to a cause of action by shareholders for breach of fiduciary duty.

(2) Committee Charters

Many corporate committees adopt charters that set out the duties, membership, and key processes whereby the committee duties are performed.

Committee charters are not required under the securities laws or corporate laws, but they are required by the NYSE and NASDAQ for the audit, compensation, and nominating committees. Charters for nominating, audit, or compensation committees are required to be presented as exhibits in SEC filings or made available on corporate websites.[67]

Committee charters do not typically operate to restrict corporate authority, as would a certificate of incorporation or bylaws. A board may confer authority on a committee to undertake actions on behalf of the board, with or without a committee charter. Actions taken by a committee outside the scope of its charter could nonetheless be valid committee or corporate actions if ratified by the board.

Depending on the level of specificity of the charter, it can provide committee members with guidance on the specific process that the committee must undertake in discharging its obligations. It is conceivable that a committee that did not abide by its charter obligations could face additional exposure to liability for breach of fiduciary duties, if shareholders were damaged as a result of the breach. In such circumstances, the charter

---

64. Exchange Act Sec. 21C.
65. Securities Act Sec. 8A.
66. SOX 1105(b).
67. SEC Regulation S-K, Item 407(a).

terms might represent evidence of a standard of due care to which the directors should be held.

(3) Whistleblower Policies

The SOX requirement that audit committees establish whistleblower policies is direct and concise:

Audit committee shall establish procedures for—

(A) the receipt, retention, and treatment of complaints received by the company regarding accounting, internal accounting controls, or auditing matters; and

(B) the confidential, anonymous submission by employees of the company of concerns regarding questionable accounting or auditing matters.[68]

Section 1107 of SOX reinforces the requirements of the whistleblower requirement policy and makes retaliation against whistleblowers a crime punishable by an unspecified fine or imprisonment not to exceed 10 years, or both.[69]

Some companies have elected to move the whistleblowing report function entirely out of the company and place it in the hands of a third party that is tasked with communicating the information to the audit committee. While such third-party processes are not required, there is the risk that a process that requires that confidential communications be delivered to management could "chill" the willingness of whistleblowers to make communications that accuse management of improper conduct.

Under Dodd-Frank 922, whistleblowing is not merely protected, it is potentially lucrative for the whistleblower. If information provided by a whistleblower generates an SEC enforcement action resulting in monetary sanctions in excess of $1.0 million, the whistleblower is entitled to collect a bounty from the SEC ranging from 10%–30% of the recovery. The bounty is also available where the information generates enforcement action by the Department of Justice, a state attorney general, an exchange or another federal agency.[70]

---

68. SOX 301(4)(A)-(B).
69. SOX 1107(a).
70. Dodd-Frank 922.

(4) Corporate Policies/Personal Trading

To prevent and detect trading in the company's securities by company personnel who possess material nonpublic information, particularly officers and directors, the board should establish trading policies. In addition to addressing deliberate misuse by insiders of confidential information, such policies can help prevent trading by insiders at times when sensitive corporate developments might cause even innocent trading, after the fact, to appear to have been a misuse of material nonpublic information. These policies should include the identification of an individual within the company, typically the general counsel or compliance officer, with whom officers and directors should preclear any trades.

The board should approve any Rule 10b5-1 trading plans implemented by an officer or director. In a Rule 10b5-1 plan, an individual may instruct a broker to make periodic sales on the basis of timing, stock price, or market conditions.[71] As long as such a plan is in writing, and it is not an attempt to avoid the prohibitions in Rule 10b-5 on trading while in possession of material nonpublic information, SEC rules would permit the use of such plans to allow members of management to diversify their individual portfolios away from company stock, even at times when the existence of material nonpublic information might otherwise prevent such trades.[72]

The board should know of, and approve, Rule 10b5-1 plans. Typically, companies will disclose the existence of such plans to their shareholders as well. Such plans could represent an exception to the company's insider trading policies and may be a waiver of the company's code of ethics or code of ethics for senior executives. If such plans do represent a waiver of the requirements of the code of ethics, the approval of such plans by the audit committee would be required and a report on Form 8-K would also be required at the time of such approval.

Under Dodd-Frank, companies must disclose in their proxies whether employees and directors are permitted to purchase financial instruments that "hedge" the risk of loss in value of company shares owned or granted as compensation to those employees or directors.[73]

---

71. SEC Rule 10b5-1(c).
72. *Id.* at 10b5-1(c)(ii).
73. Dodd-Frank 955.

(5) Corporate Governance Guidelines

The NYSE requires its listed companies to adopt and disclose corporate governance guidelines. The NYSE does not set out a model form, noting that "No single set of guidelines would be appropriate for every listed company."

The NYSE does require that the guidelines address the following items:

- Director qualification standards, including independence and other substantive qualification requirements, such as limitations on the number of other boards on which a director may sit, and director tenure, retirement and succession.

- Director responsibilities, setting out basic duties and responsibilities with respect to attendance at board meetings and advance review of meeting materials.

- Director access to management and independent advisors.

- Director compensation, including general principles for determining the form and amount of director compensation.

- Director orientation and continuing education.

- Management succession including policies and principles for CEO selection and performance review, as well as policies regarding succession in the event of an emergency or the retirement of the CEO.

- Annual performance evaluation of the board to determine whether it and its committees are functioning effectively.

An NYSE-listed company must make its corporate governance guidelines available on or through its website and disclose that fact in its annual proxy statement or other SEC filings.

C. Best Practices

"Best practices" standards of corporate governance represent a standard beyond what is merely legal or ethical. Such standards have been articulated from many sources, including institutional shareholders, such as the California Public Employees' Retirement System ("CalPERS"), or TIAA-CREF; organizations that serve institutional shareholders, such as RiskMetrics Group ("RiskMetrics), and business organizations, such as the National Association of Corporate Directors ("NACD") and the Conference Board.

Best practices recommendations provide a level of detail regarding the implementation of governance practices that would potentially be too constrictive if they were adopted as a "one size fits all" legal standard but which can serve as a frame of reference for companies adopting governance policies.

To the extent that best practices standards become commonly adopted, it is also possible that over time they would come to represent evidence of the standard of care for corporate directors, and thereby take on legal significance in fiduciary duty cases.

Each organization that has weighed in on governance has its own formulation of best practices. The core elements of director independence and oversight of management are common to all.

One excellent articulation of corporate governance principles is the "Key Agreed Principles to Strengthen Corporate Governance for U.S. Publicly Traded Companies" ("Key Agreed Principles") developed by the National Association of Corporate Directors and the Business Roundtable.[74] The Key Agreed Principles contain brief, but very thoughtful and insightful, descriptions of actions corporate boards should take, and more important, why boards should take those actions.

The Key Agreed Principles cover such topics as:

- Board responsibility for governance (establishing practices to permit the board to fulfill its duties effectively and efficiently);

- Corporate governance transparency (giving shareholders visibility into corporate processes is more important than the intent of the processes);

- Director competency and commitment (ensuring the competency and commitment of directors);

- Board accountability and objectivity (ensuring the accountability of the board to shareholders and the objectivity of board decisions);

- Independent board leadership (providing nonmanagement leadership with the board);

- Integrity, ethics, and responsibility (promoting a corporate culture of integrity, ethics, and corporate social responsibility);

---

74. NACD, Key Agreed Principles October 16, 2008. http://www.directorship. com/stuff/contentmgr/files/2/7d77608e0a8a1fb1df2d3593f94848fe/misc/ keyagreedprinciples.pdf

- Attention to information, agenda, and strategy (adopting practices that support the board in determining its priorities and focusing on strategy (and associated risks));

- Protection against board entrenchment (establishing practices to encourage the board to refresh itself);

- Shareholder input in director selection (encouraging meaningful shareholder involvement in the selection of directors);

- Shareholder communications (encouraging communication with shareholders).[75]

These recommendations on best practices are consistent with those articulated by CalPERS, TIAA-CREF, RiskMetrics, and other institutional shareholders and business organizations that have considered governance questions.

3. Conclusion

While the basic fiduciary duty of directors is still accurately described as consisting of a duty of loyalty and a duty of care, significant detail concerning the specific actions that directors must take has been supplied in recent years by SOX and the related rulemaking by the SEC and others.

Such specific requirements are directed at ensuring that the corporate actors are aware of the need to observe ethical standards and at implementing mechanisms, such as whistleblower policies, to detect and prevent misbehavior.

In addition, committee charters and management financial statement certifications encourage directors and officers to be mindful of the actions that they undertake on the company's behalf.

The world of corporate governance is experiencing an ongoing evolution, with institutional shareholders and business organizations offering "best practices" recommendations that could, over time, affect the context in which the legal standards are interpreted.

A director who does not fulfill his or her fiduciary duties faces significant personal financial exposure. While the company may promise indemnification if the director is sued, or provide D&O insurance coverage to recover litigation losses, the director would always prefer to avoid litigation by meeting the fiduciary standard.

---

75. *Id.*

The Role of Shareholders

1. Introduction

Corporate law allocates and balances risks, benefits, and decision making among management, board, and shareholders. These economic, legal, and decision-making balances have undergone continuous evolution as laws, the economy, and technology have changed.[1]

---

1. For a detailed and well articulated discussion of the relationship between shareholders and the corporation, see the "Report Of The Task Force Of The ABA Section Of Business Law Corporate Governance Committee On Delineation Of Governance Roles & Responsibilites" at 111 (Aug. 1, 2009) (*hereinafter* "Delineation Report"). The Delineation Report expertly combines a discussion of the economic, legal, and policy impacts of existing corporate law, setting out a baseline from which proposed legislative or regulatory changes in the balance of relative rights among shareholders and other decision makers in the corporation can be evaluated. The discussion of institutional investor strategies relies heavily on the scholarship and insights contained in the Delineation Report. In addition, the NYSE Commission

With the concentration of corporate ownership in the hands of institutional investors over recent decades, institutional investors have become increasingly active in corporate governance matters. By extension, the proxy advisory services that monitor governance matters for institutional investors have gained influence as well.

The failures of Enron, WorldCom, and other companies in the early 2000s triggered the adoption of corporate governance reforms in SOX. The losses suffered by investors in those companies drove home the risk of investing in corporations with weak corporate governance practices.

Institutional investor interest in corporate governance is aimed at putting the board in a better position to monitor management on the shareholders' behalf, addressing the historically recognized risk that managers will use corporate resources to enrich themselves rather than benefit the shareholders. In light of the financial crisis of the late 2000s, corporate governance processes are also addressing whether management compensation incentives encourage the adoption of business strategies that overemphasize short-term performance and underemphasize risk.

In fact, the increasing influence of institutional investors alters the "agency" dynamics originally identified by academics Berle and Means in the 1930s.[2] Rather than a dispersed and powerless group of shareholders, for whom the costs of monitoring corporate management would outweigh the benefits, institutional investors can use modern communications and the evolving models of what constitutes proper corporate governance to affect the ways boards and managements perform.

As the boundaries defining the limit of decision-making authority between shareholders and boards continue to evolve, such as in the areas of director nominations or shareholder input on executive compensation, the existing economic and legal balances will likely evolve as well.

Legislators and regulators are also redefining the distribution of established decision-making roles within corporations. In 2010, Dodd-Frank mandated shareholder voting on executive compensation, disclosure of voting decisions by certain institutional shareholders, and formation of independent compensation committees. It also authorized the SEC to establish "proxy access" rules for shareholders. Delaware adopted revisions of its General Corporation Law in 2006 that facilitated the

---

on Corporate Governance issued a report in September 2010 that offers an insightful systemic overview into the interaction of boards, managements, regulators, institutional investors and their advisors. http://www.nyse.com/pdfs/CCGReport.pdf.

2.   See the discussion in Chapter I.4.

adoption of "majority voting" rules for board elections. In 2010, the SEC issued a concept release respecting a wide-ranging review of the proxy process, which may result in regulations affecting the 600 billion shares voted in the 13,000 shareholder elections conducted in the United States annually.[3]

This chapter provides background to directors on the basic economic and legal relationship of shareholders and boards, to assist directors in addressing such questions as they arise.

2. Institutional Shareholders and Governance

Measured from 1950, when more than 90% of U.S. equity ownership was in the hands of individual shareholders, share ownership by individuals had declined by the mid-2000s to 33% or less, while ownership by institutions rose significantly. Recent estimates of share ownership by institutions place mutual fund ownership at about 27% of U.S. equity securities and public pension funds at approximately 10%.[4]

Institutional investors are a diverse group, pursuing diverse investment objectives on behalf of customers or constituents. These investors include pension funds (whether operated by public entities, unions, or private funds); insurance companies and other financial companies; investment companies, such as mutual funds; private equity funds such as venture capital funds and hedge funds; endowments for educational and philanthropic institutions; and sovereign wealth funds.

With respect to investment in any given company, not all institutional investors will pursue the same strategies or goals. Some investors are short-term traders for whom stock price volatility represents opportunity. Other investors have an interest in the "long-term sustainable risk adjusted returns" of the company.[5] Depending upon the regulations to which they are subject and the investment timelines and strategies they adopt on behalf of the ultimate owners, institutional investors can have different approaches to governance questions regarding their portfolio companies.

For example, insurance companies and pension funds tend to make long-term investments. Their beneficiaries need the proceeds of investment

---

3. "Concept Release on the U.S. Proxy System," SEC Release No. 34-62495 (2010) ("Proxy Concept Release").

4. *See* Delineation Report and sources cited therein.

5. CalPERS, http://www.calpers.ca.gov/index.jsp?bc=/about/mission/strategic-plan.xml (last visited September 25, 2010).

for retirement or other individual goals, and need stability and long-term portfolio performance. Pension funds have been active in initiating and implementing corporate governance strategies in their portfolio companies.[6]

Mutual funds have shorter investment horizons, with an average holding period of two years or less. Mutual fund performance is measured quarterly. Mutual funds compete vigorously for investment assets, and use performance comparisons with other funds to compete. As a result, longer term involvement in governance issues of their portfolio companies tends to be less important to mutual fund managers than deciding when to enter and exit investment positions.

Similarly, hedge funds tend to have short-term investment strategies, but may seek to intervene in corporate management to generate near-term investment returns, such as dividends, stock repurchases, or a sale or merger of the company.

For institutional investors with long-term investment strategies, involvement in corporate governance is necessary because they need to maintain portfolio stability, or are too large to implement nimble or risky trading strategies.

Sizable institutional investors are so large that an attempt to quickly enter or leave an investment position, even with a large public company, could move the market. Accordingly, they do not expect to achieve consistent market-beating trading gains on a portfolio-wide basis. Some investors need to hold particular positions in order to maintain adequate portfolio diversification or to duplicate the performance of a particular market, market segment, or index.

In these situations, funds establish "watch lists" or use corporate governance tools to attempt to improve performance by the board and management of the companies whose shares are in their portfolios.

For example, growing out of the need to address its constituency of public employee retirees, the California Public Employees' Retirement System ("CalPERS") has defined its investment objective to be the generation of "long-term, sustainable, risk adjusted returns."[7] Significant thought and effort are required by any investor or operating company to obtain returns that are "long-term" and "sustainable" on a "risk-adjusted" basis.

---

6. Delineation Report at 142.
7. CalPERS http://www.calpers.ca.gov/index.jsp?bc=/about/mission/strategic-plan.xml
    (last visited June 25, 2010).

Companies can find themselves under considerable pressure from near-term stock market forces to adopt strategies that generate immediately measurable returns, rather than focusing on longer term strategies.

To address this concern, CalPERS, along with other institutional investors, public companies, industry groups, and corporate governance professionals have subscribed to the Aspen Principles, which call for a focus on long-term wealth creation rather than short-term stock trading results.[8]

At the same time, for any given company, institutional shareholders can address an individual company's concerns directly only by developing an understanding of the specific issues facing that company and industry segment. The market contains thousands of public companies that could be part of an institutional investor's portfolio, and the financial and governance information about each of those companies changes regularly.

No single market participant can meaningfully acquire and manage the entire range of information on all companies, and a portion of this activity is outsourced to the proxy advisory firms. Proxy advisory firms have emerged as influential players in governance matters, tracking governance questions across thousands of companies.

Because proxy advisory firms also provide advice to companies, they face potential conflicts of interest. The role of proxy advisory firms in the governance sector has drawn SEC attention and may in the future be the subject of additional rule making.[9]

3. Shareholder Voting

In economic terms, shareholders are considered to be the claimants of corporate enterprise value after creditor claims are satisfied. Shareholders are imbued with certain key rights in furtherance of their ability to protect this economic interest: the power to vote[10] both in director elections and on key corporate issues and the power to sue individually or in the name of

---

8.   *See* Aspen Inst., Long-Term Valuation Creation: Guiding Principles for Corporations and Investors §§ 1–3 (2007), *available at* http://www.aspeninstitute. org/sites/default/files/content/docs/business%20and%20society%20program/ FINALPRINCIPLES.pdf.

9.   Proxy concept release.

10. Del. Code Ann. Tit. 8, § 212(a)(2).

the corporation for breaches of fiduciary duty by the board of directors.[11] Additionally, in support of such rights, state law typically will provide a right to inspect corporate records for shareholders meeting minimum standards, such as number of shares held.

Shareholder litigation rights relating to fiduciary duties are discussed in Chapter II.3. Chapter IV.2 examines shareholder litigation rights in the context of individual liabilities that directors might incur in connection with various securities trading activities concerning the company.

Because shareholders can, and do, enter into transactions that can separate their economic risk in a company from their voting rights in that company, the SEC is reviewing whether so-called "empty voting" is affecting the shareholding voting process, and may in the future develop rules on the question.[12]

Voting rights can be complicated, and the legal minimum requirements may be varied by corporate organization documents or agreements.

Beyond election of directors, other key corporate decisions require shareholder approval. These include:

- mergers or acquisitions, where the corporation would cease its independent existence or where significant equity would be issued;

- dissolution of the corporation;

- amendments to governing instruments of the corporation, including the corporate charter and certain corporate bylaws;

- certain compensatory stock plans;

- advisory or mandatory votes on corporate policies advanced by the shareholders under SEC proxy rules.

The basic voting power of shares is governed by state law and by the corporate charter.[13] Different classes of shares can have different voting powers. State law, or the corporation's charter documents, may provide for the use of, or limitations on, voting agreements or the use of a written consent of a majority of shareholders to affect a corporate vote.[14]

In addition, the impact of shareholder voting may be diluted by having a staggered term for the board of directors, a mechanism that is

---

11. *Kramer v. Western Pac. Indus., Inc.*, 546 A.2d 348, 351 (Del. 1988) (quoting R. Clark, Corporate Law 639-640) (1986)); *Harff v. Kerkorian*, 324 A.2d 215, 218 (Del. Ch. 1974), *rev'd on other grounds*, 347 A.2d 133 (Del. 1975).

12. Proxy concept release.

13. Del. Code Ann. Tit. 8, §§ 212–219.

14. Del. Code Ann. Tit. 8, § 218.

used for (depending on one's perspective) preserving the corporation's independence in the face of unwanted takeover bids, or entrenching existing management.

Staggered terms for directors typically involve the election of only one-third of the board in any given year. The staggered board is a form of takeover protection because a would-be acquirer cannot replace the board in a single vote and must have the patience to wait through at least two election cycles to replace two-thirds of the board.

As a point of contrast, the impact of shareholder voting may be enhanced by statutory or charter provisions providing for "cumulative voting" of directors, which may enable a minority faction of shareholders to elect at least one director.[15] The effect of cumulative voting is to permit a minority shareholder faction to obtain board representation by "cumulating" all of that shareholder faction's votes for all potential board openings and placing those cumulated votes in favor of a single board candidate. Publicly traded corporations generally do not use cumulative voting.

In public companies that have only common stock outstanding, it is rare for a single shareholder to possess sufficient voting power to determine the outcome of director elections. In private companies, or in public companies in which there is a class of super-voting stock, there may be individual shareholders or groups whose ability to control the vote foreordains the outcome of shareholder elections or where the impact of a voting agreement is pronounced.

Super-voting stock is stock that has more than one vote per share in the election of directors or other corporate matters, at a time when the common stock has only one vote per share. In public companies, super-voting stock that existed prior to the time a company became publicly listed for trading is permitted, and often arises in the context of a traditional family-owned company that has offered a class of common stock to the public while retaining family control of the board through the super-voting class.

Often in private companies, particularly those held by small groups of investors, such as venture capitalists, the parties will enter into a voting agreement to ensure that the power to vote is exercised in accordance with investors' expectations.[16] Voting agreements also are used in merger or acquisition transactions to ensure that the approval of key shareholder

---

15. *See e.g.,* Del. Code Ann. Tit. 8, § 214 (charter provision may require that all elections of directors are conducted by cumulative voting); *but see* Cal. Corp. Code §§ 301.5(a), 303(a)(1) (all corporations are required to elect directors by cumulative voting, unless the corporation is publicly traded).

16. *See e.g.,* Del. Code Ann. Tit. 8, § 218.

voting blocks has been secured prior to submitting the merger or acquisition to a shareholder vote.

Another mechanism that could result in the consolidation of shareholder voting power is the voting trust.[17] Investors may create a voting trust by entering into a voting trust agreement, in which they transfer legal title to the shares to one or more trustees and agree on voting instructions for the trustee(s). During the life of a voting trust, participating investors receive dividends but they no longer possess voting power; instead, the trustee casts votes according to the instructions in the voting agreement.

Although shareholders elect the board of directors, shareholder democracy should not be equated with the political variety, for a number of reasons.[18] Contested director elections are rare; an investor considering whether to bear the cost and uncertainty of a proxy contest in a particular company will also consider whether the money is better applied to investing in another company entirely.

One key distinction in shareholder democracy is that a director is a fiduciary to all shareholders, regardless of whether a specific shareholder or shareholder group voted in favor or against that director, and regardless of the source of that director's nomination. A director is not legally entitled to have a limited constituency whose interest the director advances at the expense of the best interests of the corporation and all of its shareholders, unlike, say, a senator who advocates for the interests of a particular state.

Moreover, unlike a political incumbent, whose only penalty for failure in office would be to lose reelection, a director faces potential personal financial liability for breaches of fiduciary duty.

Boards and nominating committees seek out directors to ensure a balance of skills, experience, and viewpoints on corporate boards, and the nominations for director should reflect the judgment of which individuals will serve the corporation's interest. The role of shareholder voting is better considered as an enforcement mechanism available to shareholders to prevent ongoing weakness on a board, rather than as a mechanism by which competing candidates vie for office.

---

17. *Id.*

18. The Supreme Court decision in Citizens United raises the prospect that control of a corporation could result in control of corporate assets donated to political campaigns. *Citizens United v. Federal Election Commission*, 558 U.S. 50 (2010). However, the members of a board that undertakes material contributions to political activities would be subject to the requirements of fiduciary duty to act in the best interests of the corporation and shareholders.

In recent years, the rules on voting by shareholders have changed. Shareholders have an opportunity to vote electronically or by telephone and to receive proxy materials electronically.[19]

Dodd-Frank prevents brokers from having the discretion to vote the shares of beneficial owners on director elections or executive compensation, and provides the SEC authority to prohibit discretionary broker voting on other significant matters.[20] Prior to enactment of Dodd-Frank, NYSE rules required that brokers have direction from clients before executing a proxy card on director elections.[21]

Historically, companies counted on management-friendly broker votes to provide support for the board nominees. As more companies adopt policies that require a board nominee to receive a majority, rather than a plurality, of votes in order to remain on the board, the need to drum up votes from institutional investors becomes more pressing. Campaigns by shareholders or proxy advisors to withhold votes from individual nominees, or to vote against them, can be highly effective in those circumstances.

Under Dodd-Frank, the SEC was provided express authority to adopt rules under which shareholders may make proposals of nominees to the board of directors, and include the identification and discussion of qualifications of such nominees in the corporation's proxy statement ("proxy access").[22] The SEC adopted proxy access rules in August 2010.[23]

In addition, Dodd-Frank requires that shareholders provide a nonbinding vote on the compensation of executives. The "say on pay" vote is required not less than every three years, with shareholders being entitled to vote at least every six years on how often the "say on pay" vote should be required.[24]

A. Voting on Key Corporate Events

In addition to voting for directors, state corporation law generally will provide that shareholders are entitled to vote on certain substantive corporate events, typically those that affect the continued existence of the corporation, such as mergers, acquisitions, or dissolutions, and for

---

19. Del. Code Ann. Tit. 8, § 212(d).
20. Dodd-Frank 957.
21. Del. Code Ann. Tit. 8, § 217.
22. Dodd-Frank 971.
23. Proxy Access Adopting Release. The SEC suspanded implementation of the rules ahead of the 2011 proxy season as a result of pending litigation.
24. Dodd-Frank 951.

the amendment of corporate charter provisions, including those relating to the number of authorized shares, but extending to any other matter set out in the corporate charter.[25]

Except for shareholder initiatives, which shareholders may commence through the proxy process for publicly traded corporations, corporate management and the board of directors typically will have considered and approved a significant corporate event before it is proposed for adoption by the shareholders.

In the merger and acquisition context, either the board will have approached or been approached by a potential acquirer and have determined that the terms of a proposed transaction are fair or it will have pursued an acquisition whose terms require the issuance of so much corporate stock that shareholder approval is required.[26]

Where shareholder approval of an acquisition transaction is required, Dodd-Frank requires a separate vote on any severance or similar compensatory benefits for executives who are part of the transaction. Like the vote on executive compensation, the "say on parachute" vote in an acquisition transaction is nonbinding, and Dodd-Frank expressly provides that the voting requirement does not change the fiduciary duties of directors.[27]

In either case, the key evaluations of the transaction, including the fairness of the terms to the shareholders, normally are reviewed by the management and board prior to submission to shareholders for a vote and are usually supported by a fairness opinion provided by investment bankers or other valuation specialists in order to provide independent confirmation that the board's decision represented an appropriate exercise of its fiduciary duties.

Shareholder votes for amendments to the corporate charter frequently occur in the context of an approval to increase the authorized number of shares, in order to implement a stock split, stock option, or other equity compensation plan. They also may involve approval of charter provisions to implement a director and officer indemnification plan under state law, or protective provisions that make corporate takeover more difficult, such as the creation of a staggered board term or ratification of a board decision to adopt a corporate "poison pill" provision.

---

25. *See e.g.* Del. Code Ann. Tit. 8, §§ 212(a)-(b).
26. Del. Code Ann. Tit. 8, § 251(c).
27. Dodd-Frank 951.

Some poison pill plans, by their terms, require periodic readoption by shareholders. In recent years, measures that are protective of corporate management, such as poison pills, have fallen out of favor. Institutional investor reviewing organizations such as ISS regard the existence of poison pills as negative factors in weighing a corporation's board.[28] In response, boards sometimes have determined not to request that shareholders approve such readoptions, allowing the poison pills to lapse.[29]

B. Compensatory Plans

If the board adopts a stock option plan that offers incentive stock options, the Internal Revenue Code requires shareholder approval of that plan within a year of board adoption.[30] Additionally, the NYSE[31] and NASDAQ[32] require that corporations obtain the ratification of their shareholders for the adoption of stock option plans.

The SEC adopted a proxy statement rule that requires corporations to disclose the total number of compensatory shares that were available for issuance, specifying which share issuances had been approved by shareholders and which had not.[33]

So long as a corporation has authorized shares available, the board is entitled as a matter of corporate law to issue additional shares for appropriate consideration.[34] Accordingly, shareholders are always susceptible to having their percentage shareholdings diluted by additional issuances.

Option plans represent something of a unique situation for the issuance of corporate securities: The corporation's commitment to issue stock at the fair market value on the date of the option grant locks the corporation into a fixed price that is expected to be lower than the fair market value at the time the option is exercised. In fact, options can only have their intended incentive effect if the employees who receive the options are able to buy

---

28. Carol Bowie, *Fewer Firms Maintain Defenses*, Institutional Shareholder Services, http://blog.riskmetrics.com/gov/2006/06/fewer-firms-maintain-defensessubmitted-by-carol-bowie-vice-president-and-director-governance-researc.html (last visited June 27, 2010).

29. Neil Henderson, *Whither the Poison Pill?*, http://www.conyersdill.com/publications/view/whither-the-poison-pill (last visited June 27, 2010).

30. I.R.C. § 422.

31. NYSE Rule 303A.08.

32. NASDAQ Rule 4350(i).

33. SEC Regulation S-K, Item 201.

34. *See, e.g.,* Del. Code Ann. Tit. 8, § 161.

the stock from the corporation at a price that represents a discount to a future, higher market price.

C. *Majority Voting for Directors*

Most state corporation laws provide that directors are elected by a plurality of the votes cast at a meeting unless a company's governing instruments state otherwise.[35] Plurality voting means that those nominees for board positions who receive the highest number of "for" votes are elected.

Under plurality voting and SEC rules, shareholders cannot vote "no" for a nominee but may "withhold" their votes.[36] Therefore, withheld votes do not count as votes against a director, and a company nominee is elected to the board as long as he or she is not opposed by another nominee and gets at least one vote.

In recent years, in response to the efforts of institutional shareholders, a substantial number of large public companies have adopted provisions to implement "majority voting" provisions for the election of directors.[37] Small capitalization companies have not followed suit, but may find themselves dealing with majority voting questions over time.[38]

In contrast to plurality voting, a majority voting standard would require a director nominee standing for election to receive support from a majority of: (1) shares voted in the election; (2) shares present at a shareholder meeting and entitled to vote (also referred to as votes cast); or (3) shares outstanding and eligible to vote.

There can be a significant difference in the outcome of an election depending upon which of these different "majorities" is specified. A standard that requires nominees to receive affirmative votes of a majority of shares voted in the election will count votes "for" and votes "against" the nominee, but votes withheld will not count. A standard that requires nominees to receive the affirmative vote of a majority of shares present and entitled to vote will count proxy cards marked "withhold" as a vote against the nominee. A standard that requires nominees to receive the affirmative vote of a majority of outstanding shares will effectively treat nonvotes and proxies marked "withhold" as a vote against the nominee.

---

35. *See, e.g.,* Del. Code Ann. Tit. 8, § 216(3).
36. *See* SEC Rule 14a-4(b)(2).
37. William Baue, Majority-Vote Director Election Shareowner Resolutions To Top 100, Dominate Proxy Season, http://www.institutionalshareowner.com/article. mpl?sfArticleId=1902 (last visited June 27, 2010).
38. http://www.directorship.com/majority-voting-for-director-elections/.

Many companies have elected to adopt policies that provide that a nominee must resign if he or she receives more than a specified number of "withhold" votes. Most of the companies adopting modifications to a plurality voting standard have done so through adoption of a corporate governance standard rather than through a charter or bylaw amendment.

Other companies have adopted what is known as a "modified plurality" standard. These policies typically state that, in uncontested elections, any director nominee who receives a greater number of votes "withheld" from his or her election than votes "for" such election must promptly tender his or her resignation following certification of the shareholder vote.

If a company adopts a policy that requires that a nominee receive more affirmative votes than "withhold" votes, this gives proxy cards marked "withhold" the effect of a vote against the nominee. In contrast, in a majority vote standard based on a majority of votes cast at a meeting, votes for and against a nominee would be counted, but proxies marked "withhold" would not be counted. By mid-2006, at least 90 companies had adopted corporate governance guidelines to provide for a modified plurality standard with respect to director elections.[39]

Delaware law was amended in 2006 to facilitate the implementation of majority voting measures by corporations.[40]

Delaware law permits shareholders to make binding bylaw amendment proposals on majority voting, although plurality voting remains the default if such majority voting provisions are not affirmatively adopted.[41] Delaware law also makes it possible to enforce a director's irrevocable advance resignation that would become effective upon failing to receive a majority of votes cast in an election.[42]

D. Advisory Vote on Compensation

Under Dodd-Frank, beginning in 2011, shareholders must be provided a chance to make an annual, nonbinding vote on executive compensation.[43] Prior to enactment of Dodd-Frank, TARP recipients were required to conduct

---

39. *See* Study of Majority Voting in Director Elections by Claudia H. Allen (the "Allen Study") (http://www.ngelaw.com/files/upload/majority051806.pdf).
40. *See* Del. Code Ann. Tit. 8, § 216.
41. *See* Del. Code Ann. Tit. 8, § 216.
42. Del. Code Ann. Tit. 8, § 141(b).
43. Dodd-Frank 951.

"say on pay" votes,[44] and some companies had voluntarily adopted "say on pay" shareholder votes.

As these votes are advisory, executive compensation is not revoked as a result of a vote against the executive compensation. Dodd-Frank expressly provides that the advisory vote shall not be binding on the company or the board of directors, and "may not be construed... as overruling a decision by such issuer or board of directors."[45]

The "say on pay" votes must occur at least every three years. Shareholders shall be given the opportunity to vote, at least every six years, on whether to conduct the "say on pay" vote annually, every two years, or every three years.[46]

Revelations of executive pay abuses in the early 2000s in companies such as Tyco provided the initial fuel for the "say on pay" movement. Revelations of huge executive compensation packages and bonuses paid by companies that were active contributors to the financial crisis of 2008 and which accepted TARP bailouts generated additional outrage around executive pay issues. The issues related not only to the size of the payments, but also to whether the structure of incentive programs induced executives to put corporate assets at risk to hit bonus targets.

Prior to the mandatory "say on pay" vote requirement in Dodd-Frank, some companies had voluntarily adopted "say on pay," or adopted it as an obligation under TARP. Most of those votes approved executive compensation, with a negative vote at Motorola in 2010 being a prominent exception.

For institutional shareholders, monitoring all elements of executive compensation is an additional strain on resources. Some investors use "red flag" indicators to try to grasp key potential risk areas quickly, such as oversized perquisite packages, lack of policies to "clawback" erroneously awarded bonuses, or pay inequality between executives and the employee base.[47]

As with shareholder proposals or proxy access, "say on pay" in practice may have its most meaningful impact as a framework in which institutional investors engage with companies regarding compensation concerns.

---

44. Release 34-613351, under Rule 14a-20.

45. Dodd-Frank 951.

46. Dodd-Frank 951.

47. See Yerger, "Red Flags for Say-on-Pay Voting" posted on the Harvard Law School Forum on Corporate Governance and Financial Regulation, at http://blogs.law.harvard.edu/corpgov/2010/05/18/red-flags-for-say-on-pay-voting/#more-9507.

Dodd-Frank requires additional disclosures in the proxy statement that call out "red flag" topics that had not previously been the subject of proxy disclosure.

Companies will be obligated to make disclosures about their policies on permitting employees and directors to "hedge" against losses in company securities that they own or have been granted as compensation,[48] as well as disclosures on the ratio of CEO pay to the average pay of company employees, and the ratio of CEO pay to corporate performance, taking into account changes in share price and dividends and distributions.[49]

Dodd-Frank also requires that companies disclose whether they have adopted policies to recover bonuses that were awarded on the basis of erroneous financial statements.[50]

4. Proxy Statements and Shareholder Proposals

For publicly traded corporations, the proxy rules establish a specific and detailed format for submitting matters to a vote of shareholders through the proxy statement, and providing specified information to the shareholders at the time the vote is solicited.[51] In addition to the specific elements identified in the SEC rules, there is a general rule that proxy statements may not contain any materially misleading statements or omit material information.[52]

Proxy statements are critical disclosure documents for publicly traded companies. Some material in proxy statements appears in no other corporate disclosures made by the corporation, and unlike quarterly and annual reports, which are only required to be filed with the SEC, proxy statements are mailed directly to shareholders.[53] As with any other corporate disclosure document, the proxy statement must be reviewed with care by directors before it is distributed to shareholders. The SEC has been willing to bring sanctions against directors for defects in the proxy statement.[54]

---

48. Dodd-Frank 953.
49. Dodd-Frank 953.
50. Dodd-Frank 954.
51. SEC Rule 14a-3; § 240.14a-5.
52. SEC Rule 14a-9.
53. SEC Rule 14a-3.
54. *In re W.R. Grace*, SEC Release 34-39156 (1997).

In addition, Delaware law has established a fiduciary duty of disclosure for directors who are communicating with shareholders regarding matters subject to a proxy vote.[55] Under Delaware law, directors must disclose all material information within their control at the time shareholder action is sought.[56] Directors (independent or not) who make deliberate misstatements or omissions in communications to shareholders that result in damage to the shareholders can face liability as a result of such breach of duty.[57]

The thrust of both the federal and state law is to prevent shareholders from approving — or declining to approve — a matter based on incorrect or inadequate facts.[58] Certain Delaware cases arose in the context of a description of a transaction in which a director was an interested party;[59] but the disclosure duty does not relate solely to interested director transactions.[60]

The SEC proxy rules in Rule 14a-8 provide that shareholders are entitled to propose matters to be included in the proxy statement.[61] The proxy statement for the corporation's annual meeting will designate a date for submission of proposals for the following year's shareholder meeting.

The corporation may exclude a shareholder proposal from the proxy statement if the proposal submission fails to meet the procedural requirements of Rule 14a-8, or if the proposal falls into one of the categories of unacceptable proposals enumerated in the rule.[62]

Shareholder proposals may be social proposals, i.e., proposals that include certain matters that have significant policy, economic, or other implications inherent in them.[63] Social proposals typically are advanced by groups advocating particular social issues who own marginal shares in the company. Most shareholder proposals on social issues are included

---

55. *ODS Techs., L.P. v. Marshall*, 832 A.2d 1254 (Del. Ch. 2003) (board of directors breached its fiduciary duty because the corporation's proxy statement was false and misleading).

56. *Malone v. Brincat*, 722 A.2d 5, 12 (Del. 1998).

57. *Id.*

58. SEC Rule 14a-9.

59. *See e.g. Malone*, 722 A.2d 5 (holding that directors breached their fiduciary duty by knowingly disseminating false information causing damage or corporate injury to an individual stockholder).

60. *See e.g. Arnold v. Society For Savings Bancorp.*, 650 A.2d 1270, 1281 (Del. 1994) (holding that corporation was required to disclose material information).

61. SEC Rule 14a-8.

62. SEC Rule 14a-8(f).

63. SEC Rule14a-8(i)(5).

by corporations, but they rarely receive more than 10% of shareholder votes.[64] For this reason, corporations often will include such proposals in the proxy statement and advise shareholders to vote against them rather than generate undue attention or expense by fighting the inclusion of the proposal. Shareholder proposals also may be advanced by economic shareholders who have specific economic or strategic directions that they would like to see the corporation take. Many proposals will relate to specific elements of board governance.

Management is entitled to dispute whether such matters are appropriate for a shareholder vote and exclude those matters from the proxy.[65] The SEC must determine whether such matters may or may not appear on a corporate proxy statement.[66] Generally, the burden is on the company to demonstrate that it is entitled to exclude a proposal.[67]

As a practical matter, a shareholder proposal request often becomes an opportunity for a company and key institutional investor to talk directly about the investor's concerns. Companies may find a way to address the concerns without recourse to a proxy vote.

In order to be eligible to submit a proposal, the shareholder "must have continuously held at least $2,000 in market value, or 1%, of the company's securities entitled to be voted on the proposal for at least one year" prior to the submission of the proposal, and "must continue to hold those securities through the date of the meeting."[68] If the shareholder holds shares in street name, the shareholder must verify that the ownership requirements have been met, using the procedures codified in Rule 14a-8.[69] This percentage ownership threshold for submitting a shareholder proposal lower than the 3% and three-year "proxy access" threshold ownership requirement under the proxy access rules.[70]

---

64. Ernst Maug, *What is the Function of the Shareholder Meeting? Evidence from the U.S. Proxy Voting Process*, June 6, 2001, http://www.fep.up.pt/investigacao/cempre/actividades/sem_fin/sem_fin_01/PAPERS_PDF/paper_sem_fin_18out01.pdf.
65. SEC Rule 14a-8(f), (g), and (i).
66. *Id.*
67. SEC Rule 14a-8(g).
68. SEC Rule 14a-8(b).
69. *Id.*
70. Proxy Access Adopting Release.

An individual shareholder may submit no more than one proposal to a company for a particular shareholders' meeting.[71] The proposal and any supporting statement may be no longer than 500 words.[72]

The unacceptable categories of shareholder proposals are those that involve:

1. *Improper under state law:* The SEC has noted that in many cases proposals are not considered proper under state law if they would be binding on the company upon adoption by shareholders but can be proper if they are cast as recommendations or requests that the board of directors take specified action.[73]

2. *Violation of law:* A proposal is improper if it "would, if implemented, cause the company to violate any state, federal, or foreign law to which it is subject."[74]

3. *Violation of proxy rules:* A proposal is improper "[i]f the proposal or supporting statement is contrary to any [SEC] proxy rule, including the [rule against] materially false or misleading statements in proxy soliciting materials."[75]

4. *Personal grievance; special interest:* A proposal is improper "[i]f it relates to the redress of a personal claim or grievance against the company or any other person, or if it is designed to benefit the [individual shareholder]" rather than the other shareholders at large.[76]

5. *Relevance:* A proposal is improper if "[i]t relates to operations which account for less than 5% of the company's total assets at the end of its most recent fiscal year, and for less than 5% of its net earnings and gross sales for its most recent fiscal year and is not otherwise significantly related to the company's business."[77]

---

71. SEC Rule 14a-8(c).
72. SEC Rule 14a-8(d).
73. SEC Rule 14a-8(i)(1).
74. SEC Rule 14a-8(i)(2).
75. SEC Rule 14a-8(i)(3).
76. SEC Rule 14a-8(i)(4).
77. SEC Rule 14a-8(i)(5).

6. *Absence of power/authority:* A proposal is improper "[i]f the company would lack the power or authority to implement the proposal."[78]

7. *Management functions:* A proposal is improper if it "deals with a matter relating to the company's ordinary business operations."[79]

8. *Relates to election:* A proposal is improper if it would affect an upcoming election for membership on the company's board of directors, except as specifically provided in the proxy rules.[80]

9. *Conflicts with company's proposal:* A proposal is improper if it "directly conflicts with one of the company's own proposals to be submitted to shareholders at the same meeting."[81]

10. *Substantially implemented:* A proposal is improper if the corporation "has already substantially implemented the proposal."[82]

11. *Duplication:* A proposal is improper if it substantially duplicates another proposal previously submitted to the company that will be included in the company's proxy materials for the same meeting.[83]

12. *Resubmissions:* A proposal is improper if it deals with substantially the same subject matter as another proposal that has been previously included in the company's proxy materials if the proposal received:

    (i)   less than 3% of the vote if proposed once within the preceding five calendar years;

    (ii) less than 6% of the vote on its last submission to shareholders if proposed twice previously within the preceding five calendar years; or

    (iii) less than 10% of the vote on its last submission to shareholders if proposed three times or more previously within the preceding five calendar years.[84]

---

78. SEC Rule 14a-8(i)(6).
79. SEC Rule 14a-8(i)(7).
80. SEC Rule 14a-8(i)(8).
81. SEC Rule 14a-8(i)(9).
82. SEC Rule 14a-8(i)(10).
83. SEC Rule 14a-8(i)(11).
84. SEC Rule 14a-8(i)(12).

13. *Specific amount of dividends:* The proposal "relates to specific amounts of cash or stock dividends."[85]

The SEC has provided additional guidance on the standards it applies in addressing requests for exclusion of shareholder proposals.[86]

5. Director Nominations by Shareholders and Proxy Access

Shareholders often have the right in a corporate charter to nominate candidates for election to the board of directors.[87] Institutional investors have long advocated to have the ability to include information about shareholder nominees in the corporate proxy statement ("proxy access"), lowering the cost to shareholders of offering alternative candidates to those offered by management, and in 2010 the SEC, under authority granted in Dodd-Frank, adopted rules under which proxy access can be conducted.[88]

Critics of proxy access argue that its objective is not to provide an electable alternative director, but to use the election and proxy statement process as a means to amplify and publicize a particular shareholder's concerns about the company to other shareholders and the public at large.[89] Proxy access proponents argue that removing barriers to shareholder participation in the election of directors provides another means to prevent management entrenchment and benefits shareholders generally.[90]

Whether or not a shareholder is seeking proxy access for a nominee, the SEC proxy rules make the corporation's treatment of shareholders in the director nomination process the subject of proxy statement disclosures.[91]

---

85. SEC Rule 14a-8(i)(13).

86. SEC Rule 14a-8(j); *see also* Amendments to Rules on Shareholder Proposals, SEC Release 34-40018 (May 26, 1998) ("Shareholder Proposal Q&A").

87. *See e.g. Harrah's Entm't, Inc. v. JCC Holding Co.*, 802 A.2d 294 (Del. Ch. 2002) (dispute regarding whether the corporation's charter allowed minority shareholder to nominate more than one director).

88. Dodd-Frank 971; Proxy Access Adopting Release.

89. *See* Grundfest, "The SEC's Proposed Proxy Access Rules: Politics, Economics and the Law," 65 Business Lawyer 361 (2010).

90. See Bebchuck and Hirst, "Private Ordering and the Proxy Access Debate," 65 Business Lawyer 329 (2010).

91. SEC Release 33-8340 (2003) ("Nominating Committee Release").

The nominating committee, or the board if there is no nominating committee, is required to disclose in the proxy statement whether it has a policy concerning consideration of director candidates recommended by shareholders.[92] If such a policy exists, the proxy statement must include a description of the material elements of the policy, including whether the committee will consider such director candidates.[93] If the nominating committee does not have a policy concerning consideration of director candidates recommended by shareholders, it must disclose that fact and specify the reasons the board considers it appropriate for the company not to have such a policy.[94]

If the nominating committee will consider shareholder recommendations for candidates, the proxy statement must describe:[95]

- the procedures shareholders must follow to submit a recommendation;

- any specific, minimum qualifications the nominating committee has set for board nominees or any specific qualities or skills that the nominating committee believes are necessary for one or more of the company's directors to possess;

- a description of the nominating committee's process for identifying and evaluating nominees for director, including nominees recommended by shareholders; and

- any differences in the manner in which the nominating committee evaluates nominees for director based on whether the nominee is recommended by a shareholder.

The proxy statement also must include a statement regarding the process whereby shareholders may communicate directly to the board of directors, or, if none exists, a statement of that fact and a statement explaining the reasons the board considers it appropriate for the company not to have such a policy.[96]

---

92. SEC Regulation S-K, Item 407(c)(1).
93. SEC Regulation S-K, Item 407(c)(1).
94. SEC Regulation S-K, Item 407(c)(1).
95. SEC Regulation S-K, Item 407(c)(2).
96. SEC Regulation S-K, Item 407(f).

Under its authority under Dodd-Frank, the SEC adopted Rule 14a-11, which provides a detailed process by which shareholder nominees for director may be included in the company proxy materials.[97]

The rule is not the exclusive method by which shareholders may propose nominees to the board. Traditional proxy contests, for which the costs or preparing and distributing a separate dissenting set of proxy materials are borne by shareholders, are still permitted.

Under Rule 14a-11, shareholders and shareholder groups who have held both investment and voting power of at least 3% of the voting power of a company's securities continuously for at least three years have the right to include nominees for director on the ballot in the company's proxy statement. The shareholders must hold the shares through the date of the meeting at which directors are selected. The ownership calculation takes into account securities transactions that can have the effect of reducing the shareholders' economic exposure to the company during the 3-year ownership qualification period. If more than one shareholder or shareholder group intends to nominate directors at an annual meeting, the access will be provided to the largest shareholding block.

Shareholders can use Rule 14a-11 to nominate not more than 25% of the board (with a minimum of one director). If the company has a classified board for which only one-third of the directors are being elected, shareholder nominees serving a three-year term will count against the 25% maximum for the following two annual meetings. A director nominated by the company after being initially proposed by shareholders would be included against the 25% maximum.

The rule will not apply to companies that have a market capitalization under $75 million until 2013. In October 2010, the SEC delayed implementation of Rule 14a-11 in light of pending court challenges.[98]

A shareholder nominee must meet any objective (but not subjective) independence requirements of the company's exchange, as well as any state or federal eligibility requirements.

Shareholders cannot use Rule 14a-11 to include director nominations in the company's proxy materials if they intend to seek a change in control of the company or to exceed the 25% of the board maximum. Nominee

---

97. SEC Rule 14a-11; see also SEC Release Nos. 33-9136; 34-62764; IC-29384 Facilitating Shareholder Director Nominations ("Proxy Access Adopting Release"), available at http://www.sec.gov/rules/final/2010/33-9136.pdf.

98. SEC Release No. 9149, available at http://www.sec.gov/rules/other/2010/33-9149. pdf.

descriptions provided by the shareholders cannot exceed 500 words per nominee.

In order to have a nominee included in the company proxy materials, the shareholders must notify the company by filing a Schedule 14N no earlier than 150 days, and no later than 120 days, prior to the anniversary of the mailing date for the prior year's proxy materials. If the shareholders intend to form a 3% shareholding group for purposes of making a nomination that could be included in the company's proxy materials, they must file a Schedule 14N notifying the company of their intent to solicit support for such a group.

In the Schedule 14N, shareholders must certify that they intend to hold shares through the date of the shareholder meeting, they do not intend to change control of the company or nominate directors in excess of the 25% maximum under Rule 14a-11, and that they believe that the nominee meets relevant director qualifications.

A company can contest the inclusion in the proxy statement of a proposed nominee using the SEC's administrative "no action" process not more than 80 days before the final proxy materials are filed with the SEC, provided that the shareholder is provided with an opportunity to correct problems identified by the company.

The SEC also adopted amendments to narrow the "election exclusion" in Rule 14a-8(i)(8) which will allow shareholders to make proposals to broaden (but not narrow) proxy access, such as a lower ownership threshold, a shorter holding period or to allow for a greater number of nominees. These amendments were also delayed in light of challenges to Rule 14a-11.

6. Communications with Shareholders

The SEC also requires that corporations provide disclosure in the proxy statement regarding the process for shareholders to communicate with board members.

The proxy statement must state:
- whether the corporation provides a process for shareholders to communicate with directors, and if not, why not;
- a description of the communication process, if the corporation has one; and

- a statement regarding the corporation's policy regarding the atten- dance of directors at shareholder meetings, including a statement of the number of board members who attended the prior year's annual meeting.[99]

Shareholders desiring to communicate directly with the board are likely to want to address a matter of corporate governance, rather than operations. Direct communication can provide board members of a company with an opportunity to understand what a key institutional investor would like to see in governance.

Corporations that adopt a shareholder communication policy need to be mindful of various legal restrictions on communications to prevent potential problems from arising. Typically, the corporation will appoint a single point of contact, such as the CEO or investment relations personnel, to speak on behalf of the corporation. For communications with the board, or with a particular committee of the board, the lead independent director or chair of the committee might be the appropriate point of contact.

Having a specified individual handle the communication helps prevent the corporation from needing to be concerned about the potential appearance or reality of conflicting or inconsistent messages being delivered. In addition, personnel who have ongoing public communications duties are aware of the need to phrase statements carefully to avoid creating an obligation to make future corrections or updates to such information.

In addition, the SEC's Regulation FD prohibits corporations from making "selective disclosures" of material information to some investors and not others. A disclosure of material information to one investor could trigger a requirement by the corporation to make a public disclosure of the information to all investors.[100]

7. Review of Governance by Third Parties

Investors, particularly institutional investors, have a multitude of sources of information available to them concerning corporate performance and evaluations of corporate governance. ISS is one widely followed service. Other services, such as Moody's, Standard & Poor's, GovernanceMetrics International, and the Corporate Library also provide governance ratings.

---

99. SEC Regulation S-K, Item 407(f).
100. SEC Regulation FD.

Because such ratings can have a bearing on the investment community's perception of the quality of a corporation, directors should be aware of the ratings of the corporations for which they serve and have some general understanding of the ratings systems.

For example, ISS provides research and advisory services to institutional investors to assess proxy proposals. ISS has established a Corporate Governance Quotient (the CGQ) rating system, based on publicly available disclosure documents, which ranks corporations against market indices and against a peer group based on the evaluation of eight key governance areas.

Other rating services also have established ratings criteria. Standard & Poor's, for instance, issues a Corporate Governance Score (CGS), which provides an assessment of how a company's governance process serves the interests of financial stakeholders based on numerous criteria and in-depth analysis. Moody's provides a Corporate Governance Assessment (CGA) as part of its services.

Boards should ensure that management is aware of one or more of these governance rankings, and highlight for board action any areas that might raise concern for company investors.

8. Conclusion

The role of shareholders in the corporate governance process has historically been relatively passive, but the past decade has seen an increasing activism by shareholders to take a larger role in governance matters. However, not all shareholders necessarily have the same interest in all companies.

At the same time, independent directors have been delegated more significant responsibilities in the corporate governance process. It is the board's obligation to act in the best interests of shareholders, and the board is entitled to use its business judgment in deciding how to do so.

Like the evolution in the standards relating to corporate governance, the evolving relationship between shareholders and companies is a development that independent directors must continue to monitor and address as circumstances arise.

Committees and Board Operations

1. Introduction

A board of directors normally will have legal authority to delegate to a committee the power and responsibility to act on specified matters. Using committees to address specific questions provides a board flexibility in convening and conducting meetings with a smaller group.

Primary corporate governance activities are given over to three key board committees, each of which must be comprised of independent directors. These committees are (1) the audit committee, (2) the compensation committee, and (3) the nominating committee. In addition to the summary description of those committees in this chapter, each is discussed in greater detail in a separate chapter in this book.

Growing out of the accounting malfeasance scandals of the early 2000s, SOX focused on the audit committee. SOX granted the audit committee broad authority, assigned the audit committee extensive and specific responsibilities, and set out membership and experience requirements for the audit committee members.

Growing out of the financial crisis of 2007-08, the governance elements of Dodd-Frank focused on executive compensation issues, independence of the directors on the compensation committee and their advisors, and on greater disclosure of compensation- related matters.[1]

Even prior to adoption of Dodd-Frank, the obligations and responsibilities of the compensation committee and the nominating committee had expanded and become more detailed and comprehensive.

In addition to the audit, nominating, and compensation committees, a board also may establish other committees for specific purposes, such as a "qualified legal compliance committee," investigative subcommittees, special litigation committees, or committees to review specific transactions or for specific limited purposes. Such committees typically require independent directors or directors who are free from conflicts of interest concerning the committee's subject matter.

This chapter discusses the roles of each of these committees, and how the committees fit in with the board governance structure.

These operational issues include how the board determines whether to separate the position of board chair from the CEO position as well as how it conducts board self-evaluations, approves related party transactions, and develops director nominations. Other aspects of board operations have also been transformed from nonmandatory or suggested "best practices" to matters that are either regulated or the subject of mandatory disclosure.

This chapter will discuss these structural and operational board level issues and how independent directors are involved in those matters.

While there were legislative proposals in 2010 to require public companies to establish separate risk committees, Dodd-Frank mandated risk committees only for financial services companies. Separate risk committees are not unusual in the financial services industry. The risk analysis function for other companies is generally addressed by the audit committee or the board as a whole. For NYSE-listed companies, the audit committee must review the company's risk assessment and risk management policies,[2] and the audit committee charter must state that the audit committee is responsible for discussing the company's risk assessment and risk management policies.[3] The SEC requires that companies evaluate

---

1.   See Dodd-Frank 951-956.
2.   NYSE Rule 303A.07(c)(iii)(D).
3.   *Id.*

the linkage of executive compensation and risk, which may be conducted by the board, the compensation committee, or another committee.

2. Audit Committee

The audit committee function is highly regulated under SOX. The audit committee's importance in corporate governance is reflected in the depth of regulation to which it is subject and the number of functions assigned to it.

The audit committee must be comprised of independent directors only. No audit committee member may be an "affiliate" of the company as defined under SEC Rule 10A-3. At least one member of the audit committee must be a "financial expert," which requires a person who has experience in preparing, auditing, analyzing, or evaluating financial statements or in actively supervising individuals who conducted such activities.

The list of required audit committee activities is lengthy (a detailed list and discussion is contained in Chapter III.2). Broadly, the categories of activities that the audit committee is required to perform are:

- Selecting, paying, and overseeing the independence, qualifications, and scope of work conducted by the independent auditors who review the financial statements;

- Overseeing management's preparation of the disclosure to the public of financial information;

- Providing a process for corporate "whistleblowers" to inform the audit committee of financial improprieties;

- Overseeing resolution of disagreements between management and the independent auditor;

- Establishing hiring policies for employees or former employees of the auditor;[4]

- Reviewing the auditor's opinion regarding management's internal financial controls report under SOX Section 404,[5] as well as critical accounting policies and practices, alternative treatments of financial information within generally accepted accounting principles, other material written communications between the independent auditor and management, and other key accounting policies and judgments;

---

4.   NYSE Rule 303A.07(c)(iii)(G).
5.   SEC Regulation S-K, Item 308(a).

- Reviewing annual audited financial statements and quarterly financial statements with management and the auditor (and internal auditor, if the corporation has one), including reviewing the corporation's specific disclosures in the Management's Discussion and Analysis of Financial Condition and Results of Operations ("MD&A") section of quarterly and annual reports filed with the SEC;[6]

- Reviewing the company's code of ethics and disclosing any waivers of the code for executive officers and directors.

3. Compensation Committee

The compensation committee reviews and establishes executive compensation, primarily the CEO's compensation, and in some cases the compensation of other senior corporate officers, as well as director compensation. Compensation includes not only salary but also bonuses, perquisites, equity incentives such as stock options or stock grants, and benefits such as salary continuation plans, severance plans, retirement plans, and the like.

The effects of executive compensation decisions can be far-reaching, as those decisions can affect the recruitment and retention of key managers.

Dodd-Frank mandates that the SEC require the securities exchanges to adopt listing requirements by 2011 that provide for an independent compensation committee.[7] Prior to enactment of Dodd-Frank, the SEC did not require that a company establish a compensation committee, but a company without a compensation committee would have to disclose why not having a committee was appropriate and identify the directors who make compensation decisions.[8] Financial services companies that accepted U.S. Treasury investment under the Capital Participation Program ("TARP recipients") must have compensation committees comprised of independent directors to undertake the obligations associated with accepting the U.S. Treasury investment.

Prior to enactment of Dodd-Frank, the NYSE required a compensation committee for its listed companies and NASDAQ did not. If a compensation committee had not been established, and the board as a whole acted on

---

6.   SEC Regulation S-K, Item 306(a)(2).

7.   Dodd-Frank 952.

8.   SEC Regulation S-K, Item 407(e).

compensation decisions, NASDAQ rules required that only independent directors could participate in the decisions.[9]

Publicly traded companies typically will establish compensation committees to deal with various tax, securities, and exchange rules that make compensation committees desirable even for non-NYSE companies. For ease of discussions in this book, the compensation function undertaken by independent directors will generally be described as being performed by the compensation committee.

The SEC requires that the dollar value of the various executive compensation elements (salary, bonuses, options, etc.) be itemized and disclosed in tables in the company's annual proxy statement.[10]

The SEC also requires that the company's compensation decisions be explained in the annual proxy statement under the "compensation discussion and analysis" section ("CD&A"). The required discussion is expected to cover each element of compensation appearing in the tables. The compensation committee is required to prepare for the proxy statement a separate compensation committee report that confirms that the compensation committee reviewed the CD&A with management and recommended to the board that the CD&A be included in the proxy statement.[11]

The compensation committee must deal with those executive compensation arrangements that are subject to legal restrictions. These restricted areas include severance compensation arrangements for executives (which are regulated under the Internal Revenue Code), compensation limits for executives of TARP recipients, option and equity payments, and restrictions on payments that have the effect of shifting compensation from one tax year to another.

Some elements of compensation, such as stock option or equity plans, must be approved by shareholders under the rules of NYSE and NASDAQ.

Beginning in 2011, Dodd-Frank mandates that public companies must provide shareholders the opportunity to vote on whether they approve of the compensation packages provided to the corporation's executives at least once every three years. The "say on pay" votes are advisory, and

---

9. NASDAQ Rule 4350(c)(3); IM-4350-4.
10. SEC Regulation S-K, Item 402.
11. A "smaller reporting company" under SEC rules is not required to include a compensation committee report in its proxy statement.

not binding.[12] Such "say on pay" votes had previously been mandatory for TARP recipients.

Dodd-Frank also mandates disclosure in the proxy statement of the ratio of the CEO compensation to the company's financial performance, including stock price and dividend policy. In addition, companies will be required to disclose the ratio of the CEO's compensation to the average compensation of the company's other employees.[13]

Review of CEO compensation also will often include review of CEO performance and whether the CEO or the corporation has achieved any targets set by the board to trigger incentive compensation. Because compensation is so intimately tied to job performance, the compensation committee sometimes also is charged with considering CEO succession issues, although those matters are sometimes referred to a governance or nominating committee.

The SEC requires that the board disclose in the proxy statement any material information to shareholders respecting the board's evaluation of whether compensation programs for executives incentivize those executives to take undue risks.[14] As this evaluation requires a review of not only compensation but also the company's risk profile, the compensation committee may not be the only committee involved in the evaluation.

4. Nominating Committee

The foremost task of the nominating committee is to develop a list of nominees for election to the board. That list typically should include incumbents. The committee also may be assigned broader governance tasks, such as determining the composition of board committees, or dealing with board operational and structural issues such as the separation of the board chair and CEO functions. The nominating committee is sometimes referred to as the "nominating and governance committee."

The SEC does not require that a company establish a nominating committee, but if the company does not, it must disclose why not having

---

12. Dodd-Frank 951. Prior to adoption of Dodd-Frank, TARP recipients were subject to "say on pay" requirements under the American Recovery and Reinvestment Act of 2009 (ARRA) Feb. 17, 2009; Interim Rule § 14a-20.

13. Dodd-Frank 953.

14. SEC Regulation S-K, Item 402(s).

a committee is appropriate and identify the process by which nominations are made and which directors are involved in those decisions.[15]

The NYSE requires a nominating committee for its listed companies; the NASDAQ does not. If a nominating committee has not been established, and the board as a whole acts on nomination matters, NASDAQ rules require that only independent directors may participate in the decisions.[16]

Publicly traded companies typically will establish nominating committees to deal with substantive nomination processes and the disclosures that are involved, which can make nominating committees desirable even for non-NYSE companies. For ease of discussions in this book, the nomination function undertaken by independent directors will generally be described as being performed by the nominating committee.

Many of the corporate governance issues raised by institutional investors in recent years have involved the nomination and election process. One issue, the election of a director who receives less than less than 50% of the votes at an annual meeting, has been resolved in practice for major U.S. corporations, a substantial number of which have adopted a requirement that a director who receives less than 50 % of the shareholder votes in an election should resign from the board.

Another significant issue relating to director nomination and elections is the question of shareholder nomination of directors. Under authority provided in Dodd-Frank, the SEC has adopted proxy access rules by which it will be possible for shareholders to include information about a shareholder nominee in the corporation's proxy materials. Under the proxy access rules, director nominations from shareholders that have certain shareholding size and longevity profiles must be included in company proxy materials.[17]

As discussed further in Chapter III.4, the SEC does not require boards to perform self-evaluations, either on the board's performance or the qualifications of directors to serve on the board, although the SEC requires proxy disclosure on the nominating committee's assessment of how the qualifications of the board match the needs of the company. Self-evaluation by the board and key committees is required by the NYSE[18] and requirements for evaluation are often included in corporate committee charters.

---

15. SEC Regulation S-K, Item 407(e).
16. NASDAQ Rule 4350(c)(3); IM-4350-4.
17. Proxy Access Adopting Release.
18. NYSE 303A.09, 303A.04, 303A.05, 303A.07.

5. Risk Committee

A risk committee reviews the company's risks and the ways the company conducts management of risk. Such committees are often found in financial services industry companies, which constantly need to monitor the stability and performance of borrowers and potential borrowers.

The list of risks to be considered by a risk committee can be quite extensive, such as the risks inherent in the business of the company, the company's risk controls, and the assessment and review of credit, market, fiduciary, liquidity, reputational, operational, fraud, strategic, technology, data-security, and business-continuity risks.

Dodd-Frank requires that risk committees be established for certain financial services companies, but stopped short of requiring risk committees for all public companies. Dodd-Frank places regulation of financial services company risk committees with the Federal Reserve, requiring such committees to be comprised of independent directors, be responsible for the oversight of the enterprise-wide risk management practices, and "include at least one risk management expert having experience in identifying, assessing, and managing risk exposures of large, complex firms."[19]

The SEC requires that the board disclose any material information to shareholders respecting the board's evaluation of whether compensation programs for executives incentivize those executives to take undue risks.[20] In addition, the company must disclose the extent of the board's role in the risk oversight of the registrant, such as how the board administers its oversight function, and the effect that this has on the board's leadership structure.[21]

The SEC does not require that companies establish a risk committee. The SEC requires risk factor disclosures as a part of disclosures in periodic reports (quarterly reports on Form 10-Q and annual reports on Form 10-K), along with disclosure on the company's quantification of certain risks, and discussion in the MD&A regarding various business risks that could affect financial results and operations. Those disclosures are obligations of the company, and are subject to certification by the CEO and CFO as to their accuracy. The audit committee is required to oversee preparation of the periodic SEC filings, meaning that typical risk disclosures will be seen by the audit committee.

---

19. Dodd-Frank 165.
20. SEC Regulation S-K, Item 402(s).
21. SEC Regulation S-K, Item 407(h).

The SEC has further advised all reporting companies that they should disclose business and financial risks that may develop as a result of regulatory developments relating to climate change, such as the impact on a business of new regulations on greenhouse gas emissions, or international accords, or as a result of changing market or physical operating conditions.

Neither the NYSE nor NASDAQ requires a risk committee, although, as noted above, the audit committee of NYSE-listed companies must review the company's risk assessment and risk management policies.

6. Qualified Legal Compliance Committee

The concept for an additional board committee called the "qualified legal compliance committee" is contained in an SEC rule that was created to implement Section 307 of SOX.[22]

Part 205 of the SEC's rules of practice ("Part 205")[23] has the potential to change the lawyer-client dynamic respecting public company reporting decisions on whether, and what, to report about a potential violation of securities laws.

There are only three possible outcomes under Part 205 once a public company's attorney becomes aware of "credible evidence" of a "material violation" of the securities laws by the company or its officers or directors:

1. the attorney must be satisfied that the company has adopted an "appropriate response" to the attorney's concerns;[24]

2. the attorney must resign, if the company's response is not appropriate or not timely; or

3. a "qualified legal compliance committee" ("QLCC") of the company must accept responsibility for determining the company's ultimate response to the attorney's concerns.[25]

The SEC still has pending a critical element of Part 205, the so-called "reporting out" or "noisy withdrawal" provision. The SEC has proposed that if an attorney who does not believe that the corporate client has delivered an "appropriate response" resigns, either (a) that attorney will notify the

---

22. SEC Release 33-8150 (2002) ("First Part 205 Release").
23. SEC Standards of Professional Conduct for Attorneys ("SEC Part 205").
24. SEC Part 205.3(b)(3).
25. SEC Part 205.3(c)(2).

SEC of the resignation,[26] or (b) the company will notify the SEC of the attorney's resignation.[27]

Under either proposed version of reporting out, a company that does not have a QLCC could encounter a situation in which it does not control the timing or content of a securities disclosure. If an attorney in a Part 205 situation resigns—rightly or wrongly—the public would have to be notified.[28]

The reporting out proposal drew considerable attention from attorneys who protested that it damaged attorney-client confidentiality, and the proposal has not been adopted, or withdrawn, since the SEC introduced it in 2002.

The SEC's development of the QLCC concept is consistent with its "gatekeeper" approach to securities law regulation (discussed further in Chapter IV.1). It would make reporting and securities compliance issues a matter of individual duty by the members of the QLCC, rather than defining compliance as an institutional obligation.

Part 205 does not impose specific experience qualifications for membership on the QLCC. A QLCC must consist of at least three independent board members, one of whom is an audit committee member; have written procedures for confidential receipt of a report of a material violation; and have specific authority from the board to investigate and resolve issues relating to securities law violations.[29]

While QLCCs do not appear to have been widely adopted, a number of companies have made the QLCC function an added responsibility of the audit committee.[30]

Conceivably, a corporation also could establish a QLCC separate from the audit committee to reduce the workload on audit committees, particularly on securities disclosure matters that are not specifically related to finance.

---

26. First Part 205 Release.
27. SEC Release 33-81-86 (2003) ("Second Part 205 Release").
28 First Part 205 Release; Second Part 205 Release.
29. SEC Part 205.2(k).
30. See Rosen, "Resistances to Reforming Corporate Governance: The Diffusion of QLCCS; 74 FORDHAM L. REV. 1251 (2005).

7. Other Committees

A. *Special Litigation Committees*

Private plaintiffs may sometimes bring claims in the name of the corporation on the theory that the board, having approved the transaction that gave rise to the dispute, would not adequately prosecute the claim. Since the plaintiffs' claims are "derivative" of those that the corporation could assert for itself, such litigation is called "derivative litigation."

Under Delaware law, a board may create an independent special litigation committee to investigate the claims alleged in "derivative" litigation.[31] The members of the special litigation committee can determine whether to prosecute, settle, or seek dismissal of those claims on behalf of the corporation, regardless of the opinion of the remaining members of the board of directors.[32]

In order for a special litigation committee to validly control the derivative litigation, the committee's actions and membership must withstand judicial review of its independence.[33]

> "The purpose of the independent committee …. is to act as an independent arm of the ultimate power given to a board of directors under 8 Del. C. § 141(a) to determine whether or not a derivative plaintiff's pending suit brought on behalf of the corporation should be maintained when measured against the overall best interests of the corporation."[34]

However, the test of director independence for purposes of a special litigation committee may be even more stringent than the typical tests imposed for purposes of determining whether a director is an interested party to a transaction, or whether the director is independent for SEC, IRS, NYSE, or NASDAQ purposes.

Delaware has determined that for purposes of a special litigation committee, factors other than financial independence may be considered

---

31. *Zapata Corp. v. Maldonado*, 430 A.2d 779, 785-89 (Del. 1981) ("Zapata").

32. *Id.; see also* Carlton Investments v. TLC Beatrice, 1997 Del. Ch. Lexis 86 (holding Special Litigation Committees may settle derivative actions).

33. *In re Oracle Corp. Derive Litig.*, 824 A.2d 917, 928 (Del. Ch. 2003) ("Oracle II"); *see also* Zapata, at 788.

34. *In re Oracle Corp. Derive Litig.*, 808 A.2d 1206, 1212 (Del. Ch. 2002).

in weighing whether the committee members are sufficiently independent. "At bottom, the question of independence turns on whether a director is, for any substantial reason, incapable of making a decision with only the best interests of the corporation in mind.... A director may be compromised if he is beholden to an interested person. Beholden in this sense does not mean just owing in the financial sense, it can also flow out of personal or other relationships to the interested party."[35]

Delaware has held members of the special litigation committee to a very high standard. In one case, the special litigation committee was determined to be not sufficiently independent to assume control of the derivative litigation because, notwithstanding that the members had not been on the board at the time of the disputed transactions, and the members did not have a direct financial interest in the transactions, the members were affiliated with a university that had been the beneficiary of the company's largesse.[36]

In another case, the independence of one special litigation committee director was held by the court to be impaired because his wife was a cousin of a defendant director; the independence of a second special litigation committee director was held to be impaired by his prior business relationship with the same defendant director.[37]

B. *Investigatory Committees and Special Committees*

From time to time, the board may designate a special committee to react to a specific circumstance, such as a report of corporate malfeasance that needs to be investigated or a related party transaction or takeover bid. To prevent conflicts of interest or to act quickly or to maintain confidentiality, the smaller committee would be vested with the authority to undertake actions on behalf of the board or to make recommendations to bring back to the full board.

Such committees would be formed by resolution of the board, which would set out the objectives of the committee and the scope of the committee's authority. Unlike a standing committee, such as an audit, compensation, or nominating committee, the special committee would not necessarily have a formal charter.

---

35. Oracle II, at 938-39.
36. Oracle II, at 945.
37. *London v. Tyrrell*, 2010 WL 877528 (Del. Ch. March 11, 2010).

In connection with the formation of a special committee, the board should consider whether the event giving rise to the creation of the committee triggers any SEC disclosure requirements. If the special committee consists of only the directors who do not have a conflict of interest, and therefore the committee's recommendation to the board would be dispositive of the question being considered, the committee's decision might also trigger an SEC disclosure requirement (a response to a takeover bid, for example).

Committees dealing with questions relating to internal investigations should work closely with counsel in determining the scope and content of their activities and any reports they make. Some companies are concerned that an investigative committee may not do more than lay the path for later investigation by governmental authorities.

Any investigations must be bona fide. The SEC is willing to bring an enforcement action against a director who claims to have conducted an investigation and instead uses the claim of an investigation to insulate management from real oversight.[38]

Where investigations are conducted with counsel, and normally might be deemed to consist of confidential and privileged attorney-client communications and attorney work product, companies have, in recent years, been asked to waive the privilege as a sign of cooperation with a governmental investigation. In at least one case, it was ruled that a "confidential" waiver of privilege to the SEC meant that confidential material was available to plaintiffs in a civil case against the disclosing company.[39]

In addition, in recent years, the Department of Justice and the SEC have been requiring corporations to waive attorney-client privilege as a demonstration of "cooperation" with government investigations. Inside and outside directors have traditionally relied on corporate counsel for legal advice. This enforcement approach puts additional pressures on the attorney-corporate client relationship.

---

38. See, "In the Matter of Info USA Inc. k/n/a Info Group, Inc.," SEC Release 34-61708 (2010).

39. *McKesson HBOC, Inc. v. The Superior Court of San Francisco County*, 115 Cal. App.4th 1229, 9 Cal.Rptr.3d 812 (2004).

8. Composition and Operation of the Board

A. *Division of CEO and Board Chair Position*

Dodd-Frank directs the SEC to establish rules for proxy disclosure on why a company has chosen to have either the same person serve as both principal executive officer and chairman of the board, or two different individuals serve in those positions.[40] SEC rules adopted prior to enactment of Dodd-Frank provide for such disclosure, and require that if the positions of board chair and CEO are not divided between two individuals, the company must disclose whether it has a lead independent director and the specific role the lead independent director plays in the leadership of the board.[41]

The proxy rules also require disclosure regarding why the company has determined that its leadership structure is appropriate in light of the company's specific characteristics or circumstances.

The proxy rules do not impose a one-size-fits-all requirement on public companies that the role of board chair and CEO be divided. Not all institutional investors believe that a mandate to divide the positions is required in all circumstances, although the arguments tend to default in favor of division, absent circumstances that make a unified chair and CEO position valuable to the company.

The lead independent director position (regardless of whether that position is also the board chair) facilitates the board's conducting executive sessions of independent directors. The SEC does not require executive sessions, but the exchanges do.[42] Periodic executive sessions are a part of the Agreed Principles and recommended by CII.

The NYSE requires regular scheduled executive sessions of "non-management directors" to be held without management, in order to "empower non-management directors to serve as a more effective check on management." "Non-management" directors are all those who are not executive officers, but would include directors who are not independent by virtue of a material relationship, former status or family membership, or for any other reason.

The NYSE notes that having regular meetings not only will "foster better communication among non-management directors, but also [] prevent any negative inference from attaching to the calling of executive sessions."

---

40. Dodd-Frank 972.
41. SEC Regulation S-K, Item 407(h).
42. See, NYSE 303A.03, NASDAQ 45605, IM-5606.2.

Under the NYSE rules, a non-management director must preside over each executive session, although the same director is not required to preside at all executive sessions. The name of any individual who is chosen to preside at executive sessions must be disclosed in the proxy statement or other SEC filings. The NYSE further requires that meetings consisting only of independent directors should be held at least annually.

The NASDAQ rules require that independent directors must have at least two regularly scheduled meetings at which only independent directors are present each year. ("executive sessions").[43]

B. Approval of Related Party Transactions

Related party transactions are transactions between a company and its officers, directors, and principal shareholders. Board members who obtain financial benefits from the transactions (other than approval of director compensation) should not be part of the approval process.

The SEC requires that companies provide proxy statement disclosure about their policies and procedures governing related party transactions. Examples of elements the related party transaction approval policies and procedures should address are:

- the types of transactions covered by the policies and procedures;
- the standards to be applied pursuant to the policies and procedures;
- the persons or groups of persons on the board of directors or otherwise who are responsible for applying the policies and procedures; and
- whether the policies and procedures are in writing and, if not, how they are evidenced.

Companies are also required to disclose in the proxy statement any related party transactions for which the policies and procedures did not require review, approval, or ratification, or where the policies and procedures were not followed, dating back to the beginning of the last fiscal year.

The NYSE requires that any related party transaction be reviewed and evaluated by an appropriate board committee or other director action, typically the audit committee.

NASDAQ requires that the audit committee or another independent body of the board review "on an ongoing basis" and approve any related party transactions.[44]

---

43. NASDAQ IM-5605-2. Executive Sessions of Independent Directors.
44. NASDAQ 5601.

As discussed in Chapter II.2, transactions with related parties can trigger fiduciary duty requirements for the board members approving the transaction, and so such transactions need to be considered with care. Moreover, a director who is "independent" prior to the approval of a related party transaction might not be a "disinterested" director for purposes of approving the transaction, and might cease to be independent once the transaction occurs.

Companies should also review the related party transaction policies and procedures to ensure that they are consistent with other corporate policies, such as any code of ethics or code of conduct policies, or policies addressing conflicts of interest.

In particular, companies should ensure that the responsibility for administering the related party transaction policies is clear and that the committee or other body bearing the responsibility has sufficient resources and access to real-time information to ensure that the policies are followed.

C. CEO Succession

The question of CEO succession may be considered by the board as whole. The question may also be addressed by the compensation committee that determines the performance measurements for the CEO as part of its compensation function, or by the nominating committee, or by a search committee formed specifically for that purpose.

Wherever the decision-making power is situated, the independent directors have a crucial role to play in the succession planning strategy of the corporation.

While CEO succession is a vital function, it typically occurs too infrequently for boards or committees to be able to do succession planning based on experience. It nonetheless is useful to have some plan, and to have some internal experience considering the issues that creating a plan forces the directors to confront, even if events ultimately do not go according to plan.

The NYSE rules do not specifically require a company to adopt a succession plan but state that "Succession planning should include policies and principles for CEO selection and performance review, as well as policies regarding succession in the event of an emergency or the retirement of the CEO."[45]

---

45. NYSE Rule 303A.09.

In cases of planned succession, such as when a CEO nears retirement age or announces retirement, the CEO can assist in the succession process and the evaluation of potential successors.

In cases of emergency succession, caused by death, incapacity, or (as happens in some cases) indictment or other legal incapacity, the board will want to have previously identified potential internal candidates who have familiarity with the company's operations and personnel and who are perceived as having the capacity to step into the CEO position.

The process of identifying potential emergency successors requires the directors to become familiar with executives other than the CEO and to evaluate the strength of the company's "bench" players.

As with executive compensation and executive recruiting, the directors may seek the advice of outside advisors to assist in evaluating potential candidates. If each internal candidate is asked who in the organization would be appropriate to replace him or her in an emergency, the evaluation provides a view of the organization that may differ from the top-down picture, provides insight into how the team works together, and offers an assessment of one another's strengths.

9. Conclusion

Since the turn of the century, federal legislation and regulation have profoundly altered board operations, requiring the delegation of substantial responsibility to board committees.

For all directors, board activities in the current governance environment require increased time and attention compared to years past. A substantial part of the burden is borne by independent directors, who are required to staff the committees.

Audit committees, compensation committees, and nominating committees each have specific and highly detailed lists of duties and responsibilities. For an independent director, mastering the list of required duties for a given committee is a task in itself, and actually performing the duties can require a significant devotion of time and resources.

The importance of committees in governance cannot be understated. The issue-driven focus of a committee makes each one a vehicle for independent directors to develop a deeper understanding of the company's needs regarding the subject matter of the committee.

Audit Committee

1. Introduction

Throughout SOX and related rule making is the expectation that when the board is independent from management, it will be less likely to act as a "rubber stamp" for management and instead act as a check if management attempts to misuse corporate assets.

The audit committee exemplifies this approach. The audit committee has broad authority and broad responsibilities under SOX, including acting as a conduit for information about potential problems.

Management is responsible for maintaining financial records and preparing financial reports. The audit committee is tasked with overseeing the process whereby a corporation's financial statements are prepared, audited, and communicated to investors. The audit committee must ensure that the process is conducted without susceptibility to challenge and that the financial statements that are the end product of that process are accurate and reflect fairly the financial position and financial results of the corporation.

For publicly traded corporations, financial information is released to the public at least once per calendar quarter, typically first in an overview form in a press release and then again in the corporation's report on Form 10-Q.

Ensuring that the financial information prepared and disseminated by the corporation is accurate and prepared with integrity requires audit committee members to devote significant time to committee activities and attend multiple committee meetings during the year, in addition to time spent on board meetings.

2. Who Can Be on the Audit Committee?

A. *Independent Directors Only*

Only independent directors may be members of the audit committee.[1] Under SOX and related rules, audit committee members may not receive any direct or indirect payments from the corporation or its subsidiaries (other than for service as a director and fixed amounts of compensation under a retirement plan, including deferred compensation, for prior service with the company).[2]

Indirect payments include payments to family members, or entities in which the director is an officer or partner, such as entities that provide accounting, consulting, legal, investment banking, or financial advisory services to the company. Other commercial relationships between a corporation and an entity affiliated with an audit committee member, such as vendor relationships, may not be deemed to be indirect compensation for purposes of measuring whether a director may serve on an audit committee, but if such relationships exist, they should be reviewed to ensure that the director's independence in fact is not compromised.[3]

For audit committee purposes, the SEC expands the definition of independence to include the requirement that the director not be an "affiliated person" of the corporation or its subsidiaries.[4] Under the SEC's

---

1.   SOX 301.
2.   SEC Rule 10A-3(b).
3.   NYSE Rule 303A.02; NASDAQ Rule 5605(c).
4.   SEC Rule 10A-3(b).

rules, an "affiliate" of a company is "a person that directly, or indirectly through one or more intermediaries, controls, or is controlled by, or is under common control with, the company."[5] Whether a director is deemed to "control" an issuer will depend upon the facts of a particular case, but the rule includes a safe harbor provision that a director who is not an executive officer or not a greater than 10% stockholder is not deemed to control the issuer.[6]

Both the NYSE and NASDAQ provide additional distinct requirements that a director must meet in order to be independent. Those independence requirements are set out in Chapter II. In addition, the NYSE and NASDAQ each impose specific requirements applicable to the audit committee and its members.

The NYSE, recognizing the time commitment audit committee participation represents, requires that if an audit committee member simultaneously serves on three or more public company audit committees, the board must make a determination (disclosed in the proxy statement) that the director's participation in multiple audit committees does not impair his or her ability to serve effectively.[7]

NASDAQ listing standards provide that an audit committee member must not have participated in the preparation of the financial statements of the company or any current subsidiary of the company at any time during the past three years.[8]

The NYSE and NASDAQ provide limited exceptions to their independence requirements. A company that utilizes these exceptions must disclose this fact to investors, as well as its assessment as to whether the audit committee is able to act independently notwithstanding membership of the noncompliant director.[9]

B. Financial Expertise and "Financial Experts"

Under SOX, an audit committee must have at least one "financial expert" (as defined by the SEC) or disclose to its shareholders why it does not.[10] The NYSE requires that at least one audit committee member have "accounting

---

5. SEC Rule 10A-3(e).
6. SEC Rule 10A-3(e).
7. NYSE Rule 303A.07(a).
8. NASDAQ Rule 5606(c)(2)(A)(iii).
9. SEC Rule 10A-3(d).
10. SOX 407.

or related financial management expertise."[11] NASDAQ requires that at least one committee member have "financial sophistication," and each audit committee member must be able to read and understand financial statements at the time he or she joins the committee.[12]

Under the SEC rules, the corporation must disclose the name of the "audit committee financial expert" and whether the expert is independent within the standards of independence set by the exchange on which the corporation's shares trade.[13] The determination of whether an individual qualifies as a financial expert must be made by the full board of directors, based on whether the director has:

- an understanding of GAAP and financial statements;

- an ability to assess the general application of GAAP in connection with the accounting for estimates, accruals, and reserves;

- either (1) experience in preparing, auditing, analyzing, or evaluating financial statements that present a breadth and level of complexity of accounting issues that are generally comparable to those that the issuer's financial statements can reasonably be expected to raise; or (2) actively supervised individuals engaged in such activities;

- an understanding of internal controls and procedures for financial reporting; and

- an understanding of audit committee functions.[14]

The financial expert must acquire this background as a result of (a) serving as, or actively supervising, a principal financial officer, principal accounting officer, controller, public accountant, or auditor; (b) experience in a position that involves the performance of similar functions; (c) experience overseeing or assessing the performance of companies or public accountants with respect to the preparation, auditing, or evaluation of financial statements; or (d) other relevant experience.[15]

The SEC rules include a safe harbor provision stating that the financial expert will not be deemed an "expert" for any purpose and that designation as the financial expert does not impose on the individual director greater

---

11. NYSE Rule 303A.07(a).
12. NASDAQ Rule 5605(c)(2)(A).
13. SEC Regulation S-K, Item 407(d).
14. SEC Regulation S-K, Item 407(d)(5)(ii).
15. SEC Regulation S-K, Item 407(d)(5)(iii).

duties, obligations, or liabilities than he or she would otherwise have as a member of the audit committee and board of directors.[16]

The rules also state that the existence of a financial expert does not affect the duties, obligations, or liabilities of other members of the audit committee or the board.[17] The rules were directed at ensuring the presence of financial expertise on the committee, not shifting the risk or fiduciary responsibilities within the committee.

The SEC safe harbor is intended to assuage the concerns of directors who might be requested to serve as a financial expert.[18] Understandably, the existence of special duties or special liability exposure would dissuade many people from wanting to serve as a financial expert.

Conceivably, litigation might arise over whether a committee or board was entitled to reasonably rely on the report of the financial expert in evaluating a challenged accounting issue, or whether the financial expert's background and experience would make his or her reliance on a management or auditor's report unreasonable as a matter of state law. The SEC safe harbor would represent evidence of a policy preference in favor of financial experts not being singled out for special treatment, and provide legal grounds for that position, but this question has not been tested by the courts.

3. What Must the Audit Committee Do?

SOX's requirements for audit committees are extensive. Implementation details in the SEC rules and exchange requirements have resulted in a comprehensive list of activities the audit committee is charged with performing. These activities include:

- controlling the corporation's relationship with the auditor;
- establishing key policies;
- performing financial disclosure duties; and
- assuming related operational responsibilities and authority.

---

16. SEC Regulation S-K, Item 407(d)(5)(iv).
17. SEC Regulation S-K, Item 407(d)(5)(iv).
18. SEC Release 33-8177 ("SOX 406 and 407 Release")(2003).

A. *Govern Relationship with Outside Auditor*

SOX restructured the historic relationship of corporation and auditor, in which the auditor was hired by, and was potentially beholden to, the management. The outside auditor now is engaged by the audit committee, and the audit committee bears responsibilities for additional multiple elements of that engagement, such as ensuring the auditor's independence.

The list of required actions for the audit committee regarding the outside auditor is generally self-explanatory, but it is not short.

With respect to the outside auditor, the audit committee must:

a. Appoint, compensate, and oversee the work performed by the independent auditor for the purpose of preparing or issuing an audit report or related work, and approve the terms of the engagement.[19]

b. Oversee the resolution of disagreements between management and the independent auditor, including any difficulties the auditor experienced in the audit (such as restrictions on the scope of the auditor's activities or on access to information).[20]

c. Review the independence of the auditor by taking into account all the circumstances in order to determine the auditor's ability to exercise "objective and impartial judgment."[21]

d. Determine if nonaudit services that auditors can perform under SOX are compatible with the auditor's independence. Generally, an auditor should not perform services for the corporation if the auditor would later be required to review its own performance in the course of an audit. Services that are not compatible with an auditor's independence include:

   • bookkeeping and other services related to maintaining the company's accounting records or financial statements;

   • financial information systems design and implementation;

   • appraisal or valuation services, fairness opinions, and contribution-in-kind reports;

   • actuarial services;

   • internal audit outsourcing services;

---

19. SEC Rule 10A-3(b)(2).
20. SEC Rule 10A-3(b)(2).
21. SEC Regulation S-X 2-01(b).

- management functions;
- human resources;
- broker-dealer, investment adviser, or investment banking services;
- legal services; and
- expert services unrelated to the audit, performed for the purpose of advocating an audit client's interests in litigation or in a regulatory or administrative proceeding or investigation.[22]

Auditors *may* provide tax compliance, tax planning, and tax advice to audit clients under SEC rules, subject to audit committee preapproval.[23] However, independence is compromised if the auditor represents the corporation in tax court, district court, or the federal court of claims.

Under the Public Company Accounting Oversight Board ("PCAOB") rules on tax services, an auditor is not independent if it plans, markets, or opines in favor of certain types of aggressive tax transactions; provides tax services for a contingent fee; or provides tax services to individuals who perform a "financial reporting oversight role" at the corporation, other than directors.[24]

e. Adopt policies governing audit committee preapproval of all audit and permitted nonaudit services to be provided by the auditor.[25] Preapproval may be made:

- for each matter for which the auditor is engaged; or
- pursuant to preapproval policies and procedures established by the audit committee, provided that: (1) the policies and procedures are detailed as to the particular service; (2) the audit committee is informed on a timely basis of each such service; and (3) the policies and procedures do not include the delegation of audit committee responsibilities to management; or

---

22. SEC Regulation S-X 2-10-(c)(4).
23. SOX 202.
24. SEC Release 34-53677, File No. PCAOB-2006-01 (April 19, 2006) ("PCAOB Tax Release").
25. SEC Schedule 14A, Item 9(e)(5).

- through delegation of authority to one or more committee members, provided that the preapprovals are reported to the full committee at each of its scheduled meetings.[26]

If the audit committee determines to engage its auditor to undertake tax services, the PCAOB has adopted additional preapproval steps for permitted tax services, including reviewing the auditor's independence, prohibiting contingent fees, and preventing the auditor from providing tax services to company insiders (other than directors) with financial reporting oversight responsibilities.[27]

The corporation must disclose the preapproval policies in its reports on Form 10-K and proxy statements.[28]

f. Establish SOX-compliant hiring policies for employees or former employees of the auditor.[29] Under SOX, an auditor may not serve a corporation whose CEO, CFO, or person with a "financial reporting oversight role" was employed by the auditor within a year of the audit.[30]

g. Review the auditor's opinion regarding management's internal financial controls report under SOX Section 404.[31]

"Internal control over financial reporting" is the corporation's process for establishing reasonable assurance that the corporation's financial reporting is reliable, including policies to (1) maintain records that accurately and fairly reflect transactions in corporate assets; (2) provide reasonable assurance that transactions are undertaken with due authorization by corporate officers and directors and are recorded so as to permit preparation of financial statements in accordance with GAAP; and (3) prevent and detect material financial misconduct by corporation personnel.[32]

Under SOX Section 404, management must prepare, for inclusion in the annual report, an assessment of the effectiveness of the corporation's internal controls over financial reporting as of the end of the most

---

26. SEC Regulation S-X Rule 2-01(c)(7)(i).
27. PCAOB Tax Release.
28. SEC Schedule 14A, Item 9(e)(5); SEC Form 10-K Item 14(5)(i).
29. NYSE Rule 303A.07(c)(iii)(G).
30. SOX 206.
31. SEC Regulation S-K, Item 308(a).
32. SEC Rule 13a-15(f).

recent fiscal year (the "SOX 404 report").[33] Management also must state whether there have been any changes that have, or are likely to have, a material impact on the internal financial controls.[34] If the corporation has one or more material weaknesses in its internal financial controls, management may not conclude such controls are effective.[35]

The auditor must provide its opinion that management's assessment in the SOX 404 report is fairly stated and that the corporation has maintained effective control over financial reporting, or include a statement that such an opinion cannot be expressed, together with the auditor's reasons.[36] In evaluating the corporation's controls, the auditor must review the audit committee's oversight of external financial reporting and internal financial controls.[37]

The SEC delayed implementation of SOX Section 404 compliance for smaller reporting companies and Dodd-Frank provides that companies with a market capitalization held by nonaffiliates below $75 million are not required to comply with SOX Section 404.[38]

h. Discuss with the auditors:

- critical accounting policies and practices;

- alternative treatments of financial information within GAAP that have been discussed with management, the ramifications of the use of such alternative disclosures and treatments, and the treatment preferred by the independent auditor;

- other material written communications between the independent auditor and management, including, but not limited to, the management letter and schedule of unadjusted differences; and

- other key accounting policies and judgments, as required under Statement on Auditing Standards (SAS) No. 61, as amended.[39]

In addition, the audit committee should inquire into whether the auditor encountered issues that required referral to the auditor's

---

33. SOX 404.
34. SEC Regulation S-K, Item 308(a).
35. *Id.*
36. SEC Regulation S-X 2-02(f).
37. *Id.*
38. Dodd-Frank 989 G.
39. SEC Regulation S-X 2-07; NYSE Rule 303A.07.

national office or otherwise required the auditor to make decisions about whether management's treatment of an item was appropriate.

i.   Receive and review, at least once a year, a report by the independent auditor describing:

   • the firm's internal quality-control procedures;

   • any material issues raised by the most recent internal quality-control review or peer review, or by any inquiry or investigation conducted by governmental or professional authorities during the preceding five years with respect to independent audits carried out by the auditor, and any steps taken to deal with any such issues;

   • all relationships between the independent auditor and the company addressing the matters set forth in Independence Standards Board Standard No. 1.[40]

j.   Review whether the auditor is complying with SOX's partner rotation requirements.[41] NYSE-listed corporations need to consider whether to change auditors periodically in order to assure continuing independence.[42]

   SEC rules require the lead and concurring audit partners to serve no more than five years, followed by a five-year period away from the client.[43] Other audit partners may serve up to seven years with a two-year period away from the client.[44]

k.   Meet to review and discuss the annual audited financial statements and quarterly financial statements with management and the auditor (and internal auditor, if the corporation has one), including reviewing the corporation's specific disclosures in the Management's Discussion and Analysis of Financial Condition and Results of Operations ("MD&A") section of quarterly and annual reports filed with the SEC.[45] The audit committee must recommend

---

40. SEC Regulation S-K, Item 306; NYSE Rule 303A.07(b)(iii)(A).
41. SOX 203.
42. NYSE Rule 303A.07(b) (commentary).
43. SEC Regulation S-X 2-01(c)(6).
44. *Id.*
45. SEC Regulation S-K, Item 407(d).

the inclusion of the financial statements in the corporation's annual report on Form 10-K.[46]

l. NYSE-listed corporations must conduct private sessions periodically with the internal and outside auditors and with management.[47]

m. Review major issues regarding accounting principles and financial statement presentations, including any significant changes in the company's selection or application of accounting principles, and analyses prepared by management or the outside auditor setting forth significant financial reporting issues and judgments made in connection with the preparation of financial statements, including analyses of the effects on the financial statements of alternative GAAP methods, regulatory and accounting initiatives, and off-balance sheet structures.[48]

In light of Enron's history, off-balance sheet arrangements received special attention under SOX and related rule making. The SEC amended its MD&A requirements to require specific discussion of off-balance sheet arrangements that have or are reasonably likely to have a material current or future effect on the company's financial condition, results of operations, liquidity, capital expenditures, or capital resources.[49]

The audit committee also will be involved in those situations in which the auditor determines in the course of an audit that an illegal act may have occurred. Section 10A(b) of the Exchange Act imposes an obligation on the auditor to determine if it is "likely" that the illegal act in fact has taken place, and if so, (a) to determine the possible effect on the financial statements; and (b) to report the act to management and the audit committee, unless the act "is clearly inconsequential."[50]

Thereafter, if the auditor determines that the illegal act materially affects the financial statements and that the company has not taken "timely and appropriate remedial actions," the auditor must report to the board if the company's failure to take remedial actions could reasonably be expected to require the auditor to depart from a standard auditor's report or force the auditor's resignation.

---

46. SEC Regulation S-K, Item 407(d).
47. NYSE Rule 303A.07(c).
48. SEC Regulation S-X 2-07; *see also* NYSE Rule 303A.07(c) (commentary).
49. SEC Regulation S-K, Item 303(a)(4); see SEC Release 33-8182 (2003) ("Off-Balance Sheet Release").
50. Exchange Act Sec. 10A(b).

The board must notify the SEC within one business day of receiving such a report and inform the auditor that the SEC has been notified. If the auditor is not informed that the SEC has been notified, the auditor must either resign the engagement or provide its own report to the SEC.[51]

Requiring auditors to report illegal acts to management and the audit committee, seek remediation of the acts, and report to the SEC if no timely remediation is forthcoming is similar to the obligation placed on attorneys under Section 307 of SOX. As is discussed in Chapter IV.1 in the section on "Qualified Legal Compliance Committees," the reporting "up the ladder" requirement for attorneys is somewhat different, and reporting by lawyers to the SEC has been proposed but not yet adopted.

B. Establish Corporate Policies; Review of Complaints

To buttress the oversight of financial reporting and auditing, the audit committee is obligated to establish internal corporate procedures to prevent and detect fraud.

i. Whistleblower Policies

The audit committee must establish procedures for the confidential, anonymous submissions by employees of concerns regarding questionable accounting or auditing matters.[52] The audit committee also must establish policies for the receipt, retention, and treatment of complaints regarding accounting, internal accounting controls, or auditing matters.[53] Upon receipt of a sufficiently credible and serious complaint, the audit committee or other committee of the board may be required to conduct an internal investigation to determine the facts.

Reinforcing the whistleblower procedures adopted by the audit committee are the enforcement provisions of SOX Sections 806[54] and 1107,[55] which protect whistleblowers. Retaliatory actions taken against whistleblowers can expose the corporation to civil and criminal penalties.

Dodd-Frank Section 922 expanded the potential benefits to whistleblowers, by providing a bounty for individual's who provide

---

51. Exchange Act Sec. 10A(b).

52. SOX 301.

53. *Id.*

54. SOX 806.

55. SOX 1107.

information on misconduct that results in a successful enforcement action. The whistleblower must voluntarily provide information "derived from the independent knowledge or analysis" of the whistleblower, not previously known to the SEC from any other source. If the information results in sanctions in excess of $1.0 million, the SEC will pay as a bounty between 10% and 30% of the recovery. The SEC has discretion to determine the exact amount of the bounty based on such factors as the importance of the information and the level of assistance provided.[56]

Internal investigations can have significant legal and securities disclosure ramifications. Such investigations should be conducted with the advice of legal counsel (perhaps even independent counsel) rather than solely through company personnel. Regulatory and law enforcement officials sometimes ask corporations to provide the results of such investigations and even to waive attorney-client privilege with respect to such investigations in order to make the information developed in the company investigations available to the authorities.

ii. Codes of Ethics

Under Section 406 of SOX, corporations are required to adopt a code of ethics for senior officers and directors. The code should promote honesty, moral conduct, and accountability to the code.[57] The code also must contain compliance standards and procedures reasonably designed to provide prompt and consistent action against violations.[58]

The audit committee must review such codes and disclose any waivers of the code for executive officers and directors.[59] Legitimate transactions in the corporation's interest may require a waiver of the code, so the waiver by itself is not an indication of nefarious conduct (although frequent waivers might indicate problems). For example, approval of a transaction between the corporation and a director or entity controlled by a director is an example of a transaction that could be entirely fair to the corporation, yet still require a waiver of the code. Also, if the corporation references its stock trading restriction policies in the code, it might require a code waiver for an officer or director to enter into a stock trading plan under SEC Rule 10b5-1.

---

56. Dodd-Frank 922 et. Seq.
57. SEC Regulation S-K, Item 406.
58. *Id.*
59. SOX 406.

For NYSE-listed companies, the code must require that any waivers for directors or executive officers can be made only by the board or a board committee and that such waivers be promptly disclosed to stockholders.[60] Each company's website must include its code and the company must state in its proxy statement that the code is available on the website and in print to any stockholder who requests it.[61]

Companies traded on NASDAQ must adopt a code of conduct applicable to all directors, officers, and employees that complies with the definition of "code of ethics" in Section 406 of SOX and any SEC implementing rules.[62]

iii. Risk Assessment and Risk Management Policies

For NYSE-listed companies, the audit committee must review the company's risk assessment and risk management policies.[63] The audit committee charter must state that the audit committee is responsible for discussing the company's risk assessment and risk management policies.[64]

The commentary to the NYSE listing standards states that companies may manage risk through mechanisms other than the audit committee but that a company's processes for managing and assessing risk should be reviewed in a general manner by the audit committee.[65]

NASDAQ does not have a similar requirement. However, to the extent that an understanding of a company's risk profile is important to an understanding of its financial position, some risk assessment is inherent in the performance of the audit committee function.

Understanding the different categories of risk faced by a specific company—business, competitive, financial, legal, regulatory, etc.—may require the audit committee to receive input from outside professionals in a relevant area, rather than relying simply on management's assessment.

Dodd-Frank requires that a risk committee be created for certain financial services companies. The risk committee must include an individual with risk assessment background,[66] similar to the requirement that the audit committee designate a person who is a "financial expert."

---

60. NYSE Rule 303A.10.
61. NYSE Rule 303A.10 (commentary).
62. NASDAQ Rule 5610.
63. NYSE Rule 303A.07(c)(iii)(D).
64. *Id.*
65. *Id.*
66. Dodd-Frank 165.

iv. *Related Party Transactions*

For NASDAQ-listed companies, the audit committee must conduct an appropriate review, on an ongoing basis, of all related party transactions for potential conflict-of-interest situations.[67] The audit committee (or another independent body of the board of directors) must review and approve all related party transactions.[68] The definition of "related party transaction" is the same as the definition used for annual report and proxy statement disclosures under SEC rules.[69]

The NYSE listing standards do not contain an analogous requirement.

The SEC proxy rules require that public companies disclose the policies and procedures they use in dealing with interested party transactions.[70]

C. Disclosure Matters

Certain corporate disclosures are either the obligation of the audit committee or involve reporting on the activities of the audit committee. In each case, the audit committee should review such disclosures for accuracy and completeness prior to their dissemination.

- The corporation must disclose its audit preapproval policies in proxy statements and incorporate such disclosures in the annual reports on Form 10-K. The disclosures may take the form of setting out the text of the preapproval policies or concise and clear summaries of the policies.[71]

- The corporation must disclose in the proxy statement the amount of audit fees that it has paid in the two most recent years.[72] There are four categories of fees that must be disclosed: (1) Audit Fees; (2) Audit-Related Fees; (3) Tax Fees; and (4) All Other Fees.[73]

- The corporation must disclose whether it has adopted a code of ethics for its senior financial officers and if not, why not.[74] If a corporation has a code of ethics, it must make that code (or the portions applicable to the CEO and senior financial officers) publicly available by: (1) fil-

---

67. NASDAQ Rule 5630(a).
68. *Id.*
69. *Id.*
70. SEC Regulation S-K, Item 404(b).
71. SEC Schedule 14A, Item 9(e).
72. *Id.*
73. *Id.*
74. SOX 406.

ing the code (or relevant portions) as an exhibit to the Form 10-K; (2) posting the code (or relevant portions) on the company website; or (3) providing a copy of the code without charge upon request. Companies that post their codes on their websites or undertake to provide copies on request must indicate in their Form 10-K reports that they intend to provide disclosure in this manner.[75]

• Companies must disclose any changes to, or waivers from, provisions of their code of ethics by filing a Form 8-K or posting the information on the company website within four days of the amendment or waiver.[76] Only amendments or waivers relating to the required elements of the code of ethics and the specified officers must be disclosed.[77]

• The audit committee must provide its annual report in the corporation's proxy statement, covering its review of the audited financial statements with management, discussions with independent auditors, and its recommendation that the audited financials be included in the company's annual report.[78]

• The audit committee must review the use of any non-GAAP financial measures (other than EBITDA) in publicly disclosed financial information.[79] SEC Regulation G prohibits material misstatements or omissions that would make the presentation of the non-GAAP financial measure misleading.[80] SEC Regulation G also requires a quantitative reconciliation of the differences between the non-GAAP financial measure presented and the most directly comparable GAAP financial measure.[81]

• For NYSE-listed issuers, the audit committee must review with management earnings guidance provided to analysts and ratings agencies.[82] As noted previously, the NYSE also requires that the board determine (and disclose in the proxy statement) that an audit committee member who serves simultaneously on three or more corporate audit committees is not impaired from performing effectively.

---

75. SEC Regulation S-K, Item 406.
76. Form 8K, Item 5.05.
77. *Id.*
78. SEC Regulation S-K, Item 407(d).
79. SEC Regulation S-X, Rule 2-07.
80. SEC Regulation G, Rule 100.
81. *Id.*
82. NYSE Rule 303A.07(c)(iii)(C).

Companies traded on NASDAQ must disclose the code of conduct applicable to all directors, officers, and employees that complies with the definition of "code of ethics" in Section 406 of SOX and any SEC implementing rules and make the code publicly available.[83] While some disclosure obligations are specifically assigned to the audit committee, the audit committee should coordinate its activities with those of the company's investor relations and securities disclosure personnel to ensure that the corporation is speaking with a consistent voice.

D. Operating Matters

i. Outside Advisors

Even though authority on the use of corporate resources resides with the Board, SOX vested separate authority in the audit committee to draw on corporate resources without the requirement of board approval.[84]

The audit committee is authorized, without board approval, to pay the auditors (who are themselves answerable to, and retained on the sole authority of, the audit committee).[85] The audit committee also is entitled to retain, and require the corporation to pay for, outside legal, accounting, or other advisors.[86] Only the audit committee has express statutory authority to require the corporation to pay for such outside advisors. As discussed below, it may be desirable for the board to vest similar authority in the compensation committee and other committees.

ii. CEO and CFO Certifications—Disclosure Controls and Procedures

Even though the certification requirements under SOX Sections 302 and 906 belong to the CEO and the CFO, the audit committee should review the underlying activities to which the CEO and CFO are certifying, particularly with respect to the corporation's disclosure controls and procedures.

These disclosure controls and procedures are separate from, and broader than, the "internal control over financial reporting." The term "disclosure controls and procedures" includes controls and other procedures designed to ensure that information reported to the SEC is recorded, processed,

---

83. NASDAQ Rule 5610.
84. SOX 301.
85. *Id.*
86. *Id.*

summarized, and reported within the time periods required by the SEC.[87] The audit committee should review that the corporation has adopted a method to ensure that information is generated on a timely basis within the corporation and reported to management, generally through an internal corporate disclosure committee involving senior management.

The PCAOB requires that the auditor evaluate the audit committee effectiveness as part of the evaluation of the company's internal control activities.[88]

iii. Committee Charter

Both the NYSE and NASDAQ require that the audit committee develop and disclose to investors a charter for the audit committee. The charter will set out the duties to be undertaken by the audit committee as defined by SOX and by the requirements of the relevant exchange, and may include specific actions that the audit committee must take in connection with performing those duties.[89]

The audit committee charter must be provided on the company's website or printed periodically in the proxy statement.[90]

The exchanges require that the board evaluate its performance and the charter annually.[91] Because the charter will set out requirements that the audit committee is supposed to perform, the self-assessment is not merely a rote exercise but is a requirement that the committee own up to any deficiencies in performance that have occurred over a prior period. Such assessments are not required to be published but would be discoverable in litigation claiming breaches of fiduciary duty; "whitewashed" self-assessments, if the committee had failed to perform, would compound any problems that existed.

As a matter of corporate law, the charter is not merely a statement of board policy or a job description for the committee; it is also a delegation of authority by the board to a committee of the board. The board may reserve various rights with respect to that delegation of authority and may change the charter and the scope of authority delegated, but the delegation of authority to the committee through the creation of the charter provides the committee with a certain autonomy as well.

---

87. SEC Rule 15d-15(e).
88. PCAOB Auditing Standard No. 5.
89. NYSE Rule 303A.07(b); NASDAQ Rule 5605(c).
90. SEC Regulation S-K, Item 407.
91. NYSE Rule 303A.09; NASDAQ Rule 5605(c).

4. Conclusion

SOX and the subsequent rulemaking profoundly altered board operations, delegating substantial responsibility to board committees generally and in specific to the audit committee.

Even though the need for audit committee reform was acknowledged prior to the adoption of SOX, the detailed statutory and regulatory requirements meant that all companies were working from a standardized set of rules. Compared to their predecessors, modern audit committees spend far more time, and have far greater involvement, in the review of financial statements and the processes by which the financial statements are prepared.

Audit committees tend to meet more often than other committees of the board, because companies report financial results quarterly, while compensation or director nomination questions tend to arise only annually.

Compensation Committee

1. Introduction

The compensation committee reviews and establishes executive compensation, primarily the CEO's compensation. The compensation committee may also establish the compensation of other senior corporate officers and as well as the directors.

Compensation includes not only salary but also bonuses, perquisites, equity incentives such as stock options or stock grants, and benefits such as salary continuation plans, severance plans, retirement plans, and the like. Each element of executive compensation for the company's most highly paid officers, including the CEO, must be disclosed in tables in the annual proxy statement ("tabular proxy disclosure").[1]

---

1. SEC Regulation S-K, Item 402.

The effects of executive compensation decisions can be far-reaching, as those decisions can affect the recruitment and retention of key managers.

Executive compensation decisions can be controversial and represent an area of reputational risk for a company. Executive compensation—particularly the approach to bonus compensation as it is handled in the financial services industry—is frequently criticized by institutional investors, academics, the press, and politicians.

Dodd-Frank requires most companies to create compensation committees comprised only of independent directors.[2] The NYSE already requires a compensation committee for its listed companies.[3] Prior to passage of Dodd-Frank, NASDAQ did not require formation of a compensation committee, but required that only independent directors participate in executive compensation decisions.[4] Financial services companies that accepted U.S. Treasury investment under the Capital Participation Program ("TARP recipients") must have compensation committees, comprised of independent directors, to undertake the obligations associated with accepting the U.S. Treasury investment.[5]

Dodd-Frank exempts a "controlled company"—a company for which more than 50% of the voting power is held by an individual, a group, or other company—from being required to have an independent compensation committee.[6] If the company does not have a compensation committee, the SEC requires that the company disclose why not having a committee is appropriate and identify the directors who make compensation decisions.[7]

Compensation committees also deal with various detailed tax, securities, and exchange rules that are more appropriately handled at the committee level than by the entire board.

The SEC also requires that the company's compensation decisions be explained in the annual proxy statement under the "compensation discussion and analysis" section ("CD&A").[8] The required discussion is expected to cover each element of compensation appearing in the tabular proxy

---

2.   Dodd-Frank 952.
3.   NYSE 303A.05.
4.   NASDAQ Rule 4350(c)(3); IM-4350-4.
5.   *See,* Interim Final Rule.
6.   Dodd-Frank 952.
7.   SEC Regulation S-K, Item 407(e).
8.   SEC Regulation S-K, Item 402(a).

disclosure. The compensation committee is required to prepare for the proxy statement a separate compensation committee report that confirms that the committee reviewed the CD&A with management and recommended to the board that the CD&A be included in the proxy statement.[9]

The compensation committee must deal with those executive compensation arrangements that are subject to legal restrictions. These restricted areas include "golden parachute" compensation arrangements for executives (which are regulated under the Internal Revenue Code), compensation limits for executives of TARP recipients, option and equity payments, and restrictions on payments that have the effect of shifting compensation from one tax year to another.

Some elements of compensation, such as stock option or equity plans, must be approved by shareholders under the rules of NYSE and NASDAQ.[10] Under Dodd-Frank, beginning in 2011, shareholders must be provided a chance to make an annual, nonbinding vote on executive compensation.[11] Prior to enactment of Dodd-Frank, TARP recipients were required to conduct "say on pay" votes,[12] and some companies had voluntarily adopted "say on pay" shareholder votes.

Companies will also be required under Dodd-Frank to adopt policies to "clawback" executive bonuses that are paid on the basis of financial statements that are later restated, regardless of whether the executives were responsible for the errors in the financial statements.[13]

Dodd-Frank requires disclosures in the proxy statement about the company's policy on permitting employees and directors to "hedge" against losses in company securities that they own or have been granted as compensation,[14] as well as disclosures on the ratio of CEO pay to the average pay of company employees, and the ratio of CEO pay to corporate performance, taking into account changes in share price and dividends and distributions.[15]

Review of CEO compensation also will often include review of CEO performance, and whether the CEO or the corporation has achieved

---

9. SEC Regulation S-K, Item 407(g). Smaller reporting companies (less than $75 million of non-affiliate market capitalization) do not have to provide reports.
10. NYSE 303A.08; NASDAQ IM-5635-1.
11. Dodd-Frank 951.
12. Release 34-613351, under Rule 14a-20.
13. Dodd-Frank 954.
14. Dodd-Frank 955.
15. Dodd-Frank 953.

any targets set by the board to trigger incentive compensation. Because compensation is so intimately tied to job performance, the compensation committee sometimes also is charged with considering CEO succession issues, although those matters are sometimes referred to a governance or nominating committee.

The SEC requires that the board disclose in the proxy statement any material information to shareholders regarding the board's evaluation of whether compensation programs for executives incentivize those executives to take undue risks.[16] As this evaluation requires a review of not only compensation but also the company's risk profile, the compensation committee may not be the only committee involved in the evaluation.

2. Who Can Be on the Compensation Committee?

A. *Independent Directors Only*

For NYSE-listed companies, only directors who meet the NYSE independence standards may be members of the compensation committee.[17] For NASDAQ-listed companies, only directors who meet the NASDAQ independence standards may be members of the compensation committee or participate in compensation decisions affecting the CEO.[18]

Dodd-Frank requires that the SEC develop rules by 2011 under which securities exchange definitions of independence for compensation committee members will address "relevant factors, including...the source of compensation of a member of the board of directors.... and whether the [director] is affiliated with the issuer, a subsidiary of the issuer, or an affiliate of a subsidiary of the issuer."[19]

For specific transactions, there are additional qualifications on compensation committee membership.

For instance, in order for executive compensation in excess of $1 million per year to be deductible for tax purposes, the compensation must be established by a compensation committee consisting of "outside directors."[20] In most circumstances, an NYSE or NASDAQ "independent

---

16. SEC Regulation S-K, Item 402(s).
17. NYSE Rule 303A.05.
18. NASDAQ Rule 4350(c)(3); IM-4350-4.
19. Dodd-Frank 952.
20. Internal Revenue Code Sec. 162(m).

director" will also qualify as an "outside director" for purposes of the tax laws. However, for purposes of the tax laws, an "outside director" must never have served as an officer of the corporation.

Also, unless the compensation committee consists of "non-employee directors" under SEC rules, directors who receive stock grants or stock options could forfeit profits on purchases and sales of company stock that occur in any six-month period. Such "short-swing profits" are prohibited under Section 16 of the Exchange Act (short-swing profits are discussed in Chapter IV.2), unless those stock grants or options are made by a compensation committee with "non-employee directors."

To be a "non-employee director" for purposes of Section 16, the director must not receive compensation, directly or indirectly, from the corporation in any capacity other than as a director, in excess of the $120,000 that would trigger reporting as a "related party transaction" in the corporation's proxy statement.[21] Under the independence standards of either the NYSE or NASDAQ, any independent director also will be a non-employee director.

If there are common directors sitting on the compensation committees of two or more corporations, the so-called "interlock" relationship is not a violation of the independence standard of NASDAQ or the NYSE, but the SEC requires disclosure of those relations in the proxy statement.[22]

The SEC requires that a public company must disclose in its proxy statements whether any of its executives serves as a director for another company, if (i) that company in turn has an executive who serves on the public company's board, and (ii) any of those individuals sits on either company's compensation committee.[23]

3. What Must the Compensation Committee Do?

A. *Establish Compensation*

The compensation decision for a corporation can be one of the most far-reaching and controversial decisions that a board can make. CEO salaries set the outer boundary for other executive compensation within

---

21. SEC Rule 16b-3.
22. SEC Regulation S-K, Item 407(e)(4).
23. SEC Regulation S-K, Item 407(e)(4).

the organization. For years, executive compensation has tended to travel upward at a pace greater than that of other corporate employees.

Compensation committees never lack for justifications to increase CEO salaries. Companies that perform well want to reward the CEO's efforts. Companies that underperform want to provide incentives to maintain the CEO in place to implement a turnaround strategy or to recruit a replacement.

In recent years, CEO pay and performance have drawn increasingly critical attention from investors and regulators. A compensation committee should ensure that the company has adopted a pay package that is an appropriate compensation for the CEO, using a process that can withstand criticism with regard to both process and result.

The compensation committee also may be called upon to establish the compensation for other key executives, such as the CFO or other senior level executives, or to approve pay grade ranges for personnel. Generally, the CEO and management are expected to establish the specific salaries for individual employees and managers and come to the board for review only in exceptional cases.

B. Report in Proxy Statement

Public companies are required to include in the proxy statements significantly detailed compensation information regarding executives and directors.

The disclosure on executive compensation includes a summary compensation table that will set out the prior three years' compensation for the top five corporate officers (the "named executive officers" or "NEOs"). This table includes information on:

- Salary
- Bonuses
- Equity-based awards (stock grants and options)
- Incentive plans
- The change in present value of accumulated pension benefits and deferred compensation
- Perquisites[24]

In addition to the summary compensation table, the company must include itemized tables on elements of executive compensation, such

---

24. SEC Regulation S-K, Item 402.

as equity awards and retirement plan benefits, and narrative disclosure accompanying the tables and describing other potential compensation sources, such as payments to executives in the event of a change of control of the company.

Compensation for directors for the prior fiscal year is to be set out in tabular form, similar to the description of management compensation.

The company is responsible for producing the section of the proxy called "Compensation Discussion and Analysis" ("CD&A"), intended to be a counterpart disclosure to the financial MD&A,[25] which will discuss and analyze the material factors underlying the company's compensation decisions, as reflected in the compensation disclosed in the tables.

The CD&A should address the goals of the company's compensation programs, what the compensation program is intended to reward and not reward, and how the company determined the amounts to be paid for each element of compensation.

The CD&A should also discuss, as applicable, the reasons for allocating compensation between cash and non-cash compensation, how equity compensation is determined, whether tax or prior compensation factors are considered, and whether the company used any benchmark measures to set the compensation levels.[26]

The compensation committee is required to provide a report in the corporation's proxy materials, stating that the compensation committee has reviewed and discussed with management the CD&A and on the basis of that review recommended that the CD&A be included in the proxy materials.[27]

Shortly after implementation of the CD&A requirements, SEC staff offered additional guidance on how companies could better comply with the CD&A requirements, based on its review of the proxy statements of 350 public companies.[28] The SEC staff encouraged companies to articulate, concisely and clearly, the company's rationales for selecting different types and amounts of executive compensation. The SEC staff also encouraged improved presentation of compensation disclosures, emphasizing material information and deemphasizing less pertinent information, as well as using plain English.

---

25. SEC Release No. 33-8732 (2006)("Compensation Adopting Release").

26. Compensation Adopting Release.

27. SEC Regulation S-K, Item 402(b).

28. U.S. Securities and Exchange Commission, Division of Corporation Finance, Staff Observations in the Review of Executive Compensation Disclosure, (2007) at http://www.sec.gov/divisions/corpfin/guidance/execcompdisclosure.htm.

Proxy disclosure must address the board's evaluation of whether compensation programs for executives incentivize those executives to take undue risks.[29] As noted above, this evaluation requires a review of not only compensation but also the company's risk profile, so the compensation committee may not be the only committee involved in the evaluation.

A company must conduct such an evaluation and disclose material risks in the proxy statement. The company should address the question affirmatively in a proxy statement, setting out the nature of its determinations about the linkage of its compensation programs and corporate risk, both to confirm that the company has undertaken the analysis and to avoid the potential that omission of a statement would be subject to open interpretations by others.

The situations that would require disclosure will vary depending on the particular company and its compensation programs. The SEC identified several specific situations that potentially could trigger discussion and analysis of compensation policies and practices:

- At a business unit of the company that carries a significant portion of the company's risk profile;

- At a business unit with compensation structured significantly differently than other units within the company;

- At business units that are significantly more profitable than others within the company; or

- At business units where the compensation expense is a significant percentage of the unit's revenues.[30]

Dodd-Frank requires additional disclosures in the proxy statement about the company's policy on permitting employees and directors to "hedge" against losses in company securities that they own or have been granted as compensation,[31] as well as disclosures on the ratio of CEO pay to the average pay of company employees, and the ratio of CEO pay to corporate performance, taking into account changes in share price and dividends and distributions.[32]

---

29. Compensation Adopting Release.
30. Dodd-Frank 955.
31. Dodd-Frank 953.
32. Dodd-Frank 953.

C. *Other Disclosures in Form 8-K*

Most decisions relating to executive compensation for NEOs will result in the corporation filing a Form 8-K report within four business days of the compensation decision (i.e., at the board meeting or committee meeting at which time the agreement is approved). While agreements regarding executive compensation must be reported on Form 8-K at the time they are made, documents reflecting the compensation agreement typically will be filed as exhibits in the next quarterly report on Form 10-Q (or Form 10-K at the end of the year).[33]

4. Charter

The NYSE requires the compensation committee to have a charter. NASDAQ does not require a compensation committee charter, nor is a charter required under SEC rules. However, the SEC-required disclosures are the functional equivalent of a charter, including requirements that the company disclose:

- the processes by which executive compensation is established,
- the scope of authority granted to the compensation committee,
- whether the committee can delegate any of its authority to others (such as an option grants committee),
- the role of executives in compensation matters, and
- the role of compensation consultants in the decision process and whether such consultants are engaged directly by the committee or by other parties.[34]

Under the NYSE rules, the compensation committee charter must address the committee's purpose and responsibilities, including the responsibility for

(A) reviewing and approving corporate goals and objectives relevant to CEO compensation, evaluating the CEO's performance in light of those goals and objectives, and, either as a committee or together with the other independent directors (as directed by the board), determining and approving the CEO's compensation level based on this evaluation;

---

33. Form 8-K.
34. SEC Regulation S-K, Item 407(e).

(B) making recommendations to the board with respect to non-CEO executive officer compensation, and incentive-compensation and equity-based plans that are subject to board approval; and

(C) preparing the Compensation Committee Report required for inclusion in the proxy statement.

The interpretative material in the NYSE rules notes that the rule is not intended to exclude the board from CEO compensation discussions by assigning the primary responsibility to the compensation committee.

The compensation committee charter required by the NYSE should also address committee member qualifications; committee member appointment and removal; committee structure and operations (including authority to delegate to subcommittees); committee reporting to the board; the need to conduct an annual performance self-evaluation; and the grant of sole authority to retain third-party compensation consultants, including establishing the payment and termination terms.

As with the charters for the audit committees and nominating committees, establishing a charter for the compensation committee would establish and communicate the specific actions the committee is expected to undertake, the corporate purposes for which the committee is expected to undertake them, and the scope of authority granted to the committee by the board.

If the compensation committee has a charter, it must be available through the company's website or included periodically in the proxy materials.[35]

A compensation committee charter is not a law or a contract. It is a delegation by the board of some of its authority to act on behalf of the corporation, which the board is free to amend or terminate, plus a statement of the actions the committee is directed to perform. Nonetheless, once a committee is committed through a charter to undertake a set of actions, it must perform them or face scrutiny as to why it failed to do so.

To ensure its policies remain current with any changes in law, the committee charter should also include a requirement for periodic review. For example, as a result of Dodd-Frank companies must adopt policies to "clawback" executive bonuses that are paid on the basis of financial statements that are later restated, regardless of whether the executives were responsible for the errors in the financial statements.[36] Under SOX,

---

35. SEC Regulation S-K, Item 407.
36. Dodd-Frank 954.

"clawback" policies were directed only at executives who were responsible for erroneous financial statements.

5. Independent Advisors

As with many other decisions in which the judgment of the directors may be questioned, compensation decisions often are referred to outside advisors who can provide a view on a compensation question based on a board range of client experiences or a broader range of experience with the executive compensation market.

Consultants will provide the clients with salary surveys that identify companies with similar operating and financial backgrounds in order to assist the corporation in determining whether its salary and benefits package is comparable to that offered by companies in the same or related industries. These surveys reflect recently reported data by comparable companies resembling the client corporation.

As a matter of fulfilling fiduciary duties, the compensation committee is entitled to reasonably rely on third-party reports in making decisions, and can use such reports to demonstrate the committee's use of due care in making compensation decisions. By obtaining data from outsiders, the committee removes the risk that it is relying on data that has been selectively sorted by management to skew the compensation decision in management's favor, by obtaining the data from a source that does not have a personal stake in the outcome.

Historically, when the selection of the compensation consultant was in the hands of management rather than the committee, there was concern whether the consultant might tilt the data in favor of the person who did the hiring. Even prior to enactment of Dodd-Frank, it was common practice (and a requirement under NYSE rules) to have the compensation committee control the hiring of compensation consultants, to mitigate the potential for bias in favor of management.

Dodd-Frank mandates that the compensation committee have sole discretion over the selection of compensation consultants, legal counsel, and other advisors (each, an "outside compensation advisor") that it uses, and may only select outside compensation advisors that are independent of the company in accordance with SEC rules. The SEC rules on independence of outside compensation advisors must address:

- the provision of other services to the company by the person who employs the outside compensation advisor,

- the amount of fees paid to the person who employs the outside compensation advisor, as a percentage of that person's total revenue,
- the conflict of interest policies of the person who employs the outside compensation advisor,
- any business or personal relationship of the outside compensation advisor and a member of the compensation committee, and
- any stock in the company owned by the outside compensation advisor.

The compensation committee is responsible for the appointment, compensation, and oversight of the work performed by its outside compensation advisors. Dodd-Frank does not require a committee to obtain an outside compensation advisor, and it expressly provides that the compensation committee may make or implement decisions that are not consistent with the advice provided by the outside compensation advisor.

SEC rule making to implement the Dodd-Frank rules on compensation committees is required by 2011.[37]

Even prior to enactment of Dodd-Frank, the SEC established proxy disclosure requirements for companies that use compensation consultants. Those requirements were similar to the requirements in Dodd-Frank.[38]

6. Conclusion

Executive compensation questions have drawn increasing scrutiny over the past decade. Complying with the requirements imposed by Congress and the SEC will mean that compensation committees need to undertake additional evaluations of executive compensation as part of the compensation setting process.

It is fair to expect that additional compensation related changes will emerge in years to come. Dodd-Frank mandates proxy disclosure about the ratio between executive pay and performance, and the ratio of executive pay to the average pay of company employees. As that data accumulates over time, it will likely provide the basis for additional legislation or regulation regarding executive compensation.

---

37.   Dodd-Frank 952.
38.   SEC Regulation S-K, Item 407.

Nominating Committee

1. Introduction

Merely having a group of directors follow a set of corporate governance processes does not create a well functioning board. The members of the board must have, collectively, the skills, knowledge, and temperament to work together effectively in meeting their obligations.[1]

The nominating committee, as the committee of the board that evaluates potential director candidates who are put forward for election by the shareholders, is responsible for putting the directors in place who can work together. The list of nominees typically should include incumbents, but the nominating committee will also look for new and replacement directors.

The National Association of Corporate Directors (NACD), in cooperation with the Business Roundtable and the Council of Institutional Investors,

---

1. *See* NACD Key Agreed Principles at 9.

developed the Key Agreed Principles to Strengthen Corporate Governance for U.S. Publicly Traded Companies (the "Key Agreed Principles"), which articulates the balance a company seeks in its board:

> A board's effectiveness depends on the competency and commitment of its individual members, their understanding of the role of a fiduciary and their ability to work together as a group. Obviously, the foundation is an understanding of the fiduciary role and the basic principles that position directors to fulfill their responsibilities of care, loyalty, and good faith.
>
> However, an effective board is far more than the sum of its parts: it should bring together a variety of skill sets, experiences, and viewpoints in an environment conducive to reaching consensus decisions after a full and vigorous discussion from diverse perspectives. While the board should reflect a mix of diverse experiences and skill sets relevant to the business and governance of the company, each board must determine for itself, and review periodically, what those experiences and skill sets are and what the appropriate mix should be as the company faces different challenges over time.
>
> Typically, a board will want some persons with specialized knowledge of relevant businesses and industries and the business environment in which the company functions who can provide insight regarding strategy and risk. Director qualifications and criteria should be designed to position the board to provide oversight of the business.[2]

In increasing the amount of required proxy disclosure regarding director nominees and the director nomination process in 2009, the SEC echoed the NACD sentiments.[3] The SEC's goal in revising the rules was to help "investors determine whether a particular director and the entire board composition is an appropriate choice for a given company," because an

---

2.   NACD Key Agreed Principles at 9.
3.   SEC Regulation S-K, Item 407(c).

effective board "must have a set of directors who collectively have all the competencies required by the board to fulfill its duties."[4]

In 2010, Dodd-Frank provided the SEC with express authority to adopt rules that would permit shareholders to bring forward their own director candidates and to include information on those candidates in the company's proxy statement ("proxy access") "under such terms and conditions as the SEC determines are in the interests of shareholders and for the protection of investors."[5]

The SEC thereafter adopted 14a-11 respecting the inclusion of shareholder nominees in corporate proxy materials.[6] As the nominating committee attempts to develop an optimum mix of skills and experience among director nominees, it will do so with the knowledge that shareholders may put forward their own nominees without reference to the nominating committee process.

In practice, proxy access may prove to be less important as a means by which meaningful or successful nominations are made than a means by which shareholder nominees are able to give voice to governance concerns of the shareholders who nominated them.[7] They dynamic of the discussions by nominating committees with investors about director nominees will be different than in prior years, since qualifying shareholders now can play the additional card of requiring the shareholder nominee to be included in corporate proxy materials.

Also in 2010, the SEC commenced a review of the entire proxy process, "seeking public comment as to whether the U.S. proxy system as a whole operates with the accuracy, reliability, transparency, accountability, and integrity that shareholders and issuers should rightfully expect."[8]

---

4. *See, e.g.,* Richard Leblanc & James Gillies, Inside the Boardroom: How Boards *Really* Work and the Coming Revolution in Corporate Governance 145 (2005).

5. Dodd-Frank 971. At the time Dodd-Frank was enacted, proposed SEC proxy access regulations were pending. Proposed Rule, Proxy Disclosure and Solicitation Enhancements, Release Nos. 33-9052; 34-60280; IC-28817 ("Proxy Access Proposing Release"), of which many, but not all, elements were finally adopted.

6. Proxy Access Adopting Release. Implementation of Rule 14a-11 was delayed in October 2010 in light of pending legal challenges. See SEC Release No. 9149, available at http://www.sec.gov/rules/other/2010/33-9149.pdf.

7. *See, generally,* Grundfest, "The SEC's Proposed Proxy Access Rules: Policy, Economics, and the Law," The Business Lawyer (American Bar Association Section of Business Law) Vol. 65 at 361 et. Seq. (2010) ("Grundfest").

8. Concept Release on the U.S. Proxy System, Release Nos. 34-62495; IA-3052; IC-29340; File No. S7-14-10 (2010) ("Proxy Concept Release").

The committee also may be assigned broader governance tasks, such as determining the composition of board committees, or dealing with board operational and structural issues such as the separation of the board chair and CEO functions. The nominating committee is sometimes referred to as the "nominating and governance committee."[9]

The SEC does not require that a company establish a nominating committee, but if the company does not, it must disclose why not having a committee is appropriate and identify the process by which nominations are made and which directors are involved in those decisions.[10]

The NYSE requires a nominating committee for its listed companies;[11] NASDAQ does not.[12] If a nominating committee has not been established and the board as a whole acts on nomination matters, NASDAQ rules require that only independent directors may participate in the decisions.[13]

For ease of discussions in this book, the nomination function undertaken by independent directors will generally be described as being a function of the nominating committee. Publicly traded companies typically will establish nominating committees to deal with substantive nomination processes and the disclosures that are involved, which can make nominating committees desirable even for non-NYSE companies.

Many of the corporate governance issues raised by institutional investors in recent years have involved the nomination and election process. One issue, the election of a director who receives less than 50% of the votes at an annual meeting, has been resolved in practice for major U.S. corporations, a substantial number of which have adopted a requirement that a director who receives less than 50% of the shareholder votes in an election should resign from the board.[14]

Boards are not required by the SEC to perform self evaluations, nor are nominating committees formally required to assess how well the skills possessed by board members match the needs of the company, but such

---

9.   *See* NYSE Rule 303A.04(a).

10. SEC Regulation S-K, Item 407(c)(1).

11. NYSE Rule 303A.04(a).

12. See NASDAQ Rule 5605.

13. NASDAQ Rule 5605(e).

14. *See* Bebchuk and Hirst, "Private Ordering and the Proxy Access Debate" The Business Lawyer (American Bar Association Section of Business Law) Vol. 65 at 331, 342 (2010) ("Bebchuk").

evaluation processes are common and often are included in corporate committee charters.[15]

Because such evaluations can be helpful in assessing the needs and performance of the board, and therefore have an impact on the director nomination process, discussion of board evaluations is included in this chapter.

Evaluations and board skills assessments conducted annually permit a board to determine whether the changes in the business environment, the nature of the business, or changes in the circumstances of individual board members make a bad match for the board and the company.[16]

2. Who Can Be on the Nominating Committee?

A. *Independent Directors Only*

The company must either (i) provide for independent director approval of director nominations[17] or (ii) have a nominating committee consisting of independent directors.[18] For a company having a nominating committee of three or more directors, NASDAQ rules will permit participation for not more than two years by one nonindependent director, in exceptional circumstances.[19]

Unlike the audit and compensation committees, the nominating committee is not required to have some or all of its members meet an additional standard beyond independence as defined by the SEC rules and relevant market standards.

In situations in which there is a shareholder with effective voting control over the election process, or where voting agreements or other contractual arrangements mandate the selection of specific directors, the NYSE and NASDAQ provide exemptions from the requirement that such nominations be approved by independent directors.[20]

---

15. *See* BoardEvals, *BoardEvals Whitepaper: Enhancing Governance Through Effective Board Evaluations*, at 2 (February 2010).
16. BoardEvals, *BoardEvals Whitepaper: Enhancing Governance Through Effective Board Evaluations*, at 6 (February 2010).
17. *See* NASDAQ Rule 5605(e).
18. *See* NYSE Rule 303A.04.
19. NASDAQ Rule 5605(d)(3).
20. NYSE Rule 303A.04 *Commentary*; NASDAQ Rule 5605(d)(3).

The terms of the U.S. Treasury investment in TARP recipients, for example, require that, upon default, the Treasury is entitled to select two directors to the board of the defaulting TARP recipient. Other examples of such arrangements would be preferred stock rights to elect directors upon a dividend default, shareholder agreements, and management agreements with third parties. In the eyes of NASDAQ, where such arrangements exist, "the right to nominate directors... does not reside with the Company, [and therefore] Independent Director approval would not be required."[21]

3. What Must a Nominating Committee Do?

The nominating committee must obtain specific information about director nominees, and perform specified actions and decision-making processes in order to comply with the SEC proxy rules.[22]

The company must disclose in its proxy statements:

1. The existence of a nominating committee or committee performing the nominating function, or, if there is no such committee, a discussion of why the company does not have one.[23]

2. The names of committee members.[24]

3. Whether the committee members meet the independence requirements set out by the NYSE or NASDAQ (or other independence standard).[25]

4. Whether the nominating committee considers director nominations offered by shareholders; and if not, why not.[26] If the committee considers shareholder nominees, the company must describe the procedures for considering such nominees, and the process by which shareholders submit nominations to the company.[27]

5. If a shareholder of more than 5% of the company stock recommends a candidate, the company must include the name of the nominee,

21. NASDAQ Rule 5605(e); IM 5650-7.
22. SEC Regulation S-K, Item 407(c).
23. SEC Regulation S-K, Item 407(c).
24. SEC Regulation S-K, Item 407(b)(3).
25. SEC Regulation S-K, Item 407(a)(1)(i).
26. SEC Regulation S-K, Item 407(c)(2)(ii)-(iii).
27. SEC Regulation S-K, Item 407(c)(2)(iv).

the name of the shareholder, and a statement by the nominating committee on whether it chose to nominate the candidate.[28]

6. A description of specific minimum qualifications for a director and specific qualities or skills that one or more board members must have.[29]

7. The process for identifying and evaluating nominees (including whether shareholder nominations are evaluated differently from candidates identified by the committee).[30]

8. For each director and any nominee for director, the particular experience, qualifications, attributes, or skills that led the board to conclude that the person should serve as a director for the company.[31]

9. A statement on the category of the source recommending candidates (e.g., management, independent director, shareholder, search firm).[32]

10. Disclosure regarding the activities of third parties paid to assist in recruiting board members.[33]

11. A statement on whether the nominating committee has a charter, and where a copy may be examined, or if no charter exists, a discussion of the company's reasons for not adopting one.[34]

The nominating committee must disclose the specific minimum qualifications and specific qualities or skills it uses to evaluate director nominees. The SEC's goal is to allow investors to compare and evaluate the skills and qualifications of each director and nominee against the standards established by the board.[35]

The SEC considered, but did not adopt, a rule to require disclosure of the specific experience, qualifications, or skills that qualify a person to serve as a committee member, noting that many companies rotate directors among different committee positions to allow directors to gain different

---

28. SEC Regulation S-K, Item 407(c)(2)(ix).
29. SEC Regulation S-K, Item 407(c)(2)(v).
30. SEC Regulation S-K, Item 407(c)(2)(vi).
31. SEC Regulation S-K, Item 407(c)(2)(v).
32. SEC Regulation S-K, Item 407(c)(2)(vii).
33. SEC Regulation S-K, Item 407(c)(2)(viii).
34. SEC Regulation S-K, Item 407(c)(2)(vi).
35. SEC Regulation S-K, Item 407(c)(2)(v).

perspectives of the company. But if an individual is chosen to be a director or a nominee to the board because of a particular qualification, attribute, or experience related to service on a specific committee, such as the audit committee, then this should be disclosed under the proxy rules as part of the discussion of the individual's qualifications to serve on the board.

Under the proxy rules, the company must disclose a nominee's directorships at public companies and registered investment companies held by each director and nominee at any time during the past five years (even if the director or nominee no longer serves on that board).[36] The SEC is seeking to provide investors information to evaluate the relevance of a director's or nominee's past board experience, as well as professional or financial relationships that might pose potential conflicts of interest (such as past membership on boards of major suppliers, customers, or competitors).

Also, the proxy rules require disclosure of certain legal proceedings involving directors dating back 10 years from the date of nomination.[37] The disclosure is aimed at providing investors with information on the competence and integrity of an individual to serve as a director. Broadly speaking, the legal proceedings that must be disclosed relate to bankruptcies or claims of fraud or securities law violations.

Finally, the SEC requires disclosure about board diversity, as defined by the company.[38] The SEC noted that if the nominating committee (or the board) has a policy with regard to the consideration of diversity in identifying director nominees, disclosure would be required of how this policy is implemented, as well as how the nominating committee (or the board) assesses the effectiveness of its policy.

The SEC noted that companies may define diversity in various ways, reflecting different perspectives.[39] For instance, some companies may conceptualize diversity expansively to include differences of viewpoint, professional experience, education, skill, and other individual qualities and attributes that contribute to board heterogeneity; others may focus on diversity concepts such as race, gender, and national origin. Under the disclosure requirement, companies are allowed to define diversity in ways that they consider appropriate and the SEC did not define diversity in the amendments.

---

36. SEC Schedule 14A, Item 22(b)(2). Instructions.
37. SEC Schedule 14A, Item 22(b)(12). Instructions.
38. SEC Regulation S-K, Item 407(c)(2)(vi).
39. SEC Regulation S-K, Item 407(c)(2)(vi).

4. Charter

While there is no single model for a nominating committee charter, there are common themes and elements in most such charters.

For NYSE companies, the nominating/corporate governance committee charter should "address the following items: committee member qualifications; committee member appointment and removal; committee structure and operations (including authority to delegate to subcommittees); and committee reporting to the board. In addition, the charter should give the nominating/ corporate governance committee sole authority to retain and terminate any search firm to be used to identify director candidates, including sole authority to approve the search firm's fees and other retention terms."[40]

The NYSE also requires that a company must make its nominating/ corporate governance committee charter available on its website and disclose in its annual report on Form 10-K that the nominating/corporate governance committee charter is available on the website.[41]

Under NASDAQ rules, each company must certify that it has adopted a formal written charter or board resolution, as applicable, addressing the nominations process and such related matters as may be required under the federal securities laws.[42]

Membership of the committee. The charter should specify the requirements for membership on the committee, including the requirement of independence by committee members.

Duties of the committee. The list of duties typically will include development of criteria for board membership, identification of potential nominees, and the evaluation of candidates. Some committee charters also provide for the committee to evaluate and report on the board's success in fulfilling the duties set out in the charter.

Some committees combine the nominating and corporate governance functions; some committees combine the executive nomination and compensation functions.

Ability to retain advisors. Some charters provide for a specific grant of authority to the committee to retain its own advisors, including search professionals and attorneys. For the reasons discussed in this section, even if the nominating committee is not granted independent authority to retain advisors, it is likely to want the board to provide access to advisors.

---

40. NYSE Rule 303A.04 *Commentary*.
41. NYSE Rule 303A.04(b).
42. NASDAQ Rules 5605(e)(2).

5. Developing a Nominating Process

The nominating committee will need to establish and articulate a nominating process.[43] The process could be set out in the committee charter, but as the charter must be approved by the entire board, the committee will have more flexibility to make adjustments over time if the process simply requires committee approval.

In accordance with its charter, the nominating committee should prepare a written list of characteristics that the board and board committees should possess, including size of the board, minimum qualifications, desired skill sets or experiential backgrounds for members, and any diversity objectives. Some qualifications may be set out in the corporation's charter or bylaws, such as a mandatory retirement age.

In this way, while not every director would possess every desired quality, the board as a group would possess the desired mix of skills and experiences.

The charter should describe the committee structure (minimum number of meetings, membership, etc.).[44] It also should set out the scope of the committee's authority, such as whether the committee will recommend CEO nominations as well as director nominations, or be involved in succession planning. It should include provisions regarding the ability of the committee to retain search firms or other professionals to advise it, and the ability of the committee to accept and review nominations proposed by shareholders.

Under SEC rules, the nominating committee must include its charter in the proxy statement or direct investors to a source, such as a website, at which the charter can be found.[45]

As an operating matter, the nominating committee should evaluate proposed director candidates, from whatever source, against the written criteria for the board, and should conduct personal interviews prior to making any director nominations. The committee should in all cases be vested with discretion to reject any candidate that it does not think will be appropriate for the board, notwithstanding that candidate's credentials, since candidates who look good on paper may be a bad fit with the board based on personality or other factors.

---

43. *See* NASDAQ Rules 5605(e)(2) ("Each [c]ompany must certify that it has adopted a . . . resolution addressing the nominations process.").
44. *See* NYSE Rule 303A.04 *Commentary.*
45. SEC Regulation S-K, Item 407(c).

6. Evaluations of Candidates

Notwithstanding the ferment in the corporate governance world in recent years, incumbent directors are not automatically disfavored. Incumbent directors have worked together and have obtained a working knowledge of the company through their prior participation on the board.

It is proper for a nominating committee to give weight to such experience in evaluating whether an incumbent should be renominated to serve as a member of the board of directors.

If a sitting director is to be nominated for a new term, the nominating committee should make sure the director qualifies for the position under the most recently developed standards for directorship, which may have changed since the director's original nomination. The nominating committee also should confirm that the incumbent has performed satisfactorily and weigh any special circumstances or considerations that could affect its view that the nomination is in the best interests of the corporation.

The list of candidates that the nominating committee will consider should consist of nominees it has identified, including incumbents, and including nominees suggested by other directors, management, or search firms, as well as nominations provided by shareholders.

As with the use of compensation advisors, if the committee rather than management is responsible for the engagement and compensation of the outside advisor in recruiting director nominees, the search more likely will be perceived as having been conducted independent of management.

In reviewing potential nominees, the committee will want to consider:

- the candidate's background, including any information that would be required to be disclosed in the proxy statements;
- whether the candidate meets the nomination committee's minimum criteria for board membership;[46]
- whether the candidate has specific skills or experience that the committee has determined is valuable for board members;
- whether any other goals (diversity, for example) would be met by the candidacy;[47] and
- whether the candidate would be a good "fit" for the board.[48]

---

46. *See* SEC Regulation S-K, Item 407(c)(2)(v).
47. *See* SEC Regulation S-K, Item 407(c)(2)(vi).
48. NACD Key Agreed Principles at 9.

The committee will want to maintain records of its proceedings that are sufficiently detailed to confirm that the committee has discharged its duties, while respecting the privacy of individual candidates.

In evaluating shareholder nominees, the committee is obligated to disclose whether the criteria it uses to evaluate such nominees differs from that used to evaluate its own nominees.[49] If factors such as the size or duration of the shareholder's interest in the company affect the evaluation process, the committee should disclose that fact. The committee will want to ensure that the relationship, if any, between the nominee and the shareholder is known to the committee and evaluated before the nomination is placed before shareholders.

The nominating committee also may consider how third-party proxy advisory groups, such as RiskMetrics Group or Glass Lewis, would view a potential candidate. The nominating committee would not want those parties to dictate its choices, but their concerns could be relevant.

The nominating committee will also want to confirm that a candidate can devote sufficient attention to board duties. "Directors need to exhibit a commitment of both time and active attention to fulfill their fiduciary obligations. Generally, that means that directors should ensure that they have the time to attend board and committee meetings and the annual meeting of shareholders, prepare for meetings, stay informed about issues that are relevant to the company, consult with management as needed, and address crises should crises arise."[50]

The board may wish to articulate guidelines that encourage directors to limit their other commitments. Such guidelines assist in communicating expectations about the commitment that is expected. Given the considerable variation in individual capacity, boards should apply their judgment and assess directors' commitment through their actions, rather than rely on rigid standards.

7. CEO Succession

The question of CEO succession may be considered by the board as a whole or by the compensation committee that determines the performance measurements for the CEO as part of its compensation function, by the

---

49. SEC Regulation S-K, Item 407(c)(2)(vi).
50. NACD Agreed Principles at 9.

nominating committee, or by a committee formed specifically for that purpose. CEO succession is discussed in Chapter III.1.

8. Board and Committee Evaluations

Since the adoption of the NYSE rules requiring regular evaluations of boards and key committees, such evaluations have become routine for public companies, even those not listed with the NYSE.[51] "According to a Pricewaterhouse Coopers survey of over 1,000 corporate directors, in 2007, 88% of public companies conducted a full-board evaluation on a regular basis, up from 33% in 2002."[52] In addition, 78% of NASDAQ companies now conduct a regular full-board evaluation, even though it is not a NASDAQ requirement to do so.[53] This trend has filtered down to board committees as well: 90% of public company board committees now conduct annual evaluations.[54]

The evaluation process can provide various benefits to a board or committee:[55]

- It can be used to identify areas in which the board regards itself to be strong or weak, permitting the board to address areas of weakness over time;
- It can be used to hold individual directors accountable for their performance;
- It can be used to help tailor the composition of the board and its committees, by identifying skills or experience areas in which gaps exist;
- It can facilitate communication within the board regarding performance and responsibilities.

---

51. *See* BoardEvals, *BoardEvals Whitepaper: Enhancing Governance Through Effective Board Evaluations*, at 3 (February 2010).

52. *See* BoardEvals, *BoardEvals Whitepaper: Enhancing Governance Through Effective Board Evaluations*, at 3 (February 2010).

53. *See* BoardEvals, available at http://www.boardevals.com/board-governance-today (last visited June 27, 2010).

54. *See* BoardEvals, available at http://www.boardevals.com/board-governance-today (last visited June 27, 2010).

55. *See* BoardEvals, available at http://www.boardevals.com/board-governance-today (last visited June 27, 2010).

The evaluation process is seen as being an important tool for ensuring individual director effectiveness, more so than mandatory retirement ages, term limits, or other devices.[56]

Directors may believe that there are one or more individual directors who are not appropriate members of the board, for various reasons, such as skills that do not match the current corporate needs, lack of engagement, lack of preparation, or lack of critical analysis.[57]

The board evaluation process typically consists of a survey, conducted by the board members anonymously to ensure greater frankness and participation.[58]

Outside parties may conduct the survey on behalf of the board, and maintain the identities of the specific responses in confidence. The process may be performed in a special session of the board, or by using an automated process.

However the survey is conducted, the critical aspect of a successful evaluation is whether it is used by the board or the nominating committee to engage meaningfully in addressing identified problems. Without follow-up engagement among board members, the evaluation process could become a "check the box" governance routine performed for show but divorced from real content.

Even areas in which the board is satisfied with its performance should be reviewed objectively to see if the board has blind spots as to its own performance.

Typical topics covered by a board evaluation would be[59]

- A Board Skills Assessment to ensure the board collectively has the right set of skills and experience to address the corporation's strategic goals.

- A General Board Evaluation to assess the board's strengths and weaknesses and the board's perception of its own performance.

- A Director Self-Assessment to permit each director to assess whether his or her contributions are at the level expected by the company.

---

56. *See* BoardEvals, available at http://www.boardevals.com/board-governance-today (last visited June 27, 2010) (PWC Chart).

57. *See* BoardEvals, available at http://www.boardevals.com/board-governance-today (last visited June 27, 2010).

58. *See* BoardEvals, http://www.boardevals.com/our-board-evaluation-process (last visited June 29, 2010).

59. *See* BoardEvals, *BoardEvals Whitepaper: Enhancing Governance Through Effective Board Evaluations*, at 12 (February 2010).

- A Director Peer Evaluation to permit candid assessments of the perceived skills and contributions of the other directors.

- Enterprise Risk Assessment to determine whether potential risks have been identified, and whether such risks are being addressed.

- CEO/Executive Director Evaluation to assess performance of the organization's leadership.

Peer evaluations in particular can represent an area in which there is a need for both follow-through and tact. Board members tend to be highly functioning individuals with records of success. Where criticism of a director's performance is merited, and fairly presented, there is an opportunity for board leadership or the nominating committee to address the questions, either directly with the individual, or through the nomination process.

Such activities require personnel who are deft at dealing with personal issues, to prevent a breakdown in collegiality that could harm the board or hinder the board's effectiveness in the future.

Some companies are concerned that the use of a board evaluation could generate legal liability. The concern is understandable, as the results of a board evaluation would be discoverable in litigation, and if a board identified areas of board weakness and then failed to address the weakness, such evidence would be damning.

At the same time, evidence of a deliberate process to identify and address any existing board issues would demonstrate that the board was exercising due care in conducting governance.

In all events, information that is contained in a board evaluation for any year will lose relevance over time, and a board should consider whether its document retention policies, in particular with regard to evaluations, provide that such evaluations are retained only for as long as is appropriate.

9. Conclusion

As discussed further in Chapter II.3, questions of majority voting, proxy access, and shareholder communication have made the relationship of shareholders and boards more complex in recent years. Legislative, economic, and technological changes have shifted the balance between the shareholders and management as well.

The core function of the nominating committee—to nominate a skilled, effective, and collegial slate of candidates for the board—requires the committee to be mindful of these corporate governance developments as it conducts its operations, and to navigate through the evolving set of rules.

SEC Enforcement

1. Introduction

Not only can directors face potential civil liability to shareholders for breaches of fiduciary duty, they can also face SEC-initiated civil or criminal actions for violations of the securities laws, including a lifetime ban from public company service.

Federal securities laws frequently are written to regulate the "issuer" or "registrant," meaning those disclosure and compliance obligations are duties of the company, rather than duties of specified individuals within the company. There is also a significant amount of SEC regulation and enforcement activity directly targeted at individuals who are pivotal in the corporate governance process, including independent directors.

This focus on individual behavior recognizes that corporate activities, in the end, are generated from the actions of the individuals who make decisions and take actions on behalf of the company.

Independence of directors from management creates a "check and balance" control process within a corporation to prevent management misuse of corporate resources. For advisors and consultants outside the corporation—such as accountants, attorneys, and consultants to the company—independence from management lends credibility to their professional advice. Investors view such independence as evidence that corporate decisions and statements are fairly made.

From time to time, the SEC commissioners and staff have used the term "gatekeepers" to refer to the non-management individuals who are central to key corporate decisions. Independent directors are high on the list of gatekeepers. The list of gatekeepers also includes accountants and attorneys who work with the company.[1]

No securities statutes or SEC rules use or define the term "gatekeeper"[2] and the term does not have an official or legal usage.[3] However, the term

---

1.   *See* SEC Speech, Stephen M. Cutler, Director, SEC Division of Enforcement,
      *The Themes of Sarbanes-Oxley as Reflected in the Commission's Enforcement
      Program* (speech at UCLA School of Law, 2004) ("Cutler 2004 UCLA"); SEC
      Speech, Stephen M. Cutler, Director, SEC Division of Enforcement, *Remarks
      at the University of Michigan Law School* (speech, 2002) ("Cutler 2002"); SEC
      Speech, SEC Commissioner Harvey J. Goldschmid, *Post-Enron America: An SEC
      Perspective* (speech, 2002)("Goldschmid").

2.   In the releases relating to its adoption of Rule 2711 relating to securities
      analysts, the National Association of Securities Dealers ("NASD") used the term
      "gatekeeper" frequently, but the term did not appear in the text of the rule. The term
      enjoys widespread, but informal, usage in the securities regulation context.

3.   Use by SEC commissioners and staff of the term "gatekeeper" differs from the
      academic view of the role of "gatekeepers" in the capital markets. *Compare* Cutler
      2004 UCLA, Cutler 2002, and Goldschmid with John C. Coffee, *Gatekeeper
      Failure and Reform: The Challenge of Fashioning Relevant Reforms,* Law and
      Economics Workshop, University of California, Berkeley, 2004 ("Coffee 2004").
      Noted securities professor John Coffee of Columbia University describes a
      gatekeeper as a party in the securities markets (institutional or individual) that puts
      its own credibility on the line on behalf of a company. In theory, the gatekeeper has
      less to gain, and more to lose, than a manager who wants to mislead the markets or
      improperly deal with the company. In that way, the gatekeeper provides a check on
      bad behavior:
      *First, the gatekeeper is a person who has significant reputational capital, acquired
      over many years and many clients, which it pledges to assure the accuracy of
      statements or representations that it either makes or verifies. Second, the gatekeeper
      receives a far smaller benefit or payoff for its role, as an agent, in approving,
      certifying, or verifying information than does the principal from the transaction
      that the gatekeeper facilitates or enables. Thus, because of this lesser benefit, the
      gatekeeper is easier to deter.*
Coffee 2004.

gatekeeper is useful shorthand for referring to individuals who are not part of corporate management but who are in a position to affect—and ensure the integrity of—corporate decisions, and that is the way the term will be used in this chapter. For example, independent directors must approve corporate decisions. The outside auditors must report on the accuracy of financial statements prepared by management. Corporate counsel has an obligation to advise the company of evidence of a material violation of the securities laws.

In this regard, the SEC regulations requiring specific individual actions are related to, but not identical to, the fiduciary duty requirements board members face. In the fiduciary duty context, board members do not face liability if they act in good faith, on an informed basis, and with due care.

SEC regulations that affect gatekeepers require observance of processes that, if followed, should produce (a) independent committee or professional judgments and (b) evidence of the independence of those judgments. Individuals who ignore the processes, or blindly follow management in disregard of the facts those processes generate, face potential SEC enforcement actions.

For example, the proxy rules require companies to make certain relatively detailed disclosures about portions of the compensation, nomination, and risk evaluation processes. Those rules are directed at ensuring that identified individuals within the company (committee members) assume the responsibility for performing specific procedures. Even if those processes are flawed or ineffective in any individual case, performing them should, in theory, generally benefit shareholders.

The SEC can act administratively to seek non-criminal penalties from officers and directors, such as obtaining money damages or obtaining injunctions to prevent specific behavior. The SEC also has the authority to bar officers or directors for life from serving on a public company.

For criminal enforcement of the securities laws, the SEC must refer a matter to the Department of Justice, which brings the case to court.

One advantage from an enforcement point of view in bringing actions against gatekeepers is that an individual is likely to be more vulnerable and command fewer defense resources than does the company. This makes the gatekeeper an effective enforcement target in the SEC's eyes, particularly in light of the SEC's relatively small resources compared to those of the companies whose activities it polices.[4]

This chapter discusses SEC enforcement actions that may be directed toward individual directors or gatekeepers, and the SEC regulations that are aimed at preserving the independence of outside advisers to the company, primarily accountants and attorneys.

2. The Evolution of SEC Enforcement

Since at least the 1970s, the SEC has focused on individual corporate actors in its enforcement actions, although the word "gatekeeper" did not come into use until the 1990s.

At least since the 1994 SEC administrative enforcement action *In re Cooper Companies,*[5] the SEC has considered members of the board of directors as potential targets for enforcement actions when the company's securities law obligations have not been met. In *Cooper*, the board was determined to have failed to act when confronted with evidence of serious wrongdoing by management in connection with trading in high yield bonds.

In 1997, the SEC brought a cease and desist action against the officers and directors of W.R. Grace.[6] In that matter, the individuals who were sanctioned were aware of certain transactions involving corporate insiders that were not included in the company's proxy statement, even though the dollar amount of those transactions should have triggered the proxy statement reporting requirements. The SEC determined that the officers and directors had the duty to go beyond the company's established reporting procedures—including relying on company counsel's review of the proxy statement—to ensure the accuracy of the report.

In 1998, the SEC proposed an overarching reform of the securities law system, including a proposal for the certification by the CEO and CFO of financial statements that were included in the company's public filings.[7] While the entire proposed rule making was not adopted in the form proposed, in the aftermath of the Enron and WorldCom bankruptcies, the

---

4. Cutler 2004 UCLA, citing SEC enforcement actions in the 1970s under what was then called the "access theory."
5. Cooper, 1994 SEC LEXIS 3975.
6. Grace.
7. SEC Release 33-7606 (Nov. 3, 1998) ("Aircraft Carrier Release"), as amended by SEC Release 33-7606A (November 13, 1998).

SEC implemented the CEO and CFO certification rule,[8] which was then incorporated into two separate sections of SOX.[9]

The role of accountants in the Enron and WorldCom bankruptcies was widely criticized as a failure of the accountants to fulfill their roles as gatekeepers. Specifically, the accountants were perceived as having neglected their professional obligations and responsibilities by acquiescing in bad or fraudulent accounting judgments of their clients, rather than putting at risk lucrative business, particularly the business of providing nonaudit services and consulting.

Prior to the Enron collapse, the SEC had recognized the risk that audit judgments could be compromised by auditors desirous of selling nonaudit services to their clients. In 2001, the SEC adopted rules that required that compensation to auditors be broken into audit and nonaudit elements and be disclosed in the proxy statement. Those rules also established that an auditor's provision of certain services would result in the auditor no longer being deemed to be independent from the client, meaning that the auditor could no longer audit the client's financial statements.[10]

In response to the corporate failures of 2001 and 2002, Congress included in SOX a number of provisions that were intended to permit—and in many cases to require—boards, professional advisors, and securities professionals to form and act on judgments independent of company management.

Such provisions included:

- Specifying elements of the audit committee function;

- Restructuring the accounting profession and establishing regulatory oversight of the profession;

- Regulating the nonaudit services auditors could perform, and structuring the relationship between the audit committee and the auditors;

- Requiring attorneys who developed concerns about corporate legal issues to make those concerns known in the company beyond management; and

- Giving the SEC expanded power to impose lifetime bans from corporate boardrooms and executive positions on individuals determined to be "unfit" for service with public companies.

---

8. SEC Release 34-46079 (June 14, 2002) ("Certification Release").
9. SOX 302, and SOX 906.
10. SEC Release 33-7919 (Nov. 1, 2001; effective Feb. 5, 2002) ("Audit Release").

Since 2004, the SEC and other government agencies[11] have further extended enforcement doctrines in connection with internal corporate investigations. In one case, law enforcement officials asserted that it was an obstruction of justice for a corporate officer to lie to the attorney hired by the company to conduct an internal investigation into fraud charges.[12] In another case, the SEC indicated that it was considering an enforcement action against an attorney whose conduct of an internal investigation the SEC considered insufficient.[13] These cases represent an even further extension of the gatekeeper enforcement approach.

SOX limited the "clawback" of bonuses to cases in which a company restated financial statements as a result of "misconduct."[14] Under Dodd-Frank, the securities exchanges must adopt rules under which listed companies will develop "clawback" policies to recapture executive bonuses on the basis of erroneous financial statements, regardless of whether the error was the result of misconduct.[15] Even before the enhanced "clawback" legislation was adopted in Dodd-Frank, at least one court had upheld the SEC's assertion of authority to seek recovery of bonuses paid to executives where financial statements are restated, even if the executive who was paid the bonus was not responsible for the "misconduct" that led to the restatement.[16]

Dodd-Frank also included a provision under which a corporate whistleblower would be able to collect a bounty from the SEC if the information provided resulted in a recovery of $1.0 million or more. The SEC has discretion to determine the size of any such bounty, between 10% and 30%.[17]

---

11. *See U.S. v. Singleton*, Criminal Action No. H 06 080, U.S. District Court, Southern District of Texas, Houston Division (Mar. 8, 2006).

12. *See U.S. v. Kumar and Richards*, indictment filed in U.S. District Court, Eastern District of New York (2004).

13. SEC Threatens Ex-Brobeck Lawyer Over Client's Probe, People Say, http://www.bloomberg.com/apps/news?pid=10000103&sid=aX0HXY74R1P4&refer=us.

14. SOX 304.

15. Dodd-Frank 954.

16. *SEC v. Jenkins*, No. CV 09-1510-PHX-GMS (D. Ariz. June 9, 2010); See SOX 304.

17. Dodd-Frank 922 et. Seq.

3. Specific SEC Enforcement Authority

A. *Cease and Desist Proceedings*

Congress provided the SEC with authority under both Section 8A of the Securities Act of 1933 and Section 21C of the Securities Exchange Act of 1934 to conduct proceedings and to issue cease-and-desist orders.

The scope of this authority is quite broad:

> If the Commission finds, after notice and opportunity for hearing, that any person *is violating, has violated, or is about to violate* any provision of this title, or any rule or regulation thereunder, the Commission may publish its findings and enter an order requiring such person, and any other person that is, was, or would be a *cause of the violation, due to an act or omission the person knew or should have known would contribute to such violation,* to cease and desist from committing or causing such violation and any future violation of the same provision, rule, or regulation. Such order may, in addition to requiring a person to cease and desist from committing or causing a violation, require such person to comply, or to take steps to effect compliance, with such provision, rule, or regulation, upon such terms and conditions and within such time as the Commission may specify in such order. Any such order may, as the Commission deems appropriate, require future compliance or steps to effect future compliance, either permanently or for such period of time as the Commission may specify, with such provision, rule, or regulation with respect to any security, any issuer, or any other person. *(Emphasis added.)*[18]

There are some important things to note about the scope of the SEC cease-and-desist authority:

- It is not limited to addressing past violations of law but permits the SEC to act in cases in which it believes a violation *may* occur.

---

18. Securities Act Sec. 8A ("Section 8A") and Securities Exchange Act Sec. 21C ("Section 21C") contain this same language.

- Unlike violations of Section 10(b) of the 1934 Act (in Rule 10b-5 cases), it does not require a specific state of mind, such as fraudulent intent. There must be an actual or threatened violation of the securities law, and a finding that the targeted individual was the "cause" of the violation as a result of his or her action (or failure to act). Sanctions can then be imposed if the party that "caused" the violation knew, or should have known, he or she would contribute to the violation.

Because this authority is broad, the SEC is able to impose cease-and-desist sanctions on parties after it has found a violation of the securities laws, even where a party sought—and received, presumably—assurances from counsel that a course of conduct was permissible.

Good faith reliance on the advice of counsel will not shield an independent director (or any other director) from being the subject of a cease-and-desist order.[19] Accordingly, directors should take care to review with counsel the relevant facts underlying potentially sensitive legal issues. In particular, if the attorney and the directors have different understandings of the underlying facts, directors should take the initiative to resolve those differences, which could have a legal impact, so that a different understanding of the facts does not become grounds for a claim that a director "caused" a violation to occur.

One consequence of treating independent directors and attorneys as gatekeepers, given the existence of an SEC sanction that can be applied after-the-fact even to good faith judgments, is that both directors and counsel have an incentive to avoid taking an aggressive legal position, even if such a position is justified under the law. Attorneys also have an incentive to advise clients that a most-conservative interpretation of law exists, so that any decisions to take a more aggressive approach that might "cause" a violation of the securities laws falls on the client—such as a board or a committee of independent directors.[20]

---

19. *See* Grace, Drummond.

20. *See e.g.,* Drummond. Drummond, general counsel for Google, Inc., prior to its initial public offering, after consulting with outside counsel, advised the board of directors that there was an available exemption for the issuance of stock options beyond the limits set by SEC Rule 701. The SEC determined that the exemption was not available, required Google to make a rescission offer, and stated that Drummond, because he had not informed the board prior to its decision of the risk that the legal position he advised might be wrong, had "caused" Google's violation—the implication being that if the board had been informed of the risk and made the same choice regarding the issuance of options, the board, rather than counsel, might have been the "cause" of the violation.

The breadth of cease-and-desist orders has been challenged successfully. At least one federal circuit court has held that the broad injunctive orders commonly sought by the SEC were unenforceable, because they generally require that the defendant "cease and desist" from breaking certain statutes or regulations, rather than identifying the specific act, such as insider trading or accounting fraud, that has been prohibited.[21] The SEC continues to seek, and obtain, broad orders.

B. Lifetime Ban from Serving as Officer or Director

Prior to SOX, the SEC possessed the power under the Securities Act and Securities Exchange Act to impose a lifetime ban preventing an individual from serving as an officer or director of a public company if the SEC determined that individual was "substantially unfit" to so serve.[22]

SOX Section 305 amended those provisions to provide that the SEC could impose the lifetime ban on anyone the SEC determined was "unfit" to serve, removing the qualifier "substantially" from the standard for imposing a ban.[23] Not unexpectedly, the SEC promptly increased its use of the lifetime ban. During its fiscal year ended September 30, 2001, the SEC obtained 51 officer and director bans under the "substantially unfit" standard; in the two years following passage of SOX, it obtained approximately 300.[24] Since that time, the SEC has sought, on average, about 125 lifetime bans per year in connection with its enforcement actions.

Cease-and-desist proceedings and lifetime ban actions may be brought by the SEC as administrative hearings for injunctive relief. Unlike a criminal proceeding, such injunctive actions do not require the SEC to involve the Department of Justice before an enforcement action can commence.

Because the SEC is able to bring administrative hearings conducted by the SEC itself, the injunctive actions provide the SEC with an effective and efficient enforcement tool.

---

21. *SEC v. Smyth* No. 04-11985, 2005 U.S. App. LEXIS 16721 (11th Cir. Aug. 10, 2005).

22. For a discussion regarding the standards relating to officer and director fitness, see Jayne W. Barnard, "Rule *10b-5 and the 'Unfitness' Question,*" 47 Ariz. L. Rev. 9 (2005); reprinted in 47 Corp. Prac. Comm. 855 (2005).

23. SOX 305, amending Securities Act Sec. 20(e) and Exchange Act Sec. 21(d)(2).

24. Cutler 2004 UCLA.

4. The Relations of Other Independent Professionals and Independent Directors

A. *Auditors as Gatekeepers; Relations with the Board*

The corporate scandals of 2002 and the financial crisis of 2008 led to major federal legislation, including SOX, and renewed the focus on outside corporate advisors.

The 2002 corporate scandals resulted in close scrutiny of the accounting and auditing profession, and the substantial restructuring of that profession under SOX. The 2008 financial crisis drew attention to the role of the credit rating agencies in perpetuating the creation of a real estate market asset bubble, and Dodd-Frank included provisions imposing additional regulation on the credit rating profession.[25]

The SEC articulated a gatekeeper rationale behind the regulation of auditors:

> Independent auditors have an important public trust. Investors must be able to rely on issuers' financial statements. It is the auditor's opinion that furnishes investors with critical assurance that the financial statements have been subjected to a rigorous examination by an objective, impartial, and skilled professional, and that investors, therefore, can rely on them. If investors do not believe that an auditor is independent of a company, they will derive little confidence from the auditor's opinion and will be far less likely to invest in that public company's securities.[26]

When SOX enacted sweeping changes with respect to public companies, it also transformed the accounting profession. The accounting profession, which prior to SOX substantially had been self-regulated, became (for those firms providing audit services to public companies) regulated by the Public Company Accounting Oversight Board ("PCAOB"), which was established by SOX and is overseen by the SEC.

Accountants who render services to publicly traded companies are obligated to register with the PCAOB. The PCAOB is empowered to enact

---

25. Dodd-Frank 931 et seq.
26. Audit Release.

rules regarding auditing, quality control, ethics, and independence standards for the profession. The PCAOB also may inspect registered accounting firms, conduct investigations, and impose sanctions for violations.

In addition to providing for the PCAOB's regulation of the accounting industry, SOX set out specific limits on the way accountants conducted business with public companies, including:

- Provision of a number of nonaudit services to audit clients was prohibited, including providing bookkeeping services, designing and implementing financial information systems, providing appraisal or valuation services, and providing internal audit, human resources, or management services. Many of those services had previously been prohibited by SEC regulation.[27]

- Provision of nonaudit services that were not prohibited under SOX or SEC rules became subject to preapproval by the company's audit committee.[28]

- SOX established a mandatory rotation of the audit firm's lead partner and concurring partner away from representation of the audit client every five years.[29]

- The auditor was required to report on a timely basis specified information to the audit committee, including (a) all critical accounting policies used by the company, (b) alternative accounting treatments discussed with management, along with the potential ramifications of using those alternatives, and (c) other written communications provided by the auditor to management, including a schedule of unadjusted audit differences.[30]

- SOX established conflict of interest provisions that prohibit an accounting firm from performing audit services for a company if key members of management have recently been employed in an audit capacity by the audit firm.[31]

- SOX also made illegal attempts by management to "fraudulently influence, coerce, manipulate, or mislead" an accountant performing

---

27. SOX 201.
28. SOX 202.
29. SOX 203.
30. SOX 204.
31. SOX 206.

audit functions for the purpose of rendering financial statements materially misleading.[32]

Beyond these statutory strictures adopted by Congress, the SEC imposed additional, detailed implementing regulations, such as further regulations defining activities that would prevent an auditor from being independent.[33] In implementing the section of SOX relating to management's influence on auditors, the SEC rules removed the requirement that management act with intent in its action to coerce, manipulate, or mislead an auditor, expanding the scope of this provision.[34]

SOX also mandated that the corporate audit committee was obligated to establish a process to receive and deal with reports of accounting fraud,[35] while auditors bear a corresponding responsibility to report information that comes to their attention that an illegal act has, or may have, occurred, regardless of whether the act has a material impact on financial statements.[36]

SOX requires the auditor, upon discovery of an illegal act or potential illegal act, to bring it to the attention of management and then to the attention of the audit committee and if necessary the board, in seeking remediation of any illegal acts that are not "clearly inconsequential."

If the illegal act has a material impact on the corporate financial statements, and the corporation has not taken remedial action, the auditor may be required to resign from the engagement and report the circumstances to the SEC.

With statutory and regulatory changes affecting both auditors and audit committees, SOX established requirements on each side of the audit relationship intended to ensure the flow of complete and accurate financial information on a timely basis within the company for preparation of public reports.

While a determined management effort to commit fraud still might be concealed from auditors or from even a vigilant audit committee, the audit environment created by SOX was intended to cast investigatory nets more broadly and with finer mesh to detect accounting problems. By making

---

32. SOX 303.
33. *See* SEC Release 34-47890 (May 20, 2003) ("Audit Influence Release"); SEC Release 33-8183A (Mar. 26, 2003) ("Auditor Independence Release"); SEC Release 33-8180 (Jan. 24, 2003).
34. *See* SEC Rule 13b2-2(b); Audit Influence Release.
35. SOX 301.
36. Exchange Act Sec. 10A(b).

a greater number of individuals, both within and outside the company, responsible for ensuring that financial reporting was timely and accurate, SOX institutionalized the gatekeeper regulatory approach with respect to accounting activities.

B. Attorneys as Gatekeepers; Relations with the Board

Section 307 of SOX did not prescribe an extensive restructuring of the attorney-client relationship, but it did require the SEC to address at least one specific concern, very much in keeping with the concept of attorneys having obligations as corporate gatekeepers:

> [T]he Commission shall issue rules, in the public interest and for the protection of investors, setting forth minimum standards of professional conduct for attorneys appearing and practicing before the Commission in any way in the representation of issuers, including a rule—
>
> 1. requiring an attorney to report evidence of a material violation of securities law or breach of fiduciary duty or similar violation by the company or any agent thereof, to the chief legal counsel or the chief executive officer of the company (or the equivalent thereof); and
>
> 2. if the counsel or officer does not appropriately respond to the evidence (adopting, as necessary, appropriate remedial measures or sanctions with respect to the violation), requiring the attorney to report the evidence to the audit committee of the board of directors of the issuer or to another committee of the board of directors comprised solely of directors not employed directly or indirectly by the issuer, or to the board of directors.[37]

In adding Section 307 to SOX, at least one Senator indicated concern that improper, and improperly limited, use of legal advice had resulted in managements of failed companies being in a position to plead ignorance of

---

37. SOX 307.

material problems and legal obligations.[38] As with accountants, attorneys were seen as having an incentive to compromise their professional judgments to make legal interpretations that would favor the managements on whom they relied for payment.

The Section 307 requirements for "reporting up the corporate ladder" promoted attorney independence from management in two ways:

- First, reporting up the ladder would make it harder for a management to assert ignorance of legal issues or the consequences of controversial actions, because close or controversial legal issues would receive increased attention and potentially the attention of the board of directors; and

- Second, faced with the prospect of justifying to the company's independent directors a controversial or narrow interpretation of law to promote management self-interest, managements and attorneys both would have incentives to avoid risky or tenuous arguments, particularly for transactions that were not necessarily in the best interests of the corporation.

However, unlike accountants, attorneys do not prepare reports for consumption by the public; they advise clients regarding potential legal risks respecting alternative courses of action. Attorneys act as advocates for clients as well as provide advice on legal compliance, and attorneys have ethical obligations to maintain client confidences. The bar is still struggling with the tensions between the role of attorneys as advocates and confidential advisors and the role of gatekeepers.[39]

The Section 307 approach reflects the understanding that an attorney's duties to a corporate client run to the organization as a whole and not simply to members of management who may have interests inimical to the interests of the organization. It also respects the legal system's fundamental principle that the client has the sole authority and responsibility to make decisions regarding the client's course of action and that attorneys are not guarantors of their clients' compliance with law.

The SEC promulgated its Part 205 rules ("Part 205") pursuant to SOX Section 307.[40] Part 205 establishes a structured sequence of disclosures

---

38. Comments of Senator Enzi, 148 Cong. Rec. S6555.
39. Corporations Committee of the California State Bar Business Section, *"At Every Peril" New Pressures on the Attorney-Client Relationship, A Public Commentary*, Nov. 18, 2003 ("At Every Peril").
40. SEC Release 33-8150 (Nov. 21, 2002) ("First Part 205 Release"); SEC Release 33-8186 (Jan. 29, 2003) ("Second Part 205 Release"); and SEC Release 8185 (Jan. 29,

between the attorney and the company regarding potential securities law violations or breaches of fiduciary duty. In crafting Part 205, the SEC developed the concept of the qualified legal compliance committee (QLCC) of the board of directors. The QLCC would be comprised solely of independent directors (at least one of whom must be a member of the audit committee) and could discharge the company's responsibilities under Part 205, provided that the QLCC had been established in advance of the referral of the specific legal matter to the QLCC. Although there are a number of companies that have adopted the QLCC, some of them by adding the QLCC function to the duties of the audit committee, the QLCC is not a universally used committee.

The starting point in the Part 205 process is the requirement that:

> If an attorney, appearing and practicing before the Commission in the representation of an issuer, becomes aware of evidence of a material violation by the issuer or by any officer, director, employee, or agent of the issuer, the attorney shall report such evidence to the issuer's chief legal officer (or the equivalent thereof) or to both the issuer's chief legal officer and its chief executive officer (or the equivalents thereof) forthwith. By communicating such information to the issuer's officers or directors, an attorney does not reveal client confidences or secrets or privileged or otherwise protected information related to the attorney's representation of an issuer.[41]

Part 205 defines "evidence of a material violation" to mean objectively credible evidence of a breach of the securities laws or fiduciary duty by company personnel.

If an attorney has made a report to the company's chief legal officer (CLO) of evidence of a material violation, Part 205 then sets out the sequence of responses and counter-responses for the company and the attorney:

1. The CLO must investigate the attorney's report, and respond to the attorney.

2003) ("Part 205 Implementing Release").
41. SEC Part 205.3(b).

2. If the CLO determines no material violation has occurred, is ongoing, or is about to occur, the CLO will so notify the reporting attorney, providing the basis for such determination.

3. If the attorney determines that the CLO has made an "appropriate response" to the attorney's concerns, the attorney's obligations under Part 205 are satisfied.

An appropriate response may be that the report of a material violation was incorrect, or that an appropriate remedial response has been adopted, or that the company, with the consent of the board or QLCC, has retained an attorney to review the reported evidence of a material violation and either: (i) substantially implemented any remedial recommendations or (ii) been advised that the company may assert a colorable defense with respect to the matter.

1. If the attorney determines that the CLO's response is still not an appropriate response, the attorney is obligated to report the matter "up the ladder" to the company's board, the audit committee, or a committee of independent directors.

2. If, at the end of the process, the attorney believes that the company has not made an appropriate response, the attorney is obligated to report the reasons that the attorney regards the response to be unsatisfactory to the CLO, CEO, and any directors to whom the attorney previously had reported the problem.

3. As an alternative to reporting to the CLO or the board, the attorney could report to a QLCC, if the company has one.

Once a matter is referred to the QLCC, the attorney's obligations under Part 205 end, including the obligation to determine whether the company has made an appropriate response to the attorney's report.

Although these provisions of Part 205 are phrased in terms of imposing duties on attorneys under the securities laws, they are consistent with existing professional duties and ethical duties of attorneys in representing corporate clients. The attorney does not merely represent management but represents the corporate entity as a whole. The obligation to maintain client (corporate) confidences is preserved.

More controversial in the SEC's implementation of SOX Section 307 were elements of Part 205 that could affect client confidentiality.

Part 205 provides that attorneys may, but are not obligated to, disclose confidential information about a client without the client's consent, where the attorney reasonably believed that such disclosure was necessary to prevent the company from committing a material violation, perjury, or an act that would perpetrate fraud upon the commission, or to correct a material violation.[42] The SEC has asserted that Part 205 would preempt state bar association restrictions on release of confidential client information, although not all bar associations agree.[43]

Attorneys are concerned about erosion of the doctrines relating to attorney-client privilege and confidentiality. In a proposed, but not adopted, provision of Part 205, the SEC asserted that disclosure of material on a confidential basis to the SEC would not represent a waiver of the attorney-client privilege.[44] The issue is not small, because a corporation's provision of materials to the SEC on a confidential basis in connection with SEC investigation might be deemed to be a waiver of attorney-client privilege that makes the materials discoverable in civil litigation. Courts are divided on this question.[45]

The SEC also has proposed, but has not adopted or withdrawn, provisions under Part 205 that would make mandatory the withdrawal of an attorney from representation in the absences of an "appropriate response" and disclosure to the SEC of an attorney's withdrawal from representation, either by the attorney or by the company (the "reporting out" proposal).[46] Such requirements to resign and report to the SEC would be analogous to the obligations of auditors who report evidence of illegal acts that are not subsequently remedied.

The bar has indicated concerns that client confidentiality would be affected by the adoption of the "reporting out" provisions.[47] The bar also

---

42. SEC Part 205.3(d)(2).

43. Giovanni P. Prezioso, SEC General Counsel, *Letter Regarding Washington State Bar Association's Proposed Opinion on the Effect of the SEC's Attorney Conduct Rules,* (July 23, 2003); Interim Formal Ethics Opinion Re: The Effect of the SEC's Sarbanes-Oxley Regulations On Washington Attorneys' Obligations Under the RPCs, Washington State Bar (2003); Ethics Alert by California State Bar Business Section (2004).

44. First Part 205 Release.

45. *Compare McKesson HBOC, Inc. v. Superior Court* (2004), 115 Cal. App. 4th 1229 (2004), and *In re* McKesson HBOC Securities Litigation (Mar. 31, 2005) (U.S.Dist. Ct., N. Dist. Cal.) LEXIS 7098.

46. First Part 205 Release; Second Part 205 Release.

47. *See, e.g.,* Comments of 79 Law Firms, April 7, 2003 (File name: 79lawfirms1. htm); Comments of Marshall L. Small, Morrison & Foerster LLP; Robert A. Epsen, Heller Ehrman White & McAuliffe LLP; Nathaniel M. Cartmell III, Pillsbury; Bruce Maximov, Farella Braun + Martel LLP; Brian L. Forbes, Gray Cary Ware & Freidenrich LLP; Ann Yvonne Walker, Wilson Sonsini Goodrich & Rosati; John C. Unkovic, Reed Smith LLP; William J. Wernz Dorsey & Whitney LLP; Thomas J. Igoe, Jr., Thelen LLP; April 2, 2003 (File name: 9cos040203.htm); Comments of

has disputed that the non-specific language of SOX Section 307, unlike the express language of Section 10A of the Securities Exchange Act requiring "reporting out" by accountants, provides the SEC with authority to expand the reach of SOX Section 307's statutory language to include "reporting out" by attorneys.[48]

In at least one reported case, the withdrawal of an attorney from representation for Part 205 reasons became public, resulting in an SEC investigation and enforcement action against the company.[49]

Although the "reporting out" provisions have not been adopted, it is worth noting that under Part 205 the QLCC made up of independent directors would represent the top rung of Part 205's "up the ladder" reporting system. An attorney who had reported material legal issues to the QLCC would have discharged his or her obligations. Even under the SEC's proposed rule to make "reporting out" by the attorney mandatory, once the QLCC accepts responsibility for a matter, the obligations regarding that matter belong to the client alone.[50]

In that respect, the QLCC model represents the intersection between governance and gatekeeping. An attorney who possesses information and advice critical to the corporate client's decision on a material legal matter has the responsibility to provide it, and the client, through the QLCC, is provided under Part 205 with the responsibility to choose a course of action in response.

Rather than asking clients and attorneys to endure unforeseen and unintended consequences of foregoing confidentiality and attorney-client privilege, the SOX Section 307 and QLCC approach ask whether the attorney and corporate client took the appropriate steps to put the client in a position to handle a material legal question.

C. *Other Professional Relationships*

Since 2002, Congress, the SEC, the NYSE, and NASDAQ have distributed corporate decision-making authority away from strict control by management through additional rule making on independence standards, the obligations

---

Timothy G. Hoxie, Chair, Business Law Section, State Bar of California; and Keith Paul Bishop and Bruce Dravis, Co-Chairs, Corporations Committee of the Business Law Section, State Bar of California, April 7, 2003.

48. At Every Peril.

49. SEC Litigation Release No. 19022 (Jan. 4, 2005).

50. SEC Part 205.3(c).

of independent directors, and the functions of compensation and nominating committees.

The audit committee was given control of the process of hiring auditors and overseeing auditor performance on behalf of the company under SOX. The compensation committee was given control over the hiring of compensation consultants, legal counsel, and other advisors under Dodd-Frank. Nominating committees are typically being given authority and responsibility for hiring the outside advisors they use, as a matter of practice, rather a direct requirement by the SEC. The proxy rules require disclosures on the extent and nature of management involvement in the selection of outside advisors who assist the board in identifying potential director candidates or with executive compensation.

The chapters on the nominating committee and compensation committee discuss the control of outside advisors by the independent directors, and the regulatory and reporting requirements associated with the hiring of such advisors.

5. Conclusion

In addition to the potential civil exposure that an independent director could face as a result of failing to meet his or her fiduciary obligations, or the requirements of the securities laws, there are significant enforcement weapons at the disposal of the SEC and other agencies that can be brought to bear against directors and companies that violate, or are believed to violate, the law.

The SEC enforcement approach identifies independent directors, along with other corporate "gatekeepers," as potential enforcement targets if management has been allowed to misuse corporate resources.

The logic underlying the gatekeeper approach is straightforward: institutions operate through individuals. Accordingly, in the securities disclosure context, it is necessary to identify the individuals associated with a company, either as management or as outside advisors, who are critical to the company's securities disclosure and compliance functions, and require those individuals to take personal responsibility for the accuracy and completeness of the disclosures. In a perfect system, the company will have aligned the individuals who have the disclosure obligation with those who have access to information, and the ability and responsibility to act on such information.

As with any civil litigation that might arise, enforcement litigation can require significant financial, time, and emotional resources to defend, putting a premium on litigation avoidance.

Securities Trading Obligations of Independent Directors

1. Introduction

No independent director should ever buy or sell securities of the corporation for which he or she serves without confirming with the general counsel, CFO, or CEO that the transaction may be conducted legally and in compliance with corporate policy.

Even though an independent director does not have a day-to-day operating role in the corporation, he or she will still have access to sensitive, nonpublic, and significant information regarding the company. Compared to the general investing public, independent directors are "insiders" for purposes of the laws relating to the trading in securities of the corporations on whose boards they serve.

The legal restrictions on securities trading by independent directors (and non-independent directors and officers) have multiple aspects. An independent director may not:

- trade company securities while in possession of material nonpublic information regarding the corporation ("inside information");

- "tip" others to trade company securities while in possession of inside information;

- trade on the basis of a tip from another person possessing inside information;

- "misappropriate" information regarding another corporation (such as a potential acquisition target) for trading in the securities of that corporation;

- make corresponding sales and purchases of the corporation's equity securities within a six-month period;

- trade company securities without making required SEC filings applicable to directors; and

- trade company securities in violation of corporate policies restricting securities trading.

All violations of trading restriction laws have potential monetary penalties, and trading with inside information could constitute a criminal offense as well. In addition, violation of corporate restrictions on securities trading could constitute a violation of the corporate code of ethics and require disclosure under the securities laws.

It is important to remember that trading of corporate securities by an insider is not automatically illegal. Shares and options are provided to independent directors and other corporate insiders as compensation for their service to a corporation, and they can only have their proper compensatory effect by being converted into cash through a sale. Insiders can, however, face significant restrictions on the timing and amount of securities they sell. Corporations establish securities trading policies so that insiders can conduct legal transactions within company guidelines.

Under Dodd-Frank, a corporation must disclose in its proxy statement whether any employee or director is permitted to "purchase financial instruments... designed to hedge or offset any decrease" in the value of the corporation's securities owned or granted as compensation to that employee or director.[1]

---

1. Dodd-Frank 956.

This chapter reviews the restrictions on trading that independent directors face as corporate insiders and the legal issues and corporate policies associated with meeting those restrictions. A significant number of these restrictions have been developed in cases involving the SEC's Rule 10b-5. Other rules, regarding the form and content of specific filings independent directors must make, result from the securities statutes and regulations.

With respect to securities trading obligations, independent directors have no duties that are different from those attaching to other directors, although their access to material information may be different.

The discussions regarding material information are applicable not only to trading restrictions under Rule 10b-5 but also apply to the considerations of corporate disclosures that directors must oversee.

2. Rule 10b-5

The essential text of Rule 10b-5 is deceptively simple: "It shall be unlawful for any person, directly or indirectly... to make any untrue statement of a material fact or to omit to state a material fact... in connection with the purchase or sale of any security."[2]

More than half a century of litigation involving Rule 10b-5, both civil[3] and criminal,[4] has established the breadth and also the boundaries of the rule's application. A claim of a violation of Rule 10b-5 can be made against the corporation or the directors or officers individually.[5]

The duty of a corporation to disclose material information is imposed by the securities laws as a matter of the registration and periodic reporting requirements and is augmented by Rule 10b-5's requirements that a company may not deliberately misstate a material fact or omit to state a fact that makes other disclosures misleading. Class action Rule 10b-5 litigation against corporations generates significant fees to the segment of the legal community that successfully brings those cases, making such suits more lucrative for civil litigants than cases against individuals.

---

2.   SEC Rule 10b-5.
3.   *See, e.g., Kardon v. National Gypsum*, 73 F. Supp. 798 (E.D. Pa. 1947) ("Kardon"); *Supt. of Ins. of State of N.Y. v. Bankers Life & Cas. Co.*, 404 U.S. 6 (1971).
4.   *See, e.g., U.S. v. Peltz*, 433 F.2d 48 (2d Cir. 1970).
5.   *See, e.g., SEC v. Texas Gulf Sulphur*, 401 F.2d 833 (2d Cir. 1968) ("Texas Gulf Sulphur").

The duty of a corporate insider or agent to abstain from trading on material nonpublic information is derived from the insider's duty to the company not to convert to personal use "information intended to be available only for a corporate purpose and not for the personal benefit of anyone."[6]

For independent directors, there are several key areas to avoid, as described below. As a matter of discharging their duty to oversee management, directors will want to ensure management does not take actions that could expose the corporation to claims under Rule 10b-5.

At its core, Rule 10b-5 is an anti-fraud rule, which means that proving a Rule 10b-5 claim requires demonstration of the accused party's fraudulent intent.[7] However, even innocent trades that occur when the general public does not have full disclosure can subject directors, officers, and corporations to litigation.

Plaintiffs in securities class actions typically use insider sales as evidence of the company's motive for making an alleged misleading statement.[8] Limiting insider trades at a time when material information has not been made public is thus a litigation avoidance strategy.

Neither the company nor the insider will want to be in a position in which an insider has made an open market trade at a time when the company had undisclosed material information (such as a pending merger) and the insider knew of the information. Such a trade almost certainly would be a Rule 10b-5 violation.[9]

Even the appearance of such a trade could encourage litigation. An insider's trade may be used as evidence of scienter in the event there is a sudden decline in the company's stock price. The theory the plaintiff likely would advance is that the price decline was due to the revelation of bad news that previously had been concealed, and that the insider traded with the knowledge that the price would decline when the bad news was revealed.

If the insider traded without knowing or using undisclosed material information, there might not be a breach of the insider's duty, but the trading public (and securities litigation counsel) monitoring the insider's trading reports would not know that until after the class action suit was filed.

---

6. *In* re Cady, Roberts, 40 SEC 907 (1961) ("Cady").
7. *Ernst & Ernst v. Hochfelder*, 425 U.S. 185 (1976).
8. *See, e.g., In re Scholastic Corp.* Sec. Litig., 252 F. 3d 63 (2d Cir. 2001).
9. *See* SEC Release 33-7881 (Oct. 23, 2000) ("Rule 10b5-1 Release"); SEC Rule 10b5-1, and discussion below regarding trading while in "possession" of material nonpublic information.

A company could have a dozen or more insiders who file trading forms with the SEC (as discussed in Part 3 of this chapter). At any given date any one of these insiders could have conducted a recent trade in the company's securities for any number of personal reasons, making it likely that a plaintiff will be able to match up an insider's trade with a sudden price decline. The key to dismissing a suit in those circumstances is having a record that there was no undisclosed information and no duty to disclose at the time of the trade.

There are some straightforward and fairly easily administered litigation avoidance tactics that corporations use to prevent market trading by insiders during sensitive periods. To ensure that the company and its insiders do not encounter problems with their market transactions, companies often adopt securities trading policies, such as trading window and preclearance policies, as discussed in Part 3 of this chapter.

A. Key Concepts: *Purchase or Sale, Company Security, and Material Information*

Insiders should bear in mind a number of key concepts that arise in analyzing a trade for potential Rule 10b-5 problems. In particular, the concept of "materiality" and "material information" is one that directors and officers encounter throughout the securities laws regarding disclosure obligations. The discussion of materiality in this section of this chapter is applicable to other securities law disclosure questions as well.

(i) Purchase or Sale

Rule 10b-5 liability is triggered by fraudulent behavior in connection with a purchase or sale of a company security, or the purchase or sale of any option on a company security.[10] Publicly traded put and call options, because they are highly leveraged, are a favorite vehicle of inside traders, and the SEC closely monitors trading in those vehicles. In addition to trades made using a broker or securities exchange, face-to-face transactions with third parties could violate Rule 10b-5.[11]

By contrast, the company's grant of stock options as part of an insider's compensation is not typically treated as a purchase or sale that

---

10. *Blue Chip Stamps. v. Manor Drug Stores*, 421 U.S. 723 (1975).
11. Kardon.

could trigger Rule 10b-5.[12] Likewise, if an insider exercises a company stock option and holds the shares, the insider has converted the form of his or her interest in the corporation from a right to acquire stock to a direct holding in a transaction between the insider and the company. These transactions are subject to securities law disclosure requirements, but usually not Rule 10b-5.

(ii) Company Security

For Rule 10b-5 purposes, the description of company security is not limited to publicly traded shares but usually includes any bonds or securities convertible or exercisable for securities that the company has issued.

However, it is important to remember that Rule 10b-5 applies to the purchase or sale of any security, which could include publicly traded options. Rule 10b-5 would apply to trading in put or call options relating to a company, even though those options were not securities issued by that company.

(iii) Material Nonpublic Information

Materiality is a critical concept not only for the securities trading restrictions under Rule 10b-5 but also for all securities law disclosure questions confronting a corporation.[13] The question of materiality can be subtle and very difficult to answer at times. Materiality depends not only on the specific piece of data but also on the context in which the data would be understood.

For purposes of the company's securities law disclosures, management and directors must make judgments about whether information is material, and those judgments are subject to being second-guessed by shareholders, exchanges, market commentators, and regulators, among others.

With regard to materiality, the legal test established by the Supreme Court is whether there is a "substantial likelihood that the disclosure of the omitted fact would have been viewed by the reasonable investor as having significantly altered the 'total mix' of information made available."[14]

---

12. However, in the 2006 option backdating cases, the SEC alleged a species of securities fraud occurred as a result of the backdating. *See e.g.,* indictment relating to Brocade Communications, Inc., *SEC vs. Gregory Reyes* (sec.gov/litigation/complaints/2006/comp19768.pdf).

13. *Basic v. Levinson*, 485 U.S. 224 (1988) ("Basic").

14. Basic at 23, *citing TSC Industries, Inc. v. Northway, Inc.,* 426 U.S. 438, 449 (1976) ("TSC").

The SEC has added its own refinements to the legal definitions of materiality, particularly in the arena of financial statements[15] and in the preparation of the Management's Discussion and Analysis of Financial Condition and Results of Operations that appears in the Form 10-K and Form 10-Q reports.[16]

Whether any given development will be material in light of the "total mix" of information available concerning the company will require an assessment unique to the company's situation at that time, taking into account the company's SEC filings, the company's other public statements, information made available by securities analysts following the company, and the types of industry and company-specific risks the company has previously disclosed.[17]

While some basic quantitative measures might be helpful to determine whether a piece of data is material (a customer that represents 10% of sales, for example, would be material), there are no quantitative measures that are reliably useful in determining that data is *not* material.[18] An individual transaction or item that affects a significant percentage of revenues, expenses, or income obviously will be material, but even a small change in an accounting reserve could be material if the change was made with an eye to the impact on the securities trading markets, such as ensuring that the corporation met analyst forecasts.

Quarterly and annual financial statements and results always will be material. Major corporate events, such as mergers, acquisitions, or divestitures that change a significant amount of assets also will be material. Sudden significant windfalls or losses will be material.

Sudden changes in products, the markets, the discovery of risks in products, and changes in key personnel may be material, or not, depending on the total mix of information already publicly available about the company.

In addition, a corporation's obligation to make disclosures of material information can be affected by the existence of prior corporate comments on the topic. For example, a corporation that denied intending to conduct a merger would be obligated to correct that statement, if the statement was inaccurate when made, or to update the statement if the statement was

---

15. SEC Staff Accounting Bulletin 99 ("SAB 99").
16. *See* SEC Release 33-8350 (December 29, 2003) ("2003 MD&A Release"); SEC Release 33-6835 (May 18, 1989) ("1989 MD&A Release").
17. TSC.
18. SAB 99.

still "alive in the marketplace" and was rendered inaccurate or misleading by later merger discussions.[19]

Whether a matter is "non-public" depends not only on whether the company has issued a press release or made some other effort to inform the public but also on whether sufficient time has passed for such information to have been circulated in the market and, implicitly, be reflected in the company's share price.[20]

B. Key Rule 10b-5 Trading Restrictions

(i) Disclose or Abstain from Trading

The board must make or ratify decisions to acquire or sell significant assets, enter into significant transactions, or make key personnel moves. Financial statements are compiled by management and the results are known to management first. Thus, insiders inherently will be aware of material corporate developments ahead of the public.

In all circumstances in which insiders are in possession of material nonpublic information, they have a duty to public investors (both the current shareholders who will sell shares to the insider and future shareholders who buy shares from the insider) not to omit such material facts at the time a purchase or sale of the corporations securities is made.[21]

The fiduciary duties of insiders to shareholders give rise under Rule 10b-5 to a duty that has been described by the courts as an obligation to disclose material information or abstain from trading in the public markets until the information has been disclosed. This rule commonly is phrased as "disclose or abstain."[22] However, unless the insider can personally direct the timing and contents of the corporation's disclosure, the result of the rule is to require the insider to refrain from trading until after the disclosure is made.

---

19. A statement that is incorrect when made can trigger a "duty to correct," *see Stransky v. Cummins Engine Co., Inc.*, 51 F.3d 1329 (7th Cir. 1995); a statement that is accurate when made but which later becomes inaccurate may be subject to a "duty to update." Basic.

20. See discussion and cases relating to tipping, and discussion of the market's incorporation into the share price of publicly disseminated information in Basic.

21. Texas Gulf Sulphur.

22. Texas Gulf Sulphur.

If the corporation has determined to withhold the disclosure of material information until a future time, the insider may not trade until the disclosure is made.

In addition to the historic "disclose or abstain" from trading interpretation of Rule 10b-5, the SEC has established Rule 10b5-1, which provides that a person will be deemed to have traded on the basis of material, nonpublic information if he or she was aware of the material, nonpublic information at the time of the trade.[23]

However, Rule 10b5-1 also provides insiders with a mechanism to conduct trades legally even if they are aware of material, nonpublic information at the time of the purchase or the sale, provided that the trading plan was established in advance.

For insiders who have not established such trading plans, company policies that establish trading windows and preclearance requirements provide insiders with a structure in which to make trades with reasonable assurance that the trades will not be conducted at a time when material non-public information has not been disclosed.

(ii) No "Tipping"

Just as an insider may not personally make a market trade while in possession of material nonpublic information, no insider may advise others—either within the corporation or without—to make a market trade in company securities at a time when material information is undisclosed.

Whether the undisclosed news is favorable (such as a takeover bid at a premium to the current share price) or unfavorable (such as significant failure to meet forecast earnings targets), if the information is of the sort that can be reasonably expected to affect the market price of the stock, insiders may not "tip" individuals to the information in advance.

The SEC has imposed the further requirement on corporations in Regulation FD that if a material disclosure is made to a single party prior to the time that the disclosure is made to the entire market, the corporation must act promptly to make the information available to the entire market.[24] In creating Regulation FD, the SEC was reacting to instances of "selective disclosure" in which the corporation would release information but only to select parties such as securities analysts, rather than to all market participants at the same time.

---

23. SEC Rule 10b5-1.
24. SEC Regulation FD.

Under Regulation FD, even inadvertent selective disclosure of material information requires a prompt general announcement.[25] Corporations tend to funnel communications of market-sensitive information through a single source so that communications that have a market impact can be screened, put into context, and not inadvertently or prematurely disclosed.

(iii) No Trading on "Tipped" Information

While the "tipper" of information has violated a corporation's confidence by disclosing material information to selected individuals, the "tippee" who receives that information is restricted from trading on it.[26]

Under the Rule 10b-5 line of cases, tippees and company agents, such as attorneys, accountants, investment bankers, etc., have a duty that is "derivative" of the duty owed by the insider from whom they obtain the information.[27] As a result of this legal "deputization" by the tipper, tippees have a duty to the company's shareholders not to use material confidential company information for individual trading, similar to the trading restrictions borne by other company agents.

In addition to the Rule 10b-5 case law, the SEC has adopted Rule 10b5-2, which defines specific situations in which a duty of confidence will be deemed to exist.[28] These situations include:

*   the recipient agrees to maintain information in confidence;

*   the parties have a history, pattern, or practice of sharing confidences such that the recipient of the information knows or reasonably should know that the discloser expects the information to be confidential; and

*   the recipient receives information from spouses, parents, children, or siblings.[29]

Under the regulations regarding tender offers, there is an analogous but slightly different set of requirements. A person who possesses material nonpublic information regarding a tender offer "acquired directly or indirectly" from the offeror, the target of the tender offer, or an officer, director, partner or employee, or any other person acting on behalf of the

---

25. SEC Regulation FD.
26. Cady; *Dirks v. SEC*, 463 U.S. 646 (1983) ("Dirks").
27. Dirks.
28. SEC Rule 10b5-2.
29. SEC Rule 10b5-2(b)(1)-(3).

offeror or the target, must not trade in target securities until the information is publicly disclosed.[30]

(iv) Inside Information from Outside the Company (Misappropriation)

In the classic cases of insider trading, a highly favorable development is known to a select few inside the company, and those few are able to buy the stock at a bargain, then sell at a premium when the news is announced. The insiders controlled the information that controlled the price and used the information for their own gain and to the disadvantage of the shareholders to whom they owed a fiduciary duty.

By contrast, in the period just prior to a tender offer, the offeror corporation controls information about the price it intends to offer for shares of the target company. Typically the price will include a premium to the prevailing market price.

The offeror corporation typically will go into the market and buy shares of the target at the prevailing market price, prior to the time it announces the tender offer, and in anticipation of the price of the target going up once the tender offer is announced. The offeror corporation controls the information that affects the future price movement of the target's stock (the offeror's intent), but it is perfectly legal for the offeror to purchase shares prior to the announcement up to the statutory limit.[31] The offeror has no duty to the target company.

However, information concerning the offeror corporation's intentions is the offeror's property: If an officer or director of the offeror used the company's information to purchase shares of the target in advance of the announcement of the tender offer, the insider would have misappropriated the company's confidential information for his or her own use in connection with a securities trade, and be liable for the violation of Rule 10b-5.[32]

Similarly, someone learning of the company's plans in confidence, such as an attorney, may not misappropriate the information for his own trading.[33]

---

30. SEC Rule 14e-3(a); *See* discussion in *United States v. O'Hagan*, 521 U.S. 642 (1997) ("O'Hagan").

31. Exchange Act Sec. 14(d).

32. O'Hagan at 654.

33. O'Hagan at 655. *See* discussion of *Chiarella v. United States*, 445 U.S. 222 (1980) in *O'Hagan, Id.* at 660-62; contrast to discussion in *Chiarella* that misappropriation theory was not before the court, *Chiarella* at 235-36.

The misappropriation liability can also apply to trading based on advance knowledge that information about a company is soon to be published. In such cases, the individual who misappropriates such information takes a securities trading position that will be profitable once the news is publicly released (for example, selling short knowing that a negative article is about to be published).[34]

3. Conducting Sales

Avoiding illegal insider trading is not only a question of corporate self-interest, it is required by law. Insiders face individual penalties for illegal trades, and corporate officials who fail to take steps to prevent insider trading could face civil actions from the SEC under the Insider Trading Sanctions Act.[35]

A. Securities Trading Policy

To facilitate legal trading and establish controls to prevent illegal trading, publicly traded corporations adopt trading policies that restrict the times at which company personnel can make market trades of company securities. A company also may want to work with insiders on establishing prearranged trading plans under SEC guidelines.

As with any corporate policy, a policy on securities trading is useful not by being established, but by being followed. Having a policy in place that the company ignores only provides fuel for litigation.

Most corporate trading restriction policies impose trading windows and preclearance of trades by insiders. Corporations also may adopt securities trading policies that prohibit insiders from conducting short sales or trading in put and call options, which tend to be speculative trades

---

34. *See SEC v. Carpenter*, 484 U.S. 19 (1987), in which information in the Wall Street Journal's "Heard on the Street" column was leaked in advance of publication to individuals who used knowledge of the column's impact on stock prices to trade profitably. The theft of pre-publication information was held to be wire fraud; the Court did not render a holding on the misappropriation theory. These information misappropriate cases are similar to the anti-"scalping" cases arising under the Investment Advisers Act, in which the investment adviser providing information to clients hides personal account information from the users of the information, profiting when the readers commence their own trading in response to the publication. *See SEC v. Capital Gains Research Bureau*, 375 U.S. 180 (1963).

35. P.L. 98-376 (1984).

that could have the appearance of trading while in possession of material nonpublic information.

Corporate insiders should expect to sign written confirmations that they have received, read, and understood the corporation's trading policies, making the policy issues not merely corporate goals, but individual obligations of employment that the corporation may enforce.

In establishing its trading policy, the company should be aware of its disclosure obligations under Dodd-Frank respecting "hedging" by employees and directors.[36]

(i) Trading Windows

One common policy is to prohibit insiders from open market trading for a period before the closing of a quarter's financial statements and until the company's quarterly results have been absorbed by the marketplace (the "window period"). The policy is intended to prevent insider trading and to avoid the appearance that anyone has traded on inside information.

A window period typically is imposed from two to four weeks before the close of a fiscal quarter until one to two full trading days after the company publicly disseminates earnings information (typically two to three weeks after the close of the quarter). This means the window period can last four to seven weeks each quarter, with the trading window consisting of the balance of the quarter, unless there is an undisclosed material development that further limits the available trading times.

(ii) Preclearance

By requiring insiders to check first with the company's CEO, CFO, or general counsel before conducting any market trade at any time, the company can prevent insiders from inadvertently violating the window period policy and can prevent trades by insiders who might be unaware that there is an undisclosed pending material development.

In addition, an insider who precleared a market trade and reasonably relied on the company's evaluation of whether material nonpublic information was outstanding might be able to use such reliance as evidence of a lack of scienter if a Rule 10b-5 challenge was mounted against the trade, even if the company's evaluation of materiality was erroneous.

Since the prohibition on insider market trades during window periods and the preclearance requirement are corporate policies and not law,

---

36. Dodd-Frank 955.

violations would be punishable by corporate discipline rather than damages or injunction. Such a penalty generally would be adequate to prevent undesired trading, although it would not prevent trading by someone who truly intended to misuse inside information and trade secretly.

The effect of such policies is to cut roughly in half the number of days per year a company insider can make open market trades. Executives for whom stock options represent a meaningful component of compensation will want to have unfettered access to the trading market for as much of the nonwindow period as is possible in order to be able to take advantage of favorable market conditions or to systematically sell in order to diversify their individual portfolios. Accordingly, maintaining up-to-date disclosure not only serves the purpose of limiting a company's exposure to securities litigation but also furthers the compensation objectives of the company's option plans.

B. Permitted Trading Using a Rule 10b5-1 Plan

Rule 10b5-1 provides that a person will be deemed to have traded on the basis of material, nonpublic information if he or she was aware of the material, nonpublic information at the time of the trade.[37] However, Rule 10b5-1 also created an exception from this presumption that permits insiders to trade in company securities while in possession of material, nonpublic information pursuant to a pre-existing plan.

Such structured selling programs operate without the insider's direct control. A trade might, by coincidence, occur at a time when the insider might have inside information, but a trade that is executed under a program based on timing, price movement, or other preset triggers could prevent a successful claim of misuse of insider information.

For a plan to be a valid Rule 10b5-1 plan, the insider needs to meet a number of requirements:

- before becoming aware of the material, nonpublic information, the insider had entered into a binding contract to purchase or sell the security, instructed another person to purchase or sell the security for the insider's account; or adopted a written plan for trading securities;

- had established instructions that: (1) expressly specified the amount of securities to be purchased or sold, and the price at, and date on, which the securities were to be purchased or sold; (2) included a written formula for determining the amount of securities to be purchased

---

37.   SEC Rule 10b5-1(a)-(b).

or sold, and the price at, and date on, which the securities were to be purchased or sold; or (3) did not permit the issuer or insider to exercise any subsequent influence over how, when, or whether to effect purchases or sales, provided that any other person who did exercise such influence pursuant to the contract, instruction, or plan must not have been aware of the material, nonpublic information;

- made a purchase or sale pursuant to the plan without subsequent interference or influence from the issuer or insider; and

- entered into the contract, instruction, or plan in good faith and not as part of a plan or scheme to evade the prohibitions of Rule 10b5-1.[38]

Rule 10b5-1 does not specify a time limit for prearranged sales plans, but such plans tend to run between six to eighteen months, with one year being typical. An insider could amend a plan at a time when the insider does not possess material nonpublic information or terminate the plan at any time.

However, an insider who terminated a plan and immediately established a new and different plan might raise questions about whether the new plan was established in good faith. Similarly, if the insider makes trades outside the plan that have the effect of hedging or otherwise altering the economic effect of the plan, such trades could violate the good faith requirement. The SEC has brought at least one enforcement action on the basis of a violation of Rule 10b5-1.

An insider who establishes a Rule 10b5-1 plan must, at the time the trades are executed, also comply with the requirements to make SEC filings under Rule 144 and Section 16 of the Securities Exchange Act discussed below.

There is no requirement that an insider establishing a Rule 10b5-1 plan make an SEC disclosure or public disclosure, but announcements of Rule 10b5-1 plans are routinely made. Other trading reports the insider is required to make, such as reports under Section 16 of the Exchange Act, can then be interpreted by the market in light of the announcement of the plan.

Before creating a Rule 10b5-1 plan, an insider should confirm that creation of a Rule 10b5-1 plan would not be deemed to constitute a waiver or violation of the corporation's code of ethics. Any such waiver or violation would have to be reported on Form 8-K.[39]

---

38. SEC Rule 10b5-1(c)(1)(i)-(ii).
39. Form 8-K, Item 5.05.

NYSE Rule 309 implies—without requiring—that companies should use Rule 10b5-1 plans to balance the benefits of having officers and directors share the shareholder's perspectives, with the need to ensure any officer and director sales are proper and made when the market has complete information.[40]

C. Section 16 Reporting

Section 16 of the Exchange Act requires that any officer, director, or 10% shareholder of a corporation who makes matching buy and sell equity trades within six months of each other must give the profits back to the corporation.[41] It was the earliest "insider trading" limitation under the securities laws, adopted in 1934. The matching trades can be a sale followed by a purchase or a purchase followed by a sale.

Unlike Rule 10b-5, Section 16 is a "no-fault" rule for which questions of intent are irrelevant.

To facilitate the enforcement of the Section 16 "short-swing" profits restriction, the Exchange Act requires that insiders file reports of their securities trades.

Company insiders are responsible for filing these reports on their acquisitions and dispositions of the company's securities on SEC Forms

---

40. 309.00 Purchases of Company Stock by Directors and Officers.
   Many shareholders feel that directors and officers should have a meaningful investment in the companies they manage. The extent of this ownership, naturally, would vary in accordance with the financial circumstances of the persons involved. As shareholders themselves, directors are more likely to represent the viewpoint of other shareholders whose interests they are charged with protecting. Similarly, officers—the executive management group—may well perform more effectively with the incentive of stock options or a share in the equity ownership of the company....
   The widespread endorsement of director and officer share ownership brings with it questions that concern the timing of their stock transactions.... One appropriate method of purchase might be a periodic investment program where the directors or officers make regular purchases under an established program administered by a broker and where the timing of purchases is outside the control of the individual. It would also seem appropriate for officials to buy or sell stock in their companies for a 30-day period commencing one week after the annual report has been mailed to shareholders and otherwise broadly circulated (provided, of course, that the annual report has adequately covered important corporate developments and that no new major undisclosed developments occur within that period)....
   In the final analysis, directors and officers must be guided by a sense of fairness to all segments of the investing public.... Particular attention is directed to Sections 10(b) and 16 of the Securities Exchange Act of 1934 and Rule 10b-5 thereunder.
41. Exchange Act Sec. 16.

3, 4, and 5.[42] Although the company is not responsible for the preparation of these forms, it is obligated to report in its proxy statement on any untimely filings by insiders.[43]

- Form 3, the initial statement of holdings by an insider, is due within 10 days of the individual becoming an insider. Section 403 of Sarbanes Oxley requires officers, directors, and owners of 10% or more of a class of a company's equity securities to file with the SEC a statement of their ownership of the company's equity securities under Section 16 of the Exchange Act, effectively disclosing their purchases or sales, within two business days of the trade or other event requiring the filing.[44]

- Form 4, which reflects changes resulting from an insider's market trades, is due within two days following the transaction.

- Form 5, which reflects stock option grants and other changes in holdings that are otherwise exempt from monthly reporting, is due within 45 days of the end of the year.

The disclosure duty created by the SEC rules regarding these forms is a duty for insiders and the company to report historic information about the specific transactions covered by the rule.

Stock option grants by the company to officers and directors, and option exercises, do not trigger a "short swing" profit calculation, if conducted in accordance with SEC requirements.[45]

Rightly or wrongly, trading patterns by insiders are viewed by a number of market observers as being indications of favorable or unfavorable trends within the company. The theory is that an insider who perceives a strong future for the company will delay selling, and an insider who has less confidence in the future will be willing to sell. Whatever interpretation the market may make of an insider's moves, the fact of the trade, by itself, typically is not forward-looking information that creates a duty for additional corporate disclosures.

---

42. SEC Form 3, SEC Form 4, SEC Form 5.
43. *See* Instructions to SEC Schedule 14A. In addition, if the company is aware that it will make disclosure of late insider filings in the proxy statement, it is required to note this fact on the face of its Form 10-K filing.
44. SOX 403.
45. SEC Rule 16b-3.

D. Rule 144

Corporate "affiliates"—a group that includes officers, directors, or anyone else in "control" of a corporation—must file a Form 144[46] at the time of a sale of company securities, and must meet other limitations under Rule 144 as to the number of shares sold and the type of transaction used.

Rule 144 provides that affiliates must sell their corporate securities only through brokers, only after having held the securities for a prescribed period, only at times at which the corporation is current with its SEC reporting (other than filings under Form 8-K), and only in amounts that, in any three-month period, do not exceed the greater of (a) 1% of the corporation's then-outstanding securities of that class or (b) the average weekly reported volume of trades in those securities during the four weeks before the sale.[47]

Historic SEC policy treated company insiders and significant shareholders as "presumptive underwriters" whose sales were being conducted on behalf of the company, even if the insiders had purchased shares that were part of a registered public offering or in the open market. The SEC's goal was to ensure that promoters did not use a loophole to make an illegal distribution of securities. While the "presumptive underwriter" doctrine was eventually abandoned, elements remain in Rule 144, and in Rule 145, which applies Rule 144 trading restrictions to the shares acquired in a corporate merger or reorganization.

The primary role of Rule 144 is to provide a means for investors to resell shares that were acquired from a company or affiliate of the company without a registration statement, so long as the investor has held the shares for sufficient time and so long as sufficient information regarding the shares is available to the investing public.

The operation of Rule 144 can be complex. For example, a gift by an insider, such as a gift to a family member or a charitable donation, will not be a sale that triggers a requirement to use Rule 144, but the recipient could find itself restricted in its subsequent resales.[48]

E. Insider Trading Sanctions Act

The Insider Trading Sanctions Act (ITSA) provides that the SEC can bring a civil action against an employer whose employees trade using inside

---

46. SEC Form 144.
47. SEC Rule 144.
48. SEC Rule 144. *See* SEC Release 33-6099 (Aug. 2, 1979) ("Rule 144 Release").

information, if the employer "knew or recklessly disregarded the fact" that the employee was "likely" to trade illegally and the employer "failed to take appropriate steps" in advance to prevent such trading.[49]

Establishing a securities trading policy will assist management and the board in ensuring that it has taken appropriate steps to prevent illegal trading.

Enforcing the policy is critical: A company that adopts a policy that it does not enforce creates a record that suggests the company knew what the law was and then acted in disregard of the law and its own policies.

F. Additional Restrictions

SOX Section 306 responded to a particular factual element of the Enron fraud by banning trades by insiders during periods in which a corporation prohibits its employees from trading the same securities through a pension or benefit plan sponsored by the corporations.[50] Insiders who violate this provision must surrender any profits made to the corporation, a remedy similar to that found under Section 16 for "short-swing" trades.[51]

4. Conclusion

Directors and officers devote significant time and effort to expanding the value of the company, and that growth, sooner or later, should be reflected in the share price. Directors and officers will typically have share ownership in the companies they serve and ultimately convert that share ownership into cash at some point by selling the shares.

With appropriate attention to the securities law restrictions that relate to their trades, insiders are permitted to make share purchases and sales and receive a financial reward for their efforts.

---

49. Exchange Act Sec. 21A.
50. SOX 306; *see also* SEC Regulation BTR, Rule 101.
51. SEC Regulation BTR, Rule 103.

CHECKLISTS AND SAMPLE CHARTERS

Independence Factors for NYSE Companies

1. Subjective Determination for NYSE Companies	Yes/No
The Board must affirmatively determine that director has "no material relation" with the Company that would prevent independence NOTE: Focus of test is independence from management NOTE: Automatic Exclusions from Independence are in Section 3	
2. Factors to be Considered	
The following factors are not automatic disqualifications, but require review by the Board: Large stock ownership position by director or affiliate Social relations with management Charity relationship with director and Company (must disclose publicly if Company donations exceed $1 million to charity with which director is affiliated)	

3. Automatic Exclusions from Independence	Check if applicable
A. Employment by company in last three years NOTE: Not independent while serving as interim CEO, but after interim CEO position ends, no three-year look back for independence evaluation	
B. Receipt of fees from the Company of more than $120,000 in last three years NOTE: The calculation of fees does not include board fees, pensions. Exception: board fees, pension, or deferred compensation that does not require continued service on board are not counted in determining the $120,000 threshold.	
C. Audit Relationships: Automatic exclusion from independence for (i) Current partner or employee of auditor (ii) Persons who worked on an audit of Company in last three years	
D. Compensation committee interlock: Automatic exclusion if director (or immediate family member) is employee of entity on which Company executive serves as compensation committee member, or vice versa	
E. Business Relationship in last three years of either $2 million per year or 2% of gross revenues of entity that employs director	
F. Affiliate: A person controlled, controlled by, or under common control with the Company is not independent. NOTE: Large shareholder does not lead to presumption of control	
G. Immediate family member has: • Served as executive officer of Company in prior three years • Received fees of $120,000 or more in the past year (excluding board fees, pensions, or deferred compensation that is not dependent on continued service) • Worked on audit of the Company in prior three years	

4. Additional Compensation Committee Factors	
Never have served as an executive officer of the Company if involved in approving "golden parachute" for an executive officer	

Determining Director Independence Factors for NASDAQ Companies

1. Subjective Rule for NASDAQ Independence	Yes/No
An independent director is "a person other than an Executive Officer or employee of the Company or any other individual having a relationship which, in the opinion of the Company's board of directors, would interfere with the exercise of independent judgment in carrying out the responsibilities of a director.	
2. Automatic Exclusions from Independence	Check if applicable
A. Employment by company in last three years NOTE: Not independent while serving as interim CEO, but after interim CEO position ends, no three-year look back for independence evaluation if interim CEO service was less than one year and Board determines independence is not compromised	

B. Receipt of fees from the Company of more than $120,000 in last three years Exception: Board fees, pension, or deferred compensation are not counted in determining the $120,000 threshold.	
C. Audit Relationships: Automatic exclusion from independence for (i) Current partner or employee of auditor (ii) Persons who worked on an audit of Company in last three years	
D. Compensation committee interlock: Automatic exclusion if director (or family member) is employee of entity on which Company executive serves as compensation committee member	
E. Business or Charity Relationship In last three years, Company has provided either $200,000 per year or 5% of gross revenues of entity that employs director (excluding non-discretionary charitable matching funds or investment gains).	
F. Affiliate: A person controlled, controlled by, or under common control with the Company is not independent. NOTE: Large shareholder does not lead to presumption of control	
G. Family member has: • Served as executive officer of Company in prior three years • Received fees of $120,000 or more in the past year (excluding board fees, pensions, deferred compensation, or pay as a non-executive employee of the Company) • Worked on audit of the Company in prior three years	
## 3. Additional Compensation Committee Factors	
Never have served as an executive officer of the Company, if involved in approving "golden parachute" for an executive officer	

4. Additional Audit Committee Factors	
Shareholder with 10% or more of the Company's stock is not prohibited from Audit Committee, but Company must disclose.	

Sample
Audit Committee Charter

I. Purpose

The Audit Committee (the Audit Committee) is appointed by the Board of Directors (the Board) to assist the Board in monitoring the integrity of the financial statements of the Company, the independent auditor's qualifications and independence, the performance of the Company's internal audit function and independent auditors, and the compliance by the Company with legal and regulatory requirements.

The function of the Audit Committee is oversight. Management of the Company is responsible for the preparation, presentation, and integrity of the Company's financial statements. Management and the internal auditors are responsible for maintaining appropriate accounting and financial reporting principles and policies, and internal controls and procedures designed to assure compliance with accounting standards and applicable laws and regulations. The outside independent auditors are responsible for planning and carrying out a proper audit of the Company's annual financial statements, reviews of the Company's quarterly financial statements prior to the filing of each quarterly report on Form 10-Q, and other procedures.

Members of the Audit Committee are not full-time employees of the Company, and do not perform the functions of auditors or accountants. Each member of the Audit Committee shall be entitled to rely on the integrity of those persons and organizations within and outside the Company from which it receives information absent actual knowledge to the contrary (which shall be promptly reported to the Board of Directors).

II. Composition of the Audit Committee

- The Audit Committee shall be comprised of at least three directors, each of whom is "independent" under the rules of the exchange on which the Company's shares are listed for trading and in accordance with applicable laws and Securities and Exchange Commission regulations.

- No Audit Committee member may accept any consulting, advisory, or other compensatory fee from the Company other than in his or her capacity as a member of the Board or any committee of the Board.

- No Audit Committee member may be an "affiliate" of the Company or any subsidiary of the Company, as such term is defined in Rule 10A-3 under the Securities Exchange Act of 1934, as amended (the "Exchange Act").

- All members of the Audit Committee must be able to read and understand fundamental financial statements, including a company's balance sheet, income statement, and cash flow statement. The Audit Committee shall have at least one member who has past employment experience in finance or accounting, requisite professional certification in accounting, or other comparable experience or background so that such member may be deemed a "financial expert" for purposes of the Commission's rules.

- No director may serve as a member of the Audit Committee if such director serves on the audit committees of more than two other public companies unless the Board of Directors determines that such simultaneous service would not impair the ability of such director to effectively serve on the Audit Committee, and discloses the determination in the Company's annual proxy statement.

- The members of the Audit Committee shall be appointed annually by the Board on the recommendation of the Chairman of the Board and shall serve at the pleasure of the Board and for such term or terms as the Board may determine.

- The Audit Committee shall elect a chair who shall be responsible for ensuring that the Audit Committee fulfils its obligations under this Charter.

- The chair of the Audit Committee may recommend removal of a member of the Audit Committee as the chair deems appropriate provided, however, that removal shall be made only by the Board of Directors.

- The Audit Committee will evaluate its performance and the Audit Committee charter annually. Members of the Audit Committee shall conduct an honest and critical assessment of the Audit Committee's performance, and the performance of individual members, including acknowledgement of any areas in which improvements are useful or necessary. Such assessments are not required to be published.

III. Meetings and Structure

- The Audit Committee shall meet as often as it determines, but not less frequently than quarterly.

- The Audit Committee shall meet periodically with management, the internal auditors, and the independent auditor in separate executive sessions.

- The Audit Committee may request any officer or employee of the Company or the Company's outside counsel to attend a meeting of the Audit Committee or to meet with any members of, or consultants to, the Audit Committee.

- The Audit Committee shall be entitled to establish such subcommittees or temporary or ad hoc subcommittees as it may from time to time find necessary or useful, provided that no actions or determinations of such subcommittee shall be binding upon the Audit Committee unless the Audit Committee expressly delegates the authority to such subcommittee for such actions or determinations. The Audit Committee may ratify actions or determinations of any subcommittee. Any actions or determinations delegated to a subcommittee or ratified by the Audit Committee shall be deemed to be actions of the Audit Committee.

IV. Specific Responsibilities and Authority

The Audit Committee shall have authority and responsibility in the following areas:

- *Independent Auditor*

    o **Appointment and Oversight.** The Audit Committee is responsible for the appointment, compensation, retention, oversight, and preapproval of services provided by the Independent Auditor in connection with the annual audit report and such other audit, review, or attest services relating to the Company's financial statements. The Independent Auditor shall report directly to the Audit Committee.

    o **Evaluation.** The Audit Committee shall annually evaluate the qualifications, performance, fees, and independence of the Independent Auditor, including an evaluation of the lead partner of the Independent Auditor. The Audit Committee shall report its findings to the Board.

    o **Annual Report on Quality Control and Independence.** The Audit Committee shall receive and review, at least annually, the Independent Auditor's report on the Independent Auditor's independence and quality of internal controls. The Audit Committee shall review all relationships between the Independent Auditor and the Company (including any significant fees for any anticipated nonaudit services), including those required by Independence Standards Board Standard No. 1. The Audit Committee shall establish policies respecting rotation of the lead partner of the Independent Auditor in accordance with SEC requirements, and the hiring by the Company of current or former employees of the Independent Auditor.

    o **Independent Auditor Plan.** The Audit Committee shall review with the Independent Auditor and management the plan and scope of the annual financial audit and quarterly reviews, including the Independent Auditor's fees. The Audit Committee shall be responsible to preapprove audit, nonaudit, and any other services to be provided by the Independent Auditor.

    o **Audit Reports and Reviews.** The Audit Committee shall review the results of the annual financial audit and limited quarterly reviews of the Company's financial statements, and any other matters required to be communicated by the independent auditors, including any significant accounting, auditing, and internal control issues identified by the Independent Auditor (the Independent Auditor's management or internal control letter). The Audit Committee will review with the Independent Auditor any problems or difficulties the Independent Auditor encountered in the course of its work, including any restrictions on the scope of the Independent Auditor's activities, access to information, or significant disagreements with management and management's responses to such matters. The Audit Committee is responsible for the resolution of any disagreements between management and the Independent Auditor regarding financial reporting.

- *Internal Audit*
  - o **Internal Auditor.** The Company's internal auditor shall report directly to the Audit Committee, which shall have the authority to hire and terminate any internal auditor, which may be an employee of the Company or an outside party. The role of the internal audit function shall include auditors of operational, financial, information technology, and compliance matters.

- *Financial Reporting*
  - o **Form 10-K.** The Audit Committee shall review, with advice from management and the Independent Auditor, the Company's annual financial statements, the Independent Auditor's report, Management's Report on Internal Control over Financial Reporting, and the Company's disclosures under Management's Discussion and Analysis of Financial Condition and Results of Operations ("MD&A") to be contained in the Company's annual report on Form 10-K, prior to such Form 10-K being filed with the SEC. The Audit Committee shall recommend to the Board the inclusion of the Company's financial statements in the Form 10-K following such review.
  - o **Form 10-Q.** The Audit Committee shall review, with advice from management and the Independent Auditor, the Company's interim financial statements (including disclosures under MD&A) prior to the filing of any Quarterly Reports on Form 10-Q with the SEC.

○ **Scope of Review.** The Audit Committee's review of financial reporting shall include:

- review of management certifications in connection with the filing, including regarding any significant deficiencies or weaknesses in the design or operation of the Company's internal control over financial reporting and any fraud, whether or not material, involving management or other employees who have a significant role in the Company's system of internal control;

- review of issues regarding the presentation of the Company's financial statements;

- review of issues regarding the Company's accounting principles, including material changes in the Company's selection or application of accounting principles;

- review of the effect of off-balance sheet structures on the Company's financial statements; and

- review of communications by the Independent Auditor, including matters required to be communicated to the Audit Committee under Generally Accepted Accounting Principles (GAAP).

- *Earnings Releases and Non-GAAP Financial Information*

  ○ **Review of Releases.** The Audit Committee (or Chairman) shall discuss with management and the Independent Auditor each of the Company's earnings releases prior to its issuance.

  ○ **Use of Non-GAAP Financial Information.** The Audit Committee shall review and discuss with management and the Independent Auditor the presentation and information use in the Company's earnings press releases (including, but not limited to, "pro forma" and "non-GAAP financial information").

- *Compliance, Internal Controls, and Risk Management*

  ○ **Compliance Program.** The Audit Committee shall establish and recommend for adoption by the Board Standards of Business Conduct and Code of Ethics. The Audit Committee shall oversee the Company's compliance program. The Audit Committee shall also establish procedures for (i) the receipt, retention, and treatment of complaints received by the Company regarding accounting, internal accounting controls, or auditing matters; and (ii) the confidential, anonymous submission by the Company's employees of concerns regarding questionable accounting or auditing matters.

o **Internal Control.** The Audit Committee shall review major issues as to the adequacy of the Company's internal controls and any audit steps taken in light of material control deficiencies.

o **Risk Assessment.** The Audit Committee shall review with management the Company's major financial and other risk exposures, the Company's risk monitoring and management policies, and management's implementation of those policies. The Audit Committee shall require that management periodically, and at least annually, report to the Audit Committee management's assessment of the Company's exposure to financial and other risks.

o **Executive Compensation.** As requested by the Board or the Compensation Committee, the Audit Committee shall provide analysis and advice to assist in determining whether the compensation programs for executives incentivize undue risk for the Company.

• *Qualified Legal Compliance Committee*

o The Audit Committee is also appointed to serve as the Qualified Legal Compliance Committee (the "QLCC") of the Board of Directors. In its capacity as QLCC, the Audit Committee shall: (i) receive, review, and take appropriate action with respect to any report made or referred to the Audit Committee by an attorney of evidence of a material violation of applicable U.S. federal or state securities law, material breach of a fiduciary duty under U.S. federal or state law, or a similar material violation by the Company or by any officer, director, employee, or agent of the Company, (ii) otherwise fulfill the responsibilities of a QLCC pursuant to Section 307 of the Sarbanes Oxley Act of 2002 and the rules promulgated thereunder and (iii) perform such other duties as may be assigned to it, from time to time, by the Board.

o The Audit Committee shall adopt written procedures for the confidential receipt, retention, and consideration of any oral or written reports received in its capacity as QLCC. In its capacity as QLCC, the Audit Committee shall have the authority to establish procedures in order to fulfill its obligations under this Charter and under applicable law, rules, and regulations, and shall meet wherever circumstances warrant as determined by the Chair.

o   In its capacity as QLCC, the Audit Committee has the authority and responsibility to act, by majority vote, to take all other appropriate action, including the authority to notify the SEC in the event that the Company fails in any material respect to implement an appropriate response that it has recommended to the Company.

o   The Audit Committee shall report to the Board on a regular basis regarding any QLCC matters.

Sample Compensation Committee Charter

I. Purpose

The purpose of the Compensation Committee is to aid the Board of Directors in meeting its responsibilities with regard to oversight and determination of executive compensation. The Committee shall review, recommend, and approve all elements of compensation to the Company's executive officers.

II. Composition of the Compensation Committee

- The Compensation Committee shall be comprised of at least three directors, each of whom is "independent" under the rules of the exchange on which the Company's shares are listed for trading and in accordance with applicable laws and Securities and Exchange Commission regulations.

- In connection with transactions implicating Section 162 of the Internal Revenue Code or Section 16 of the Securities and Exchange Act, the Committee shall determine if its members require any additional qualifications other than independence as defined by the exchange on which the Company's shares are listed.

- The members of the Compensation Committee shall be appointed annually by the Board on the recommendation of the Chairman of the Board and shall serve at the pleasure of the Board and for such term or terms as the Board may determine.

- The Compensation Committee shall elect a chair who shall be responsible for ensuring that the Compensation Committee fulfils its obligations under this Charter.

- The chair of the Compensation Committee may recommend removal of a member of the Compensation Committee as the chair deems appropriate; provided, however, that removal shall be made only by the Board of Directors.

- The Compensation Committee will evaluate its performance and the Compensation Committee charter annually. Members of the Committee shall conduct an honest and critical assessment of the Compensation Committee's performance, and the performance of individual members, including acknowledgement of any areas in which improvements are useful or necessary. Such assessments are not required to be published.

III. Meetings and Structure

- The Compensation Committee shall meet as often as it determines, but not less frequently than two times per year.

- The Compensation Committee may request any officer or employee of the Company or the Company's outside counsel to attend a meeting of the Committee or to meet with any members of, or consultants to, the Committee.

- The Compensation Committee shall be entitled to establish such subcommittees or temporary or ad hoc subcommittees as it may from time to time find necessary or useful, provided that no actions or determinations of such subcommittee shall be binding upon the Compensation Committee unless the Compensation Committee expressly delegates the authority to such subcommittee for such actions or determinations. The Compensation Committee may ratify actions or determinations of any subcommittee. Any actions or determinations delegated to a subcommittee or ratified by the Compensation Committee shall be deemed to be actions of the Compensation Committee.

IV. Specific Responsibilities and Authority

- *Establish Executive Compensation*
- *The Committee shall*

  o review and approve corporate goals and objectives relevant to all elements of CEO compensation, including salary, incentives, severance, bonus, deferred compensation, and perquisites; evaluate the CEO's performance in light of those goals and objectives, including evaluating performance against any previously established measurements; and determine and approve the elements of the CEO's compensation level based on such evaluation.

  o make recommendations to the board with respect to non-CEO executive officer compensation, and incentive-compensation and equity-based plans that are subject to board approval.

  o evaluate, in establishing the elements of executive compensation, whether the Company's compensation programs encourage those executives to take undue risks. Such evaluation may, in the Committee's discretion, be undertaken in consultation with the audit committee or any other committee, adviser, or other party the Committee determines may be relevant to such evaluation.

  o recommend to the board a policy to recover executive bonuses that are paid on the basis of financial statements that are erroneous ("clawback policy") and whether officers and directors may "hedge" Company securities they own or have been granted as compensation ("hedging policy").

  o ensure compliance with law for executive compensation arrangements that are subject to legal restrictions, such as "golden parachutes," [compensation limits for executives of

TARP recipients], option and equity payments, and restrictions on payments that have the effect of shifting compensation from one tax year to another.

- *Oversee Required Disclosures and Shareholder Approvals*
  - ○ The Committee shall review the Compensation Discussion and Analysis for inclusion in the Company's proxy statement, and shall prepare any required Compensation Committee report for inclusion in the proxy statement.
  - ○ The Committee shall also ensure that the proxy statement includes required disclosures relating to compensation, including
    - A periodic non-binding vote on executive compensation ("say on pay") by shareholders;
    - Not less often than every six years, a shareholder vote on the frequency of "say on pay" votes by shareholders;
    - A vote, in connection with any applicable merger or acquisition, of the compensation arrangements triggered in connection with such transaction;
    - Applicable disclosures on the Company's hedging policy;
    - Disclosures on ratios of CEO pay to company performance and average company employee pay; and
    - Disclosure in the proxy statement of any material information to shareholders respecting the Board's evaluation of whether compensation programs for executives incentivize those executives to take undue risks.
  - ○ The Committee shall ensure the Company makes prompt disclosures on Form 8-K relating to compensation decisions and arrangements.
  - ○ In connection with the adoption of stock option or equity plans, the Committee shall ensure that the board has taken steps to have such plans approved by shareholders.
- *Engage and Oversee Independent Advisers*
  - ○ The Compensation Committee shall have sole authority to retain and determine the terms of any engagement with any consultants or legal counsel respecting compensation matters, provided that such outside advisers are "independent" under any relevant SEC rules.

The Committee shall be responsible for the oversight and compensation of such advisers. The company shall provide the Compensation Committee with resources for such purposes.

- *CEO Succession*
    - o If the Board delegates authority to the Compensation Committee to establish policies and contingency plans respecting CEO succession, the Committee shall establish such policies and procedures to conduct such activity as it determines in its sole discretion.

Sample
Nominating Committee Charter

I. Purpose

The Nominating Committee (the Committee) is appointed by the Board of Directors (the Board) to assist the Board in identifying, evaluating, and recommending to the Board of Directors nominees for membership on the Board of Directors, and for membership on committees of the Board, and for recommending to the Board the adoption of policies respecting the governance of the company and structure and operations of the Board.

II. Composition of the Nominating Committee

- The Nominating Committee shall be comprised of at least three directors, each of whom is "independent" under the rules of the exchange on which the Company's shares are listed for trading and in accordance with applicable laws and Securities and Exchange Commission regulations.

- The members of the Nominating Committee shall be appointed annually by the on the recommendation of the Chairman of the Board and shall serve at the pleasure of the Board and for such term or terms as the Board may determine.

- The Nominating Committee shall elect a chair who shall be responsible for ensuring that the Nominating Committee fulfils its obligations under this Charter.

- The chair of the Nominating Committee may recommend removal of a member of the Nominating Committee as the chair deems appropriate provided, however, that removal shall be made only by the Board of Directors.

- The Nominating Committee will evaluate its performance and the Nominating Committee Charter annually. Members of the Committee shall conduct an honest and critical assessment of the Nominating Committee's performance, and the performance of individual members, including acknowledgement of any areas in which improvements are useful or necessary. Such assessments are not required to be published.

III. Meetings and Structure

- The Nominating Committee shall meet as often as it determines, but not less frequently than two times per year.

- The Nominating Committee may request any officer or employee of the Company or the Company's outside counsel to attend a meeting of the Committee or to meet with any members of, or consultants to, the Committee.

- The Nominating Committee shall be entitled to establish such subcommittees or temporary or ad hoc subcommittees as it may from time to time find necessary or useful, provided that no actions or determinations of such subcommittee shall be binding upon the Nominating Committee unless the Nominating Committee expressly delegates the authority to such subcommittee for such actions or determinations. The Nominating Committee may ratify actions or determinations of any subcommittee. Any actions or determinations delegated to a subcommittee or ratified by the Nominating Committee shall be deemed to be actions of the Nominating Committee.

IV. Specific Responsibilities and Authority

- *Establish and Implement a Director Nomination Process*
    - ○ The Committee shall establish operating policies by which it will conduct its operations. It will evaluate its process at least annually and shall make such adjustments as it may determine from time to time are necessary or useful, and shall make such disclosures of its nomination process as may be required under the proxy rules or otherwise.

    - ○ In establishing a nomination process, the Nominating Committee shall prepare a written list of characteristics that the Board and Board committees should possess, including size of the Board, minimum qualifications, desired skill sets or experiential backgrounds for members, and any diversity objectives.

    - ○ In evaluating candidates recommended by any source (whether from the Committee, management or Board members, by shareholders, or recommended by paid advisors), the Nominating Committee shall evaluate such proposed candidates against the written criteria for the Board.

    - ○ The Committee shall conduct personal interviews prior to making any director nominations of nonincumbent directors.

    - ○ In developing a slate of nominees to be proposed by the Company, the Committee has discretion to reject any candidate, proposed from any source, that it does not think will be appropriate for the Board, notwithstanding that candidate's credentials, with consideration given to the collegiality and working relationships with Board members.

    - ○ The Committee shall:
        - ▪ Review and recommend to the Board, from time to time but not less than annually, the desired characteristics of the composition of the Board—including size, competencies, experience of members, diversity, age, and other appropriate qualities;
        - ▪ Assist the Board by identifying, attracting, and recommending qualified candidates for membership on the Board, consistent with such characteristics.
            - • Such candidates may include, if the Committee deems it advisable, candidates recommended by the Chief

Executive Officer, other members of the Board, and shareholders (where such shareholder recommendations have been offered in accordance with procedures established by the Committee and relevant law);

- Review members standing for reelection, evaluate such members on the basis of contribution, change of status, and commitment to the Company, and make recommendations to the Board for reelection of members;

- Review from time to time, but not less than annually, whether members of the Board meet the standards of independence, financial expertise, and other competencies required under exchange requirements and all other applicable legal requirements and advise the Board as to the conclusions reached by the Committee as a result of such review;

- In reporting to the Board, include information to assist the company in fulfilling its proxy disclosure requirements respecting evaluation of the nominees for the Board.

   o In conducting evaluations, the Nominating Committee may, in its discretion, consider the evaluations of proxy advisory organizations.

   o The Committee shall consider level of commitment of time and active attention a director nominee can provide, including any guidelines limiting other commitments by Board members.

V.   Review Board Structure and Operations

- The Committee shall:

- conduct an evaluation process that takes into account the mix of skills, experience, and intangible factors that make a good Board, including the diversity of the Board;

- review the structure of the Board and its committees and make recommendations for any changes and the basis for such recommendations;

- review whether the roles of chairman of the Board and CEO should be separate, and make recommendations to the Board and the basis for such recommendations;

- nominate a lead independent director, in the event that the Board chair position is held by the CEO;

- Periodically review the Charter, and submit the Charter to the board of directors for approval and publish the Charter in accordance with any applicable regulations.

- *Oversee Required Disclosures and Shareholder Approvals*

  o The Committee shall review the disclosures of nominees for director and discussions respecting the nomination process for inclusion in the Company's proxy statement to ensure accuracy, completeness, and compliance with relevant law.

  o The Committee shall ensure the Company makes prompt disclosures on Form 8-K relating to director and executive appointment matters.

- *Engage and Oversee Independent Advisers*

  o The Nominating Committee shall have sole authority to retain and determine the terms of any engagement with any consultants or legal counsel respecting the identification and qualification of nominees.

  o The Committee shall be responsible for the oversight and compensation of such advisers. The company shall provide the Nominating Committee with resources for such purposes.

- *CEO Succession*

  o If the Board delegates authority to the Nominating Committee to establish policies and contingency plans respecting CEO succession, the Committee shall establish such policies and procedures to conduct such activity as it determines in its sole discretion.

- *Shareholder Nominations*

  o If the Nominating Committee determines that it shall evaluate nominees provided by shareholders using criteria different from that used for nominees of the Committee, it shall include a statement setting out the difference and the basis for such difference in its written evaluation criteria.

  o The Nominating Committee shall develop policies for dealing with nominations made by shareholders, including nominations, as applicable, made pursuant to applicable SEC regulations under which information on shareholder nominees must be included in the company's proxy statement.

○ The Nominating Committee shall report to the Board on any recommendations by shareholders for nominees to the Board.

Sample Evaluation Questionnaire to be Used for Board or Committee Self-Evaluation

The Board or committee should score the following questions on a range of 1-10, with 10 representing "Strongly Agree" and 1 representing "Strongly Disagree."

IMPORTANT NOTE REGARDING USE OF EVALUATIONS:

Obtaining the scores of directors on the following matters is not an end in itself.

The objective of the evaluation process is to identify areas for improvement in the Company's processes or execution of Board and committee activities, using the scores as indicators of the Board's cumulative assessment. The evaluation questionnaire represents only the starting point in a review process. The Board or committee has to discuss and address any identified areas of weakness.

Organization of Board (committee)

The Board (committee) is the right size.

Selection of members of the Board (committee) is handled appropriately.

Current committee assignments are appropriate.

The members of the Board (committee) have a sufficient mix of skills, business and life experience, and differences in perspective to promote effective and vigorous review of Company policies.

The Company's decision on whether to divide the role of Chair and CEO is appropriate.

The respective roles of directors and management are clearly understood, by the directors and by management.

Meetings and Information

The number of meetings each year is appropriate.

The attendance at meetings of all directors is appropriate.

The agenda and necessary information are available prior to meetings.

The board is provided adequate materials on a timely basis in advance of meetings.

Directors are prepared for meetings.

Adequate time is provided at meetings for complete discussions of agenda items.

The independent directors demonstrate their independence in deliberations on Company matters.

Directors vote according to their view of the Company's best interest and not simply to "go along."

The executive sessions of the Board are effective.

Management's presentation of information is objective and balanced, not slanted in favor of management's suggested positions.

Directors have adequate access to management and outside advisors to fully inform their understanding of matters brought to the board.

Management is responsive to director requests for additional information.

Strategy and Risk

The Board reviews the Company's strategy at least annually to adjust for changes in business and economic circumstances.

Each director understands the Company's strategy.

The Board (committee) uses appropriate measurements to determine if the Company's strategy is being implemented effectively.

Management adequately apprises the Board (committee) regarding all known factors that bear on the Company's ability to compete effectively, including factors that are within the Company's control and factors that are not.

The Board (committee) understands potential threats and opportunities it faces.

The Board (committee) has discussed contingencies, including crisis management and merger and acquisition opportunities, and is prepared to respond to unforeseen events.

Organization and Compensation

The Board regularly reviews with management the appropriate management structure for the Company.

The Board (committee) establishes annual performance objectives with the CEO and monitors performance through the year.

The CEO provides balanced and objective reports to the Board (committee) regarding the performance of other executives.

The Board (committee) has access to members of management other than the CEO.

The process for determining executive compensation is appropriate.

The process for determining director compensation is appropriate.

Committee Operations

Each committee has access to management and other employees necessary to fulfill its duties.

Management and directors both understand the scope of the committee's duties.

Outside advisors understand the scope of the committee's duties.

Each committee chair has been effective in ensuring the committee has met its obligations under its charter.

Access to outside advisors is adequate.

Performance by outside advisors has been adequate.

Committee members pay appropriate attention to matters that arise; any "red flags" are given proper attention.

Sample Checklist for Securities Trading by Officers and Directors

This sample checklist is intended to be used by the Company in connection with its pre-clearance of securities trades by officers and directors of the Company.

The list is intended to be a model only, and should be adapted to the Company's specific pre-clearance and securities trading policies. Not all of the elements shown on this list will necessarily be consistent with the policies of all companies.

Introduction

The goal of the pre-clearance policy is to permit the Company to review the compliance by its officers and directors with the Company's security trading policies and restrictions, including the observance of the company's "window" period restrictions on trading, and to ensure that there is no inadvertent failure by a director or executive to comply with the securities laws.

IMPORTANT WARNING: Pre-clearance of a trade by the Company does not represent legal advice to the individual.

The pre-clearance policies are established for the benefit of the Company and not primarily for the benefit of individual officers or directors. Most securities laws restrictions on trading are personal obligations of the individual conducting the trading. It is the responsibility of each director and executive to ensure that any personal trades are made in compliance with the securities law, and pre-clearance of a transaction by the Company does not imply that the officer or director has complied with the law.

1. Establishing or amending an automatic transaction plan ("Rule 10b5-1 Plan")

Before the Company clears a Rule 10b5-1 Plan for an officer or director, the Company shall receive a written confirmation from the individual (and shall separately confirm with information in the Company's possession and reasonably available to the person conducting pre-clearance):

- That the individual is not in possession of material nonpublic information about the Company.

- That the Rule 10b5-1 Plan is established during a "window period" in which trading is permitted for Company personnel.

- That the creation or amendment of the Rule 10b5-1 Plan is made in good faith and not with the intent to evade the requirements of Rule 10b5-1 or any other securities law.

- That if the individual previously has entered into a Rule 10b5-1 Plan, the individual has not stopped or terminated any scheduled transactions under that Rule 10b5-1 Plan (which may result in the prior plan being deemed terminated).

- That the individual acknowledges that the Company reserves the right to disclose the Rule 10b5-1 Plan with the SEC.

- That the individual is responsible for all SEC filings, including without limitation filings on Form 4 or under Rule 144.

Sale or purchase of securities not as part of a Rule 10b5-1 Plan

Before the Company clears a transaction not involving a Rule 10b5-1 Plan for an officer or director, the Company shall receive a written confirmation from the individual (and shall separately confirm with information in the Company's possession and reasonably available to the person conducting pre-clearance):

- That the individual is not in possession of material nonpublic information about the Company.

- That the transaction is conducted during a "window period" in which trading is permitted for Company personnel.

- That the individual is responsible for all SEC filings, including without limitation filings on Form 4 or under Rule 144.

- That the individual is aware that any "matching" trades made within the prior six months or next six months will expose the individual to forfeiture of gains under Section 16 of the Securities Exchange Act ("matching" trades are sales followed or preceded by purchases, or vice versa, other than exempt compensatory option transactions).

- The individual is aware of the Company's policies on employee "hedging" risks of loss in the value of the Company's securities held by them or granted as compensation.

- In a sale, any restrictive legends on the individual's accounts or share certificates will be removed as appropriate for the new owners, but continue on the certificate share balance.

- In a purchase, any accounts or share certificates are subject to having a restrictive legend placed on them to prevent trading in violation of the securities laws.

Index

About the Author

Bruce F. Dravis is a partner at Downey Brand LLP. He has practiced corporate and securities law for 25 years, as outside corporate counsel and as General Counsel for a publicly traded semiconductor manufacturer that was acquired by Intel Corporation. He is former Co-Chair of the Corporations Committee of the California State Bar's Business Section and is Publications Chair for the Corporate Governance Subcommittee of the American Bar Association Section of Business Law. He has taught mergers and acquisitions for the University of California; and writes and speaks frequently on securities, business, and governance topics. He graduated with honors from Boston University School of Law and practiced law in Boston before returning to his native California. His email address is bdravis@downeybrand.com.